AF281102

# Change in the mind of the strategist

a book about development, competitiveness and how we can realise potential that requires a little more

Pontus Wadström

**Change in the mind of a strategist**

a book about development, competitiveness
and how we can realise potential that requires a little more

ISBN 978-91-527-6283-7
© 2023 Pontus Wadström

Front cover photo: Jr Korpa on Unsplash
https://unsplash.com/photos/_af0_qAh4K4 [Last retrieved 20220914]

Print: BoD - Books on Demand, Norderstedt, Germany
Publisher: **V8** - Verb Scribblings | Wadstrom Management AB

**Copying prohibited**

This work is protected by copyright law. Infringement of the author's rights
under copyright law may result in penalties (fines or imprisonment),
damages and seizure/destruction of the unauthorised material.

www.pontuswadstrom.com
info@pontuswadstrom.com

To my mother, because she taught me that one of the differences between being intelligent and being smart is being kind. Without being kind - that abused word - we don't get real change. No one stands up for someone he dislikes. And many of us need to stand up when we want to realise a potential that requires a little more.

# Content

# List of figures

## About the Author

Pontus Wadström works as an independent advisor, lecturer and researcher. He has previously worked as a strategy and management consultant and as a manager responsible for strategy and change issues in various organisations. In addition to his practical activities, he is an affiliated researcher at the Department of Industrial Economics at the Royal Institute of Technology in Stockholm, where he obtained his PhD in strategy. He is also a visiting lecturer in entrepreneurship and innovation management at Uppsala University. His undergraduate education consists of an MBA and degrees in Business Administration and Behavioural Science.

Pontus' knowledge is based on practical experience from over 200 organisations in most industries, as well as deep theoretical knowledge from a variety of research domains that are not usually associated with each other (e.g. strategy and psychology).

His expertise, in practice and academia, is in how organisations work practically with strategy in order to become better at adapting, changing and succeeding over time. His work has been published in academic journals such as the *Journal of Strategy and Management* and the *Journal of Business Strategy*, and in books such as *Advancing strategy through behaviour psychology* and *Strategi: arenor, affärer, arbetssätt, ansvar, avsikter.*

# Foreword

It is with some pleasure that I write this foreword. This book has been near completion for a long time and, unfortunately, I have had to tell colleagues, clients and friends that "it's on its way". But now it has arrived.

One of the reasons I've delayed finishing it is that I've been thinking about what to call the book and how to place it in context. Change in the broadest sense is probably the most critical thing for any organisation that wants to be successful over time. However, change is also probably one of the world's most overused and worn-out words. It doesn't nearly reflect the weight it carries for organisational success.

So, what can you call a book about what is perhaps the single most important thing for the long-term success of organisations when the word that should describe it is so utterly meaningless and watered down?

I initially thought this book was about change management. A handbook on pushing through things that 'require a little more'. That's certainly true, but it's not the whole truth. As the title reveals, it's about change from the strategist's perspective (to play on Ohmae's classic)[1]. A strategist is a person who devotes most of his or her work to *strategising*. Strategising aims to improve an organisation's ability to be successful over time. That's what I do. This book is no exception. The book thus gives my perspective on change with the advantages and disadvantages it entails. Moreover, a starting point is that organisations that want to be successful over time need to become good at linking the two. In reality, these organisations are few.

Many organisations talk broadly about strategy, change and strategic change. They have a new transformation programme every nine months, but real change is rarely seen, especially not the kind of change that benefits their ability to be more successful over time. Change does not permeate the way they operate, but is driven by something else, such as savings or political considerations. Other organisations do not talk much about change. Yet, when we look at what they do and the progress they have made, change must be built into the way they operate. Consciously or unconsciously, they have managed to navigate the borderland between strategy and change that I write about in this book.

To succeed as an organisation, I think we need to let change wash over us. It's not enough to dip our toes. We need to be prepared to do what it takes to transform. This may entail moves that are unconventional or even 'hard' means. One quotation that I carried a long time comes from an interview with Malcolm X in *The Village Voice* in 1965:

> The greatest mistake of the movement has been trying to organize a sleeping people around specific goals. You have to wake the people up first, then you'll get action.[2]

This 'awakening' was a starting point for me for a long time. If I want get people to change, I need to wake them up. Then we can talk about goals. In a change cliché, this is sometimes called creating a *sense of urgency*. Waking someone up first can be necessary sometimes. However, I'm too chastened to believe that a leader can communicate some 'one-off urgency' to wake up the commitment of a sleeping people, and then it'll be resolved. Today, I also see a more nuanced side to starting to make a change: people can, and must, be awakened in different ways.

When I was younger, listening to my parents talk about their jobs, I realised that my mother often managed to realise major changes. At first I thought it was because she was so nice that people did what she said. For those of you who don't know my mother, I can tell you that she is the archetype of a mother as described in fairy tales: kind, sweet, small, loves children and tries endlessly to take care of everyone.

As I got older and started working on strategy and change, I got a complementary view of my mother. I personally felt that others were not doing what I said. Even though I thought I was being kind (and even though I was the boss). My mother had something more. She had an ability to get others to do things they might not initially want to do. What's more, she made them believe it was their idea. I suspect that 40 years of leadership in areas where everyone has an opinion about what is being done - the school world, childcare and social services - honed her skills. My twisted insight into this was that my mother is more street-smart than I am.

As a semi-academic, and for the sake of my battered hip-hop ego (where smartness carries weight), I wanted to understand this better. So I talked to my mom. What she did concretely was plant a seed of some improvement in a number of people, and then water that seed periodically by asking about it to make the idea grow. After a while, co-workers often suggested that they would like to do what she had suggested. They also thought it was their idea and were very engaged. Mom, as the boss, then just had to say, 'Yeah, sure. That's great! Do it.'

Mom woke a 'sleeping people' differently than Malcolm did. Smarter? She didn't do badly, which is an obvious risk if we move too aggressively. The circumstances for Malcolm and Mom are different, of course, but no one wants to stand up for someone he dislikes, and the outcome of change will be less if we can't mobilise more of both 'us' and 'them' who might influence the change.

Someone might consider it manipulative to plant an idea and water it. So be it. Then I lean on Malcolm X again and think: "change, by any means necessary"[3]. If we want to change something, we want to change it, don't we? If not, why pretend, waste energy on it, or even talk about it? Energy in organisations is a scarce resource that should be used carefully.

Conclusively, managing change requires a little more than managing operations. It requires a combination of the patience Mom showed to give as many people as possible the chance to take responsibility, with the willingness and courage to do what it takes, as Malcolm X demonstrated. A good change manager, then, behaves like a somewhat bizarre combination of a civil rights campaigner in 1960s America who is prepared to resort to violence to achieve set goals and a cute and meek mother who cries when children and puppies on TV get hurt.

I realise this sounds strange, but as we will see in the book, much of what is required if we want change is not 'either/or'. It's 'both and'. It's not either Malcolm or Mom. It's Malcolm *and* Mom. It's not revolution or evolution. It's revolution *and* evolution.

This book is therefore written for those who believe that we need to combine the hard with the soft to succeed in making a change, those who don't want to create another tired PowerPoint presentation with fluffy messages about change that don't make a difference, those who don't want to see potential go to waste when we don't do what it takes, those who realise that if behaviours don't change, nothing really changes, those who want to see concrete and measurable results from the changes that are realised, and those who realise that kindness is a must.

In short, this book is written for those who are serious about change. If that's you, welcome! Pleased to meet you.

*// PW. 2022-12-02

# Acknowledgements

This book is the result of my last 10 years of work as an adviser and educator, things I have read, and my own research. It is difficult to list everything that has contributed. Nevertheless, I would like to thank three groups:

The first group consists of the people I was working with when the first sketch of the ideas presented in the book took shape over a decade ago: Mikaela Jensen, a better 'right hand' does not exist. Björn Flygare, a sounding board in big and small ways. Jennifer Eklund, for insights on competence development. Ida Dahlbäck, for contributions on change communication. Mattias Hellichius, for reasoning on benefits and business case management. Stefan Sundberg, for talks on project management methods.

The second group consists of several courageous leaders in various organisations where, in one way or another, together we have successfully realised rather substantial changes. This work has helped to refine the reasoning and to ensure that the book works in practice as the handbook I initially intended it to be. You know who you are, thank you!

In this group, one person stands out: Mattias Magnell, responsible for leadership development at Skanska and chairman of the SIS committee for ISO certification of Human Resource Management. Together with Håkan Björding and Johan Lundström, we have trained nearly 500 people to use the ideas in the book in making changes. The effects of the efforts are impressive. He is happy to tell you about them. Just get in touch with him and say hello from me.

The third group consists of people who have read and provided valuable feedback on the book during the work. Many thanks to: Eva Åkesson, Maria Anjou, Robert Winneborn, Patrik Hamann, Jörgen Svonnni, Thomas Kalling, Jörgen Dahlström, and Per Wilhelmsson.

Finally, Karin, my wife and best friend, a special thank you for all the support in the work on the book and help in a series of both large and small choices.

# 1. Brief introduction to the book

All organisations must continually adapt to changing circumstances. These changing circumstances can be both external and internal, and the changes that must follow can be both large and small to organisations.

This book is essentially a handbook on how to manage such large and small changes. More broadly, it is about learning how to lead and realise 'things' that are a little more challenging than the 'usual' and that contribute to increased competitiveness and success. It is one thing to manage a business. It's another thing to change it. It is changing a business that we are looking at in this book.

The word I use to describe when something is different from today is *change*. Actually, it doesn't matter what we call it. Evolution, transformation, etc. What does make a difference, however, is that it requires a slightly different approach when we lead. Sometimes we use the term *change management* for the type of management that involves leading towards something that is different. That is also the word I use.

When we have to push through changes of various kinds, especially if they are of a major or strategic nature, the stakes are often high, the risks high and the chances of success quite uncertain. Despite such poor conditions, we sometimes must change our organisations. When faced with a fact that requires us to change, much of what is involved in management, governance, leadership, decision-making, personal relationships, will and motivation, measurement and monitoring, accountability and structure is put to the test. So how do we lead and realise such changes?

There's a lot we don't know about leading change. There are no tried and tested one-size-fits-all solutions. However, some we do know with pretty good support. We know that change is a slog. Most people who have been responsible for leading major change, or have been involved in it, can attest to how much effort is required and how often it still feels like we are doing too little. In addition to being a slog, change management is a "full-contact

1

sport", as my friend Jan Lindvall at Uppsala University likes to say. In fact, there aren't many words that explain change management better. It is an ordeal quite few people have the patience and energy to pursue as it should be done to have an effect.

In all honesty, it's most fun in the very early stages when we're trying to understand what to do, and towards the end, when we see positive results. It's not always fun trying to sell the changes because it often meets resistance. It's rarely fun when we're in the middle of it because there's so much for which we don't have the time. It's not even always fun when we're done, even though we see positive results. There's almost always someone who's got it worse and may hold us accountable to some extent.

Despite this, we sometimes need to change our organisations to be better equipped to meet the demands placed on us by customers, society or the environment. But not to make it look all dire, some elements involved in leading a change are fun - insanely fun - if we do it properly. If we do it right, there are few things that are as educational and enriching for anyone who wants to become better at creating thriving, high-performing organisations or who wants to be a better leader. Moreover, organisations are often starved of people who are good at driving through change in a structured and systematic way. So, a good change manager can get both recognition and do enjoyable assignments.

We also know from decades of well-established research that change is hard to achieve. One reason is probably that it is daunting, and we don't always have the knowledge and tools to succeed. In addition, it often requires a more substantial effort than initially seemed reasonable. Trying to push something through with too little knowledge, the wrong tools or too few resources is, of course, incredibly challenging and not much fun.

The researcher in me feels that organisations are not taking advantage of the knowledge that exists about how we should do things. Unfortunately, I quite often see organisations neglecting things that research points to as crucial. I don't think people are stupid, mean or bad. On the contrary. Most people I have worked with are smart, friendly and competent. However, I think the knowledge of change management and the understanding of how that knowledge can be applied in practice is too shallow and narrow. This is because the experience of leading a major change is limited. Few have done it.

So with this book, based on both my experience and my research, I want to develop the knowledge both broadly and deeply, and encourage more people to take change management seriously; to work with change management in a way that is supported by research; to show practical ways to use what we know from studies of change and apply it in practice.

## Purpose of the book, structure and how to read it

The purpose of this book is to offer knowledge on how to understand, prioritise and manage change in organisations in a systematic and structured way, and with a strategy perspective, change that has to do with how organisations best use limited resources to create success over time.

My hope is that by treating strategy and change as two sides of the same coin, I can help ensure that we weigh in strategy considerations when we change our organisations. I also hope that the strategy perspective helps focus on the realisation of the benefits that change aims to deliver.

To achieve this, I have built the book around a number of overarching areas that research and experience suggest we need to address. We can think of them as *Lego pieces* about strategy work and change management that we need to know, each one separately, and how to put them together in different ways. The pieces represent the issues we need to address if we are to succeed in driving through change and ensuring that change leads to some form of success over time. They are questions that, by their answers, ensure that we have an idea of what outcomes we want to achieve, what we want to change and how we can go about it.

In fact, there are quite a few things we need to think about before we tackle change. There are many questions that need to be answered to lead major and strategic change. It's not something we can do on a whim and expect to be successful over time. It makes for a lot of Lego pieces.

Because there are so many Lego pieces and because we can't possibly go through them all at once - we must take them one by one - you can get the feeling that 'Wow, is all this really necessary?' This is particularly true of Chapter 7. The work of the change manager, which is about the work of the Change manager. In fact, that's what's required. You can't wrap up the message. Sometimes it requires 'a bit more' than leading the usual. Sometimes it requires substantially 'much more'. Yet, as we learn more about change and strategy, the content of the book will feel less overwhelming. Ploughing through this volume should be seen as the first step in a journey, not the last.

The fact that there are many parts that we go through one after the other can also make you as a reader feel that you sometimes don't understand the context, that you feel that you are missing some part or that you wish you remembered an earlier part. This is perfectly normal. The book is written that way. I want you, the reader, to have the chance to draw conclusions for yourself as much as possible. Then your learning will be stronger. In other words, you won't be able to draw all the conclusions until you've read the last page. The 'Lego figure' isn't complete until we've put all the pieces together. Only then will you feel that it all fits together.

To help you, I have therefore tried to write as straightforwardly as possible. On the other hand, this makes the book quite 'dense' - there is a lot on every page.

The structure that will guide and constitute the Lego pieces and their related discussions gives the book the following layout:

1.  **Brief introduction to the book** paints the background and purpose of the book and describes how we can read it to assimilate the content in a good way.

2.  **Change!?** tries to preserve what change and change management is, and what it is not, how we can understand change in a way that enables us to work with it and bring about improvements. The chapter also defines some key concepts that help us better to understand and apply the rest of the book's content.

3.  **Pressures for change in large and small** explores issues related to what pressures for change are, how they can be analysed and understood, what types of pressures for change exist and how they affect organisations.

4.  **Organisations' results and changed behaviours** answers questions about the difference between results, benefits and behaviour, and describes how these are interrelated. It also describes how we can understand these relationships to understand what leads to what when change takes place.

5.  **Magnitude and stakeholders** provides answers on how we can understand who our different stakeholder groups and key stakeholders are. This allows us to get an idea of the magnitude of our change.

6.  **Tackling change** describes how we can combine different approaches and strategies to bring about change.

7.  **The work of the change manager** answers what change managers need to do to ensure that a change actually leads to evolved behaviours and realised benefits, i.e. improved organisational outcomes.

8.  **Organising change** presents how we can organise change in different ways depending on, for example, the type of change and the resources available for change management.

9.  **Summary and conclusions** present the main points of the book and provide suggestions for further reading in the form of notes for those who wish to delve deeper.

Given this structure, it is natural that we can read the book in different ways. However, I have an original thought in the way it was written.

In a construction project, work preparations are made for various complex elements. The purpose of a work preparation is to identify future difficulties and thus to know better how to carry out a task in the best possible way. It is a way of trying to think through what to do to avoid problems later. It goes without saying that there are many things to keep track of when building something with many parts and people involved. Just such an obvious thing as that we must think about where different conduits go so that water and electricity lines don't collide with each other - underground, in walls and in ceilings, or that the concrete base slab might have to dry for several weeks and then many other parts of the operation can mostly wait.

> The natural way to read the book is from top to bottom. This gives us a natural flow that helps us think through change from different perspectives and logically helps us avoid problems later. Moreover, if we apply the content to an actual change we are dealing with today, the insights are deepened, and we learn how to apply 'work preparation for change'.

To help with the application, I have broken down in each chapter concrete questions that I think we need to answer to get the effects of change. These questions are linked to each area - and therefore chapter - and numbered. In total, there are 39 of them. I've also added an empty page for your personal reflections after each chapter.

In the last chapter - in Figure 9.1 - all questions are collected. By answering them, we make a working preparation for the change. When we do that, it becomes clear what we are facing and how we should approach the change. So, anyone who is about to start a change, is in the middle of one, or has just finished one, can answer these questions on an ongoing basis to deepen his learning.

As I mentioned, the book has a bias towards strategy, strategic change and therefore comprehensive change. Much change of this type is driven, led or coordinated to some extent from the centre. Those who are faced with driving strategic or large-scale change are therefore likely to gain more from certain parts of the book (e.g. pressure for change, reasoning about goal analysis and benefit realisation and how we can organise change). Those who are about to tackle large-scale and/or strategic change need to be well grounded in the answers to these questions, or aware that the answers do not exist and then start looking for them.

Those who want to tackle a smaller or more limited change, for example in their group, do not need to answer all the questions equally exhaustively. Nor does that person need to convince as many other people as possible of the purpose and value of the change. Some questions, probably about the range of involvement and the transfer of change to the business, may seem less applicable in such cases than, for example, questions about change activities. Details about the work of the change manager probably do too. However, whatever the type of change we are pursuing, all questions need to be answered - albeit in the shortest possible manner.

In addition to working with the book practically, and working with the questions, we can read parts of the book in which we might be particularly interested: stakeholder analysis, change strategy, models, methods or communication in change, organising change, etc.

Regardless of how we read the book, my ambition and hope is that in the future we can use it as a workbook and reference book when working with change in our organisations.

# 2. Change!?

Change. It's the word on almost everyone's lips, but what does it really mean? Is change something we are exposed to? Is it something we drive ourselves? Is it both? Whichever way we look at change, we can see that the world is changing, markets are changing, organisations are changing and people are changing. If we look at the atomic level, change is a force of nature, and it can probably be felt at the 'human' level as well. Just by the passage of time, changes occur in different ways and at different levels. All organisations and their members have to deal with this in one way or another. At least if we want to remain successful or relevant.

The Russian philosopher Nikolai Berdayev has a vivid way of describing change, and of relating to the changes that are constantly taking place around us:

> What you need to do in every moment of your life is to put an end to the old world and start a new world.[4]

This is a philosophically beautiful formulation. What makes it particularly appealing is that, in addition to its painterly description, it is also correct in substance. Every day we need to learn something new and 'unlearn' something old. This learning and unlearning also applies to organisations because they are populated by people. However, to address how we can work with change in organisations, learning and unlearning, we need to be more precise about a few things related to change as a concept and as a phenomenon.

In this chapter, we will therefore clarify how we see change in general and how we need to take it seriously, as well as how change relates to change management and other concepts floating around in this universe of constant evolution.

# Change in a big way and in earnest

This book is about change. About change for real. Change with real impact. Although I am an advocate of change and believe that anything less than change is impossible for an organisation that wants to become and hopefully remain successful, I am sceptical about change. Or perhaps more correctly, because of my seriousness I am sceptical. Change is the most common management tool to solve a problem, but it is far from certain that change is the best solution. Often it may be a matter of doing what we said we would do instead. If sales are poor, sell more! If quality is poor, work on quality. Change may not be the answer. Instead, keep at it. Work on the things that need improvement. But it's not as popular to press ahead. It doesn't sound like as much fun. Change is more fun. Then there is *innovation*, which in my conceptual world is included in change because it aims to turn a creative idea into something that finds its use or market[5]. Sounds like fun, but innovation is not a one-size-fits-all solution either.

Change and innovation feel more exciting than pressing ahead or scrimping, more creative. It feels more efficient too. We're doing something, right here and right now. That creates some engagement (hopefully). So, we launch another change initiative, transformation programme, or develop a new innovation framework. Why not? That's interesting. Yes, but is it relevant?

This reflects an all-too-common view, even though I'm mocking. As we shall see, there are several problems with this view.

Change is simply in vogue. Hardly a day goes by when I don't hear someone say that change is happening so fast right now. One change after another is considered both revolutionary and rapid, perhaps radical.[6] Or why not *disruptive*.[7] Sometimes it seems that few things are as important as having read about Joseph Schumpeter's concept of *Creative destruction*.[8] It is certainly true that change is massive and rapid from some perspectives. There is support in the literature that this is so and that the conditions for success in organisations over time have been affected by increasing pressures to change.[9] However, it could also be that 'not everything is going faster, but the amount of change is increasing'.[10]

One explanation for why it feels like it's moving fast, one I personally like, is that maybe it's not the speed of change that's increasing. Maybe it's the quantity. *Combinatorics* is the branch of mathematics that deals with how different parts combine and relate to each other. If there are 20 things that need to change, it probably feels like change is happening fast. However, it's not clear that it is happening faster than it was five years ago, or that each of these changes is going fast or accelerating.

From this point of view, we could therefore talk about *combinatorial change*: many changes are interconnected. The reason why faster change and combinatorial change are important to keep apart is that the solutions to the two problems are slightly different. If the *pace of change* increases, we face an acceleration problem and need to solve it by increasing the speed. If the *variety of change* increases, we face a selection problem and need to prioritise and, not least, de-prioritise, i.e. express what we should *not* do. That is different from trying to change faster. By de-prioritising, we also create the opportunity for ourselves to invest more time and increase the pace of the few changes we choose to tackle.

That said, the speed of technological development is hard to overestimate.[11] There is no doubt about that. Still, how much impact does change really have on the way organisations fundamentally operate? We don't always know. There is an impact, no doubt, but is it decisive? Do we have to manage change? Do we have to do it now? What about forces other than the evolution of technology? Globalisation has slowed or stalled according to many experts.[12] So has urbanisation, at least in the traditional Western world, with access to the internet enabling, for example, teleworking and other things needed to move citizens out of urban areas. Covid-19 and an increased focus on sustainability have weakened both globalisation and urbanisation, which until now have been seen almost as laws of nature. What are the implications for organisations?

At a time when change is on everyone's lips, it is important to decide what change is. We often use words like change, development or transformation. Everyone should be working on change, on development and everyone is in the midst of a major transformation. What these terms mean in different contexts is often unclear. And it is equally unclear whether we get any impact from all these change efforts. Are we getting happier customers? Better quality? Increased competitiveness? Better care? Unfortunately, we rarely know what the effects are. For some reason, the results of change often seem less interesting than figuring out what the future will look like. We need to come to grips with this.

All these concepts of change that we're waffling on about can be examined, but not out of academic interest, we can do that another time, but because we want to get better at this 'change thing'.

I therefore want to be clear that this book does not aim to sort out previous research definitions, contrast perspectives and debate, and then set a common definition on which everyone can agree. I will give my view - with the strengths and weaknesses that implies.

> My view of change is rooted in much of the research. My experience of having worked in strategy, governance and change for over 20 years and with nearly 200 organisations also plays a major role. I don't believe my picture is 'the truth'. I don't believe there is a truth. Apart from that, I will try to clarify a couple of things I think are important to clarify to make sure that change gets real in organisations.

We can certainly argue that in all modern times, individuals with some kind of responsibility for an organisation have found that change is fast paced. Electrification undoubtedly had a major impact on organisations. So did school reform, railroads, automobiles, processors, and international trade agreements. There is no doubt that environments have changed for organisations throughout the ages. Nor is there any debate about whether organisations should change. Everyone knows they need to do so.

What is perhaps different is that historically the important questions about change have been about *what* should change and, to some extent, *when* this should happen. The closer we get to today, the *what* question has become more important because of the variety of change. The focus has also become increasingly on *how* change should be led. The answer to the question when is often given: preferably yesterday.

Today, it is relatively easy to identify external threats and opportunities that drive change. The analysis itself is not a complex task. However, we can see that precisely because it is relatively easy to identify external threats and opportunities, or organisational strengths and weaknesses, priorities and de-prioritisation become more important. The variety of change in different combinations means that in most organisations we have a selection problem. As a result, the big questions about change are a little different today than they were just 20 years ago.

> Today I feel that the most burning issue regarding change is: How will we find the time to change enough and fast enough? What and how should we (de-)prioritise? How do we speed up change? How can we drive change all the time without chaos? To manage these, an organisation needs a common language for change.

## Adapting and driving change

In her book *Change Masters*[13], the American change researcher Rosabeth Moss Kanter distinguished between 'Change to us' and 'Change by us'. That is, changes in the external world that affect us and changes that we try to drive in or from the internal world. Just by using two different prepositions together with change ('to' or 'by') she makes two things clear: First, she shows that we can see change from two different perspectives, that which drives us and that which we drive. Secondly, and less explicitly, she helps us to understand how much difference there is in organisations' views of change. Some organisations see change as something they are essentially affected by and must deal with. Others see change as something they own and can harness to their advantage. The first example has a more reactive approach and the second a more proactive one. Are we affected by change, or do we drive change? Is change essentially an ally, or is it essentially an enemy? It does not need to be justified that many organisations that see change as an ally are also generally more successful at both managing change reactively and driving it proactively.

However, of course, an organisation does not only work with proactive or reactive change. What is important for organisations to learn is which issues they need to manage proactively and which they can manage more reactively. The more proactive is not more right, although some may think it sounds better. On the contrary we need to learn to understand and use both perspectives. However, there is a perception that it is cooler to be a 'game changer', that it is cooler to be a 'first mover'. It's definitely cooler to be a change agent than a laggard - the one who stands by and waits. However, is it necessary for everyone to be the first mover? That everyone should be an industry leader? That everyone should be 'disruptive'? Of course not. [14]

Somewhere here, in a hype about change that sometimes lacks balance, much of change loses what should be the most important thing when it comes to developing an organisation and ensuring its success over time: a strategy perspective.

What do I mean by that? Well, to understand whether change is necessary or beneficial to realise - reactively or proactively - we need to understand what creates success for the organisation over time with the limited resources available. If change does not help the organisation to become more successful, then scepticism is clearly justified. The conformist plays a crucial role. In other cases, for example if a new law (such as GDPR) has been introduced and we need to ensure that we are complying with that law, there is no room for questioning. Different changes have different motives and purposes.

> Strategy, I tend to define in a simplified way as the work of creating an organisation that is successful over time with the limited resources available.[15] From this perspective, strategy should lead change. We therefore need to understand an organisation's strategy to assess whether change is necessary or not.

Some organisations need to be at the forefront. They may have a so-called resource-based approach. They have a valuable and rare, resource that is difficult to imitate, and that suits their business and that they can exploit to create competitiveness.[16] These may be organisations working to maintain product leadership; working in research and development and needing to find ways to proactively change products and services to maintain a *temporary monopoly*. In such cases, change - or innovation, which is perhaps a more common term in these types of organisations - needs to be a central part of how the whole organisation works. For others, who may be in less volatile and/or technologically advanced, or research-intensive markets and industries where the pressure to change is lower, for example because the industry is more mature or the business is local in geographical terms, it may be less relevant. Why should anyone rush to be first out if it is not necessary? Changing an organisation to be first to market takes a lot of resources, and no organisation has unlimited resources. Being a 'trail blazer' involves many risks and does not contribute to the competitiveness of all organisations.

## Strategy, change and fit

Strategy work aims to ensure that we as an organisation stay relevant. The strategic fit between the world around us, the market we are in, and the organisation we are, with all that that implies, is absolutely critical.[17] Lack of fit is the same as a *change gap*. In practical terms, such a gap means that we as an organisation are not delivering what customers or citizens want and/or are entitled to receive. Anyone who does not pay attention to what is expected of customers will sooner or later be left without customers or at least be subjected to massive criticism (assuming he has a monopoly-like position, as some public services do).

One way to understand this fit between an organisation and its environment is to take advantage of linear algebra. In mathematics, we learn that a straight line can be described mathematically as $y = kx + m$. In the formula, $k$ is a constant that corresponds to the slope of the line. It is also called the coefficient of direction. $m$ is a constant corresponding to the value where the line intersects the y-axis. *The x and y variables* in the function give the points for x and y on the graph.

In figure 2.1 below I try to illustrate this.

Figure 2.1 Fit and change gap between environment, industry and organisation

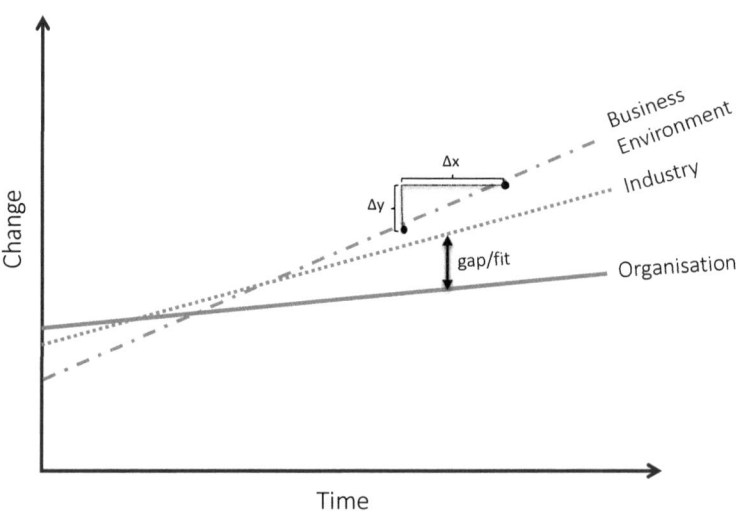

What does this mean in relation to changes in the world and for our organisation?

Changes occur over time. Translating the equation into 'change language' we can put change on the y-axis and time on the x-axis. $k$, the slope of the line is the pace of change. The steeper the slope, the more extensive and rapid the change. Change in mathematics is also called 'delta' (after the Greek letter $\Delta$ as a capital letter and $\delta$ as a lower case). The steeper the slope, the greater the change on the y axis, and thus, the greater the delta ($\Delta y$).

In practice, the lines are not straight. Change happens in different ways - jerky and steady, increasing and decreasing, seasonal, etc. Moreover, we know from physics that disorder in the world (entropy) is constantly increasing.[18] This is what I was referring to at the beginning of this chapter when I said that change at the atomic level is a law of nature. The law of nature is the second theorem of thermodynamics, to be precise. Nothing gets less messy with time at the particle level. However, in my example, it's easier with straight lines.

My feeling is that this increasing messiness is something that many people feel in organisations as well. I have that feeling myself at times. The mathematical formula for entropy - the order of a system - includes delta, the sign of change, and shows how it is continually increasing. For the mathematically inclined, the formula looks like this: $\delta S/\delta t \geq 0$.

To illustrate increasing change and the gap in change that occurs between an entity that is changing and one that is not changing at the same pace, the image serves a purpose.

We can see in Figure 2.1 that both the outside world and the industry have a steeper slope than the organisation. This means that both are changing faster than the organisation. By extension, this means that the *change gap* between the organisation and the outside world and the industry will increase if the organisation does not act. In other words, this means that the products or services the organisation provides, their way of working, their values, etc. are becoming less and less relevant every moment. And that's what it looks

17

like for most organisations. Few organisations are likely to change faster than their customers change their needs, expectations and requirements.

The implication of this is that whether or not we ourselves believe we need to change as an organisation, we always need to look at the outside world (e.g. society at large) and the industry (e.g. customers, competitors, suppliers) in one way or another and see what they expect of us. Otherwise, we risk quickly becoming irrelevant and eventually going out of business.

What can also be explained by this picture is that old organisations that have existed for a longer period almost always have a change gap. The gap is that the solutions developed, the way they have organised themselves, etc. were developed many years ago and in those years the world and the industry have changed. Unfortunately, the disaster does not end there. The longer an organisation operates without addressing the major structural or cultural changes that are necessary, the greater the *strategy debt* it incurs. The gap widens. Fit (relevance) diminishes.

If we are an old and large organisation with a proud heritage, a strong culture, a lot of structures, processes and systems that have evolved over time, change will therefore be more difficult than if there is not so much existing to break with.[19] What complicates things further for old, existing and dominant organisations (incumbents) is that when a new player enters the market, they do not enter at the point where the incumbent organisations are ($m_0$). They enter at the level that is expected by the outside world and the market at a given time ($m_1$). They have probably done an analysis of the customer's needs today and tried to meet them as best they can. In other words, new entrants usually have a smaller change gap than the old ones and are therefore likely to be better adapted to deliver what the market wants at that moment. It is then up to the incumbent to drive change that benefits from the advantages of being an incumbent, perhaps in being large and heavy. Such things might be brand loyalty and the credibility that comes from having been around for a long time, a track record, or economies of scale and costs

18

that a smaller company can never achieve. In such a situation, strategic change becomes something quite different from that of a challenger start-up.

Changes must therefore be related to the actual situation and strategy of the organisation. In some cases, neither the industry nor the world around it may change significantly. Do we then need to pursue something as difficult as change, which may cost more than it seems worth?

From a strategy perspective, we need to understand that change is not just about passively adapting to external factors (change 'to' us). We can increase competitiveness, or as in the public sector, get more out of it in the long run, if we make the right changes (change 'by' us). However, there must always be an argument for why we should change. The argument cannot be 'because we need to change'. In the science of logic, and in the world of Excel for that matter, we call it circular reasoning. We need to change because we need to change. This is just weird, and it's soon seen for what it is. Another wacky argument I also hear is that others are doing it. That kind of 'teenage motivation' (everyone else does it) doesn't sit well with a strategy perspective. So we need to understand more about the purpose, the benefits of the change and its impact on competitiveness if we are to take change seriously.

## Change management

I believe that an organisation's ability to manage change is one of the most important capabilities for long-term success. Another basic assumption is that a structured and systematic approach is sometimes a prerequisite for change to generate specific improvements in performance. This certainly *does not* mean that all change that occurs in organisations is managed in a systematic, or even conscious, way, or that change is managed at all. On the contrary, most of organisations' overall change is probably rather unconscious, and just happens on an ongoing basis as employees learn new things and develop their ways of working or offerings to customers - without any particular effort being made to do so. That's amazing, of course. Who doesn't want to improve without having to make an extra effort?

> The most effective changes are therefore often those that have not been given special attention, but which nevertheless increase the organisation's performance or competitiveness by teaching employees new and more functional behaviours.

Creating an organisation that is constantly learning and evolving is essential for long-term success. I've written about this before in the book *Advancing strategy through behavioural psychology*.[20] However, in this book, the focus is not on how we create learning and smart organisations. Instead, we concentrate on how we can lead or drive through changes that require a little more care, systematicity or consideration.

The approaches, methods and models we use in organisations for this type of intervention, which are designed to deliver specific improvements in performance, can be called *change management*. In other words, we invest resources (e.g. hours worked, money, materials) in initiatives and/or projects that aim to change employee behaviours; behaviours that in turn generate actual benefits (improvements in organisational performance) that would not have occurred if the investment in resources had not also occurred.

The reason I describe how I see this is that I feel we interpret and use the concepts in many different ways. We need to clarify and understand these concepts better to be better at leading change.

## Change management and related concepts

Many things that are generally considered as change are for me rather tools to bring about 'the real change'. A reorganisation or the introduction of a new IT system - to take two common examples - are tools to get employees to change their behaviour. They are not the change itself. Neither a reorganisation nor a system change creates benefits on its own. In fact, to ensure that the benefits reach the customer or the business, employees have to change what they do, their behaviour. For example, start working in the new system. This means that we must get down to a behavioural level when we change a business. Change management is fundamentally about changing people's behaviour.

A common misconception is that change management is something soft and fluffy. This is what we sometimes call *'the soft sides of change'*. In order to achieve real change, i.e. to change behaviour and secure benefits, a change process must also have 'hard' parts. A structured process with frequent follow-ups on real data is a prerequisite. So, something completely different from soft and fluffy. If we do not measure and follow up, we cannot possibly say whether benefits have been realised or not. A little communication, training and an enthusiastic inspirer won't be enough even halfway.

Furthermore, working with change and change management is perceived as creative. If nothing else, it sounds creative to say that you work with change. This too is, at least in part, a misconception. A creative change manager is likely to be more successful than an 'uncreative' one. However, this is true, as far as I can tell, in many professions. Creative salespeople are certainly more successful in creating value for customers and for their own organisation than uncreative ones. Creative footballers are likely to produce better results on the pitch than those who are not creative. The list of professions could go on and on.

So, what is change management? Change management, like strategy work, is an art and a craft that requires systematics, persistence and patience.[21] It is not possible to realise real change without doing the job properly and involving a crucial part of the people affected. The creative part is finding new ways to progress. It is about being creative about how we work in the future and finding new ways to motivate others to change. Defining how an organisation will change, the target image for the future, is a very small part of change management. Perhaps it is even more accurate to say that defining the vision is rather part of the early strategy work. And the perception that it is soft probably lies in the fact that we need to understand what people can and want if we are to help them change. If we don't get employees to learn and change, then we won't get any improvements either. Fortunately, change management is something we can become good at by practicing, like any other craft. No one is born to be a good change manager. It takes a great deal of experience and *deliberate practice*[22] to become an expert at it.

Change management, in this book, is therefore used for a structured and systematic approach to moving an organisation from one point to another: in Figure 2.1 above, it means one point on the graph to another point on the graph, to the right - because time only goes in one direction. Ideally, we also want to be higher up the Y-axis (a higher $m$) and with a smaller gap to the outside world and the industry than before.

The *organisation* we want to relocate does not have to be seen as a large or whole organisation, such as a company, group or government agency. Organisation in this context is best understood as at least two people with a common purpose or goal, who need to work together in one way or another to achieve that common purpose or goal. It does not need to be more sophisticated than that. In practice, the 'organisation' we want to change may have 10, 1000 or 100,000 employees, be located in one country or in 100 countries, have a relatively simple structure or have an extremely complex corporate structure. These are the kinds of factors we need to consider when thinking through change, how to approach it and how to ensure that benefits are realised. However, it does not determine how we define organisation as a concept. Analysing and understanding how different organisations affect change is something we will learn later in the book.

A concept related to change management is *business improvement*. It usually includes all activities, initiatives or attempts to develop one or more parts of a business.[23] Business development is thus broader and describes more or all the things we do to develop the business in some way.

*Business development* is another term that usually refers to a set of tasks aimed at creating growth within and between organisations.[24] By growth we traditionally talk about growth at the top or bottom line of the income statement: increasing turnover (revenue, sales) or profit (profitability, return). Business development is thus close to economic growth in some form and not infrequently sales are part of this. Acting in a systematic and structured way to achieve this growth is likely to be an advantage, but not a requirement.

A modern term, which may make sense to us, is *business transformation*. Business transformation generally has two characteristics. It deals with deep structures and it is typically driven by a change in the world around us.[25] Business transformation thus has a somewhat reactive approach and is likely to involve change of a more substantial nature.

Finally, in some contexts there is a tendency to confuse change management with project management. *Project management* is a discipline or a way of organising work to initiate, plan, implement, follow up and complete work by delivering something specific.[26] Projects are often managed based on what is to be delivered - 'deliverables' - and whether the delivery is made on time, at the right cost and with the right quality.

In change management, the aim is to achieve an improvement in performance. This means that we manage for benefits, not for deliverables. In simple terms, we can say that project management aims to 'put stuff on the quay' and change management is about 'carrying stuff in from the quay' and ensuring that it starts to be used by people in the organisation. So, it's quite different. However, certainly there are changes that are driven as projects. It's even common. Then, in addition to deliverables such as a new organisation, a new process or a new system, the project, which then becomes a *change project*, needs to ensure that concrete benefits are realised as a result of the deliverables.

What I focus on in this book is change management, leading and driving through change: a structured and systematic approach to moving an organisation from one stage to another and thereby achieving performance improvements.

To work suitably with change management, a number of criteria must be met. The purpose of the criteria is to provide descriptive features required for real change to occur and concrete results to improve. If we want to create positive impact on results, there is good support in research and proven experience that we need to do the following things.

We need to:

* Identify the organisational outcomes we want to influence and get an idea of how much we want to influence them, i.e. define the benefits.

* Specify which behaviours of which employees affect these results positively and negatively, so we know which behaviours we want to influence.

* Involve the key stakeholders and critical mass of the organisation required to change the behaviours that deliver the desired performance improvements.

* Involve these stakeholders as early as possible to allow them to take ownership of our common change. Ask many people if they understand where we are going and how they can contribute and ask often.

* Perform skills development interventions targeted at improving the specific behaviours that affect the outcomes we want to improve and evaluate the impact of the interventions.

* Create a business case built on benefits that are the effects of changed employee behaviours. Set the benefits against the costs associated with changing these employee behaviours.

* Check with the business and any management team/steering committee on an ongoing basis to ensure that they believe in the solution and the benefits the change will bring. Update the business case based on the input from the reconciliations.

* Ensure that your change activities are targeted at clarifying expectations, developing competencies, creating opportunities and/or reinforcing the deficit behaviour of one or more stakeholders. Otherwise, change resistance is created.

* Evaluate and reflect on an ongoing basis on the change activities carried out and their impact on the change, and on the results (realisation of benefits).

* Generate change activities based on what evaluations show has worked - not what you think needs to be done in advance. Don't plan too much; plans quickly become invalid. When planning, plan from the end, decide what will be delivered when and count backwards. Then decide what to do here and now.

* Offer feedback in an educational and appealing way - preferably visually - to the business as to what is happening in the change work, what results it has produced so far and how the people in the business can help.

If we do this, we have a good chance that the benefits that are the purpose of the hard work of change will be realised.

Words have a meaning. To avoid talking past each other in organisations, it is good to be strict in the choice of words and to have a common language. That's why we've looked at a couple of terms related to change. The relevant thing is of course not what something is called 'really' but whether it helps us to develop our organisations. Whatever words we choose, there is a benefit in having the same words for things that we put under the umbrella of management, leadership and governance within an organisation. Having common words helps us to avoid misunderstandings about concepts and responsibilities, and we can instead focus on the things in the business we want to change and improve.

In this book, the investigation of words also serves a purpose for our further learning. We need to set some definitions to understand and be able to apply what is in the book.

## Change and concrete improvements

Change management thus aims to create something new. Sometimes we talk in organisations in a way that makes me think that change itself is the goal. When we do, we allow ourselves to become vague and unclear about what we expect from the organisation and its people in to contribute to the overall purpose or goal of the organisation. Clear expectations are an important component in getting employees to want and be able to contribute to the development of their organisation and its success. As I mentioned above, change needs to have other goals than changing something. Change needs to realise concrete improvements that reduce the change gap, for example developing better products or providing better care. We need to be clear about what the change will lead to.

> There are studies from different fields of research that examine what change is and is not, how we succeed, why we fail, etc. A common conclusion, which we often know from our own experience, is that organisations rarely succeed in achieving the results they want from their changes. We don't get there for a variety of reasons. Many initiatives are not completed with the same enthusiasm with which they were started. We don't get there. We need to fix that.

There is strategy research that shows that organisations lose large parts of their competitiveness and profits precisely because they fail to realise their ideas.[27] There are other studies that show that between 70 and 90% of all strategic changes fail to achieve their goals.[28] There are organisational studies that show that culture change fails to achieve the desired changes 90% of the time.[29] There are studies that find that change projects involving new technologies fail 40-80% of the time. Studies in business management show that 90% of all governance, measurement and KPI-related changes fail and that changes involving the introduction of Lean in various forms fail in about 80% of cases.[30] In conclusion, the sage of leading change and Harvard professor John Kotter states what we ourselves can deduce from the above example: 7/10 changes never get realised as intended, nor do they lead to the results as intended.[31]

Regardless of the field of knowledge, the research shows that organisations have a hard time realising the ideas for improvement that are identified. One reason for the low target achievement may be that we in organisations are bad at setting targets for change and therefore miss the target in so many cases. In some cases, this is certainly true. However, in many cases it is probably that we are not leading change in a way that maximises our chances of success. Whatever the reason, there is clearly room for improvement for many.

What these studies reflect is what a layman would express as 'change is hard'. I hear that quite often. However, difficult is a difficult concept, which I personally have difficulty with (to play with words). It's very vague. What does difficult really mean? It must be put in relation to something.

I think there is a need to nuance 'the difficult' in relation to change. Because my experience is a bit different. Personally, I don't perceive change as difficult. Difficult for me is close to complicated, convoluted, difficult to understand, unravel, get a grip on, etc. I do not consider change to be that. At least not usually. Above all, I don't think that's why we fail to change to the extent that the studies indicate. However, I do think it is demanding. It's about 'working the floor'. Going out into the business and pushing. It often takes longer time and more resources of various kinds (commitment included) than we initially envisage to get through what we want to get through, and thereby get the benefits of the change.

For those who are to lead change, what Angela Duckworth, a psychologist and professor at the University of Pennsylvania, calls *grit* is therefore important.[32] Grit and similar traits have been studied under many names, over many decades:[33] Some examples of concepts are *persistence*, *perseverance* and *self-efficacy*. I personally think 'thick forehead' is an apt description. The Finnish concept of *sisu* is also a word I like in this context.

> Whatever we call 'grit', I see it as a declared willingness and determination to work towards long-term goals, an ability to buckle down and keep going, and not give up despite setbacks, fears or failures.

Or why not be inspired by the Irish writer Samuel Becket in his novel *The Unspeakable*: "I cannot go on, I'll go on."[34]

Then, of course, there is the risk of becoming too attached to your goal and not giving up. That's when a systematic approach can help us decide whether it's worth holding on to or whether it's time to give up. I think it is difficult to make that choice without structure and a systematic approach. It leads us to underestimate or overestimate the factors that come into play in both the short and long term. For example, a common problem is that we overestimate the situation as it is here and now and lose the long-term perspective when we make choices based on intuition. It also causes us to lose the link between change and strategy.

I understand if the insights delivered above: that organisations rarely succeed in change, that it is demanding and that an extraordinary effort is critical, feel discouraging and burdensome. Humans are evolved to take the path of least resistance. Evolution has drilled us in it – physically and cognitively. But we can see an upside for those individuals and organisations that become good at leading change. And this book aims to do just that: to improve our ability to lead that which requires a little more.

# Summary: Change?!

In this chapter, we have discussed how we view change broadly and seriously, and how change relates to change management.

### How do we look at change broadly and seriously?

⋆ The world is changing, markets are changing, organisations are changing and individuals are changing. Change is a force of nature. An organisation that wants to be successful over time needs continually to change in order to remain relevant to those it serves (e.g. customers, users, society). Learning is then critical.

### How does change relate to change management?

⋆ Change can be understood from two different perspectives: change on the 'outside' that organisations 'suffer' and change on the 'inside' that we try to lead to adapt the organisation to what is happening in the outside world. Change management is a systematic and structured way of moving an organisation from one stage to another. It is a way of trying to maintain a 'fit' with the ever-changing world outside the organisation (to remain relevant).

# Reflections: Change!?

# 3. Pressure for change in large and small

Once we have defined the concepts of change and change management, and can relate them to each other, we can understand what drives change. Our world is changing. There is no doubt about it. There is also no doubt that we need to relate to the changes that are happening around us.

The need for change that the world we operate in creates can be called pressure for change. Pressures for change exist both externally (the world and industry) and internally (organisations and people). We understand pressures for change by paying attention to what is happening around us. Austrian-American neurologist and Nobel laureate in physiology or medicine, Eric Kandel can teach us something about our attention. He writes:

> I would like to develop a reductionist approach to the problem of attention
> by focusing on how place cells ... create an enduring spatial map only when
> an organism pays attention to its surroundings.[35]

The place cells Kandel is referring to are the neurons in the hippocampus of our brain that become active when we arrive at a particular place in a particular environment. Place cells are thought collectively to create a cognitive representation of that place in that environment. We sometimes call this a *cognitive map*,[36] or layman's 'mental image'. Place cells have the unique ability to change the way they send impulses based on how the environment changes. In short, they help us to understand our place in a context. For an organisation, this kind of understanding is crucial. If organisations become better at paying attention to their environment and their place in that environment, individuals are likely to send different signals to each other.

In this chapter, we therefore explore how organisations can understand the world and its impact on organisations; the dynamics and impact of different sectors on organisations; the evolution of organisations over time; how people's learning creates pressure for change in organisations; and finally, how the pressures for change at these different levels interact.

# Business environments' influence

Different organisations experience pressures for change differently. Pressure can come from a variety of factors. Organisations in different sectors, countries etc. naturally experience pressure for change from different sources in different ways. Nevertheless, there are general descriptions that help us understand how to analyse and manage the pressures for change that we face. In this book, I explore change pressures at four levels: environment, industry, organisation and individual.

## PEST and macro factors

At the most overall level, we can talk about pressures for change in the business environment. What in economic terms are called *macro factors*.[37] Macro factors are large, fundamental trends or tendencies that affect all organisations, in one way or another. This means that no matter what industry we are in, what type of organisation we are or what geography we are in, we are affected to some degree.

One way to analyse the world to understand macro trends is to carry out a so-called PEST analysis (sometimes called PESTEL, or similar variants).[38] PEST is an acronym for Political, Economic, Socio-cultural (Social) and Technological factors. The point of the framework is that it helps us to categorise different factors in the world around us and thus gain a better understanding of what is exerting pressure for change and how.

> The PEST factors that affect an organisation, affect its ability to conduct its business in the way it intended. In doing so, they create the conditions for how the organisation needs to operate, and place demands on the organisation to change.

*Political factors* consist of things that affect the organisation and relate to the political situation, governance in a country, political security, elections or other situations related to politics and legislation in a particular region or country. A politically governed organisation is likely to be affected by many political factors to a greater extent than others. The same is true for organisations doing business with politically controlled activities (Business to Government, B2G). Some examples that many have been affected by in recent years are the way governments and agencies are trying to get at Big Tech (the big tech organisations Google (Alphabet), Facebook (Meta), Amazon, Microsoft) and their near monopoly positions, environmental legislation at EU level, the uncertainty and conflicts in Russia and its neighbourhood. At a more local level, we can see increased political activity and willingness to regulate for a more sustainable society and an increased circular economy, as well as increased national protectionism.

*Economic factors* relate to the economic growth of countries and regions, trade agreements and balances between countries and regions, inflation, currencies, interest rates, commodity prices and other economic factors that drive or inhibit development. Just as political organisations are affected by political factors, so organisations of an economic or financial nature: banks, insurance companies and other financial actors have a greater need to change in response to pressures for change from economic factors. We have seen, for example, the introduction of the Basel and Solvency regulations to ensure that banks and insurance organisations have a stable capital base and good liquidity or backing. These regulations have evolved in different versions since the mid-1990s and exert pressure for change on financial institutions to meet the requirements. Another important factor in our global society is currencies. For exporting organisations, the rise and fall of currencies is an important factor affecting their financial situation and thus their ability to develop.

*Social (socio-cultural) factors* have to do with things like demographics, values, income distribution and trend sensitivity. Organisations that sell products or services directly to private end consumers (Business to Consumer, B2C) are often strongly influenced by these types of factors. Two

33

examples are clothing and fashion in general. There it is of course important to know where and how we position our brand and what we think we can offer based on the values or income distribution of an area, an area we can then call market. It is equally important to know how old or young the people in that market are. The reason for the pressure for change on organisations producing consumer products is simply put that end users are generally more sensitive to trends than organisations. We wear the clothes, the watch or drive the car. The products say something about us as people. We want them to represent us. However, it is not as important to the purchasing department of a hospital or public transport company if workwear is 'trendy'. However, the one influence that does exist, even for large heavy industrial organisations selling to other companies (business to business, B2B), and which relates to demographics is, for example, the availability of trained staff. Northvolt's battery factory in Skellefteå in northern Sweden (which is just one of many ventures in the region) presents a challenge in finding enough skilled people fast enough. Not because the skills are not available in the region, but because the demand for well-educated people in the region exceeds the supply. Skellefteå municipality and industrial companies even go on 'recruitment campaigns' to Stockholm to attract workers. Demographics matter.

*Technological factors* have to do with access to research, technical solutions, types of technology and the like that allow us to offer something unique or to do work in new, smarter ways. When we have access to technology, it puts pressure on us as an organisation to change. The same is true when others have technology we do not have. Technological factors are particularly driving for organisations operating in technology-intensive, research-heavy organisations or organisations that are at the forefront of technological development where access to the latest technology is needed to fulfil missions. There is no doubt that technology affects all organisations. Digitalisation, a technological factor born out of automation and which will eventually help to lead us into robotisation, has made enormous strides since the turn of the millennium. Digitalisation presents both opportunities and threats for many organisations. We can also see that Covid-19 in 2020-2022 brought major changes to the way we collaborate within and between organisations. For example, with the help of various digital solutions such as Teams, Zoom and Google Meet.[39] Arguably, education, in primary and secondary schools and universities, took greater steps towards digitisation in two years than they did in the previous 20 years. This clearly creates pressure for change.

## Macro trends and megatrends

All these types of factors affect all organisations - large and small. In most studies and in the media, specific macro-level trends are sometimes singled out for special attention, such as globalisation, digitalisation, urbanisation and the circular economy. We can call these *megatrends*[40] or perhaps even gigatrends. These are trends that have developed in a macro-environment over a long period of time and can therefore be considered relatively stable over time. We can then refine, nuance, adapt them to our organisation or sort them into one or more of the PEST headings.

It is worth mentioning that although PEST factors, and thus megatrends, have so far been described as separate factors, they interact in many different ways. Access to capital is a prerequisite for advanced technological development (economic and technological factors interact). Similarly, social trends and tendencies in society, such as values, are a breeding ground for policies in a given region. Scattered unemployment combined with low economic growth in an area creates difficult conditions to escape from a difficult situation for many who live there. This easily leads to dissatisfaction with the prevailing conditions and sets the stage for political trends and laws that have far-reaching consequences for many. Brexit is an example of something similar.

It's probably impossible to keep track of all these connections, and that's not the point. We need to understand the factors that affect our organisation and how they relate to us. My thought is that when we do a PEST analysis, or environmental analysis using the PEST framework, we need to ask ourselves how these factors affect us and how they interact.

A common way to do such an analysis is to try to describe, for example, PEST factors to create a snapshot of what is happening in the world and then sort them under the respective headings. If a particular 'heading' (e.g. Political) has no trend, we can use deduction to realise that there should probably be some sort of trend there too. In this way, the various P, E, S and T factors help us to create a complete picture (as far as possible) of world trends. The next question then becomes: What factors do we see and how do they affect us? It is not wrong to make such an assessment, but there is also a point pondering the time perspective. Trends and tendencies evolve (and indeed 'decay') over time. We therefore need to understand how factors change over time. Now we are back to the line of the linear equation. What we then also need to ask is how the trend has developed over time and how it will develop over time. For an example see Figure 3.1.

Figure 3.1 PEST analysis

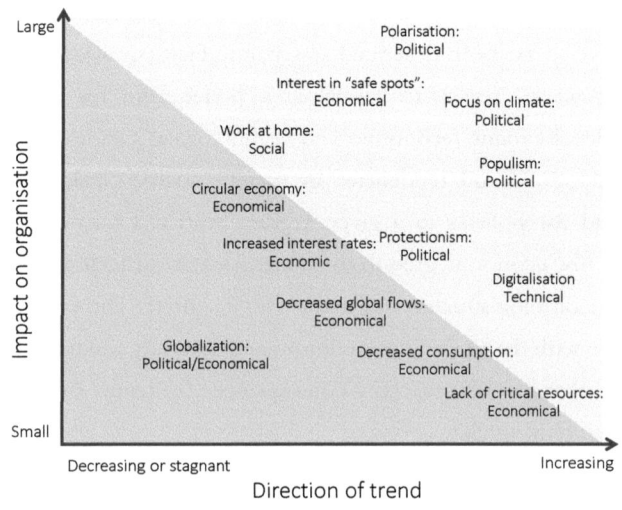

36

This figure shows parts of an analysis we produced for the board of a real estate company that was a joint venture between a municipality and a contractor.

There we can see how the impact is evaluated on the vertical axis and the direction on the horizontal axis just to get a feel for what it looks like going forward. Each pair of concepts was then followed by a short description to help in future discussions on priorities.

## Pressures for change and the business environment

When we try to understand the business environment, we want to know a little more specifically: What factors/trends affect us a lot or a little? Which ones play into our hands (create opportunities)? Which ones create problems for us (pose threats)? Which ones reinforce, weaken or cancel each other out? If we don't have answers to these questions, we probably need to find out to know how to change going forward.

To understand the pressures for change that the world is exerting on us, we therefore need to answer these five questions:

1. What is the trend?
2. How much pressure does it exert on us to change?
3. How has it changed over time (e.g. in the last 3-5 years)? Has it increased or decreased (has the slope become steeper or flatter)?
4. How do we think it will evolve over time (e.g. 3-5 years)? Will it increase or decrease (will the slope become steeper or flatter)?
5. How does it interact with other trends and/or tendencies? Reinforce? Weaken? Cancel each other out?

By being a little more precise in what trend we see and how we think it has evolved over time we get an understanding of the slope of trends and relationships between trends. We also get ideas about the change gaps that exist in our organisation. Once we have answers to this, we can create an idea of what we could change to get a better fit with the business environment (close the gap). In addition, if we work together to quantify our perceptions, we can get a visually educational picture of what is affecting our organisation that we can discuss and hopefully come to a relative agreement.

## Industry dynamics

One step closer to our organisations, we have different industries and the pressures for change in them. The discipline of economics that deals with this is *microeconomics*.[41] For simplicity, we can call the trends and tendencies that prevail at this level microtrends. They are therefore linked to a specific branch of industry or sector. Usually these are not as long-lasting and stable as macro-trends, but they may well have sprung from them.

> While the environmental analysis aims to describe the business environment at large, regardless of the sector we are in, the industry analysis is a tool to understand a specific industry and its unique challenges.

The PEST analysis was a tool to understand macro trends. *The Five Forces Analysis* by Harvard professor Michael Porter, arguably one of the world's best-known strategy researchers, is a tool for understanding the pressures for change in a specific industry.[42] Or, in his words, the possibility of becoming profitable in an industry. We'll come back to that. Based on nearly six decades of data, the Five Forces Model is one of the most researched and well-established strategy models. Despite this weight, like all tools, it has limitations, and we will go through them also.

What we can conclude is that the pressures for change in a specific industry affect companies operating in that industry and their ability to make money or use their limited resources efficiently. It is a reasonable conclusion that the higher the pressures for change, the greater the need for organisations to invest resources in change to prevent the change gap from widening. The steeper the industry slope is, the steeper the organisations lope needs to be.

> The more time we spend on driving change in our organisation, the less time we spend on running and improving our business: talking to customers, talking to colleagues, developing new solutions, products and services that create more value for customers. In short, less time for our organisation to do what we should be doing (unless change is what we should be doing).

Moving from a position where we may have a big change gap, to a position where we have a better fit, is always costly. So, although the model is originally an analysis of how different industries are reasonably profitable, it is an excellent tool for understanding the pressures for change.

The Five Forces Analysis describes how the pressure for change, or dynamics, in an industry is made up of five different forces. These five forces are: 1.) bargaining power of suppliers, 2.) bargaining power of buyers, 3.) entry barriers for new entrants, 4.) threat of new substitutes, and 5.) internal competition in the industry in which the players operate (See Figure 3.2).

Figure 3.2 Five force analysis

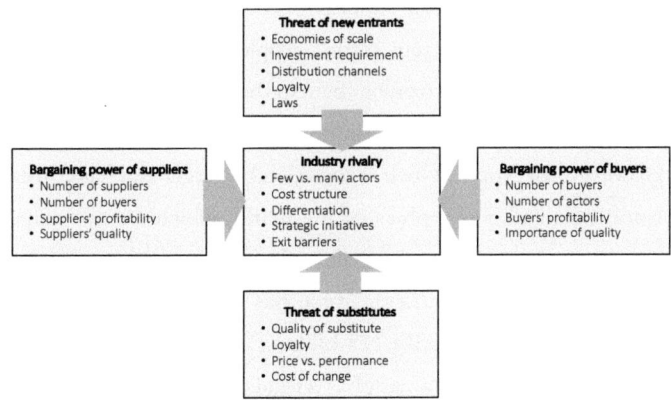

Source: adapted from Porter (1980)[30]

## Bargaining power of suppliers

*The bargaining power of suppliers* consists of their ability to influence or make demands on the players in the sector. This strength depends on the number of suppliers, the number of actors buying the suppliers' products and services, the profitability of the suppliers, the unique quality of the suppliers' products and services, etc. Generally speaking, the fewer the suppliers and the more actors, the greater the bargaining power of the supplier, who can then choose his customer. If there is only one supplier, then that supplier maintains a *monopoly*. If there are only a few large, heavy suppliers (*oligopolies*), they can dictate the terms and conditions of those who buy from them with relative ease. We can see in most industries that a few giants are becoming more and more common.

By looking at the consumer electronics industry, we can learn something about the bargaining power of suppliers. We can see that it is large, and we can understand the consequences of that. Suppliers such as Apple, Samsung and Siemens are often many hundreds of times larger than the consumer electronics chains that exist in different countries. This does not mean that the consumer electronics chains are small by definition, but their suppliers are usually much larger.

The relationship between supplier and buyer is therefore a factor to consider. To put it in concrete terms: Apple is bigger than Elgiganten. Elgiganten is a dominant electronics chain in the Nordic region with a market share of over 20%.[43] This is a clear dominant position, regardless of the sector. However, for Apple, which is considerably larger and has considerably more customers in all geographies of the world, which are also larger than Elgiganten, Elgiganten becomes a small, and to be blunt, insignificant partner for Apple globally. In comparison, Apple has over 150,000 employees and annual revenues of around USD 115 billion.[44] Elkjøp, which is the Nordic group of which Elgiganten is a part, has a total of about 12,000 employees in all Nordic countries and total sales of about USD 5 billion.

In terms of size, Apple and Elkjøp play in completely different leagues, and this has implications for bargaining power. Apple dictates the terms. We need to understand this to decide what we want to change and what we don't. Apple, in addition to its size, is also hugely profitable. In addition, they have a quality that is unique. Many people who have bought Macs, iPhones or iPads don't want anything else and Apple is the only one who keeps them. In other words, Apple has an incredibly strong bargaining position with those who want to buy Apple products. They are unique. Few organisations have as much bargaining power as Apple and that is precisely why they serve as an educational example.

## Bargaining power of buyers

If we look at the opposite side of the value chain, we have the buyers and *bargaining power of the buyers*. Just as the number of suppliers has an impact on the pressure for change in the industry, so does the number of buyers. If there are few buyers, they affect the pressure for change in the industry. All actors then compete for the few buyers that exist. This assumes, of course, that the total demand from buyers is not greater than the supply from all actors. However, this is rarely the case. When it does, it is usually in a market that has not yet matured but will do so fairly soon. The reverse is more common. In most industries, we have excess capacity, more supply than demand, and this creates competition for buyers and pressure for change on the actors in the industry.

For example, if we are working on large infrastructure projects: railway construction, tunnel construction, large roundabouts, on-ramps and bridges, in any given geographical region there are a small number of buyers: The Transport Administration and to some extent the large municipalities and occasionally larger organisations. Then there are no more buyers. This means that if the buyers play their cards right, they will have a strong negotiating position. There are in fact several suppliers who can and want to build a large bridge, for example Vinci, Skanska, Bechtel, Larsen and Tobru, ACS and

Power China to name a few large actors. All of these can provide what the different national Transport Administration wants.

Another thing that affects the bargaining power of buyers is whether the buyers are profitable or not. Buyers will have a stronger bargaining position if they are not dependent on a particular actor to develop their own profitability or financial situation. Buyers who are not dependent on a particular actor to influence their financial situation (such as Transport Administrations or a municipalities) can make demands and thereby exert pressure on the actors in the sector. These organisations that do not have to deliver quarterly profitability to a financial market and can take advantage of this in the negotiations by taking somewhat of a wait-and-see approach.

A further factor affecting the bargaining power of the buyer is the requirement for a certain quality linked to a particular actor. The more unique quality a buyer depends on, the less bargaining power the buyer has. This is the same reasoning that applies to suppliers. In the consumer electronics sector, it can be observed that private customers who buy a new TV from a consumer electronics chain are neither dependent on a new TV to secure their financial situation, nor on a unique quality that Fnac or Mediamarkt have. Private buyers therefore have more bargaining power in this case.

## Threat of new entrants

Looking at the next force, *threat of new entrants*, there are a few underlying factors. First, we can look at *economies of scale* in the industry. Economies of scale mean that there are opportunities for actors in the industry to reuse their solutions multiple times, thereby making it difficult for new entrants to compete. In simple terms, they do not have to reinvent the wheel while new entrants must do just that. The more opportunities there are to reuse different types of solutions, the cheaper it will be to produce and deliver something to a buyer, and the more difficult it will be for another player to enter that market. The ability to take advantage of economies of scale in an industry reduces the pressure to change. The reverse is also true. The lower the ability to replicate solutions, the easier it is for new entrants to enter and hence the higher the pressure to change.

It's not easy to get into the car business. Designing and building a new car is incredibly complicated and expensive. It's easy to get into the organisational consulting business. Anyone can open his own 'consultancy shop' at any time.

Another factor is the *investment requirements* for setting up. The more money organisations need to invest in terms of time or resources, the higher the barrier to entry for new entrants and the lower the pressure for change. Once again, we can contrast the automotive industry with the consulting industry. Investment in production lines, design and development of a car is in the billions of euros. The investment to set up a consultancy shop may be almost nothing. As a consultant, we need a computer (maybe) and a telephone (maybe). We don't even need to set up a limited company, we can run everything as a sole trader. It is thus easy to understand why the consultancy sector has many players while the car sector has far fewer.

Another factor is *distribution channels*. These grant access to established channels for purchasing, distribution, transport and logistics. If it is difficult to establish distribution channels and thereby ensure that we can deliver our services or products to a particular buyer, then this means higher barriers to entry for new entrants and lower pressure on the industry to change. The consultant only distributes itself, sometimes perhaps even digitally. The automotive sector has extensive global supply chains and logistics networks to develop and maintain. Automotive industries have barriers to entry linked to distribution channels and thus lower pressure to change.

In some industries, there are also *laws* that regulate the business. In most countries, there are laws and regulations governing who can conduct financial activities and is therefore under the supervision of some kind of financial supervisory authority. In other industries, there are laws and/or requirements of other kinds that make it difficult for a new player to establish itself. There may also be different certification requirements, such as ISO, which require investment to operate.

The more laws, restrictions, certification requirements and the like, the higher the barrier to entry for a new entrant. This in turn reduces the pressure for change, and not infrequently the rate of change in the industry. Banks, for example, which enjoy legal protection are rarely the most change-prone organisations, and based on logic, why should they change? After all, they make tons of money anyway, and since many of them are limited companies, making money for their owners is their purpose. We might have moral or ethical qualms about this, but that's another issue.

A final parameter that creates barriers to entry for new entrants is the *loyalty* of buyers to a particular actor. Loyalty means that buyers always turn to a particular actor because they are loyal to it for various reasons. These reasons can range from established personal relationships, understanding of your business or a unique competence of the actor in question. Whatever the reason, loyalty to an existing player makes it more difficult for new players to enter the industry. It therefore reduces the pressure on the industry to change.

Looking at the consulting industry again, we can see that it is difficult to take advantage of economies of scale. There is no direct 'output' that can be scaled up. The solution is often uniquely tailored to the client's needs. In addition, there is no direct need for distribution channels - you 'distribute' people and can even do much of the work via digital channels (e.g. Teams, Zoom). Loyalty is perhaps the only factor a consulting organisation really has to work with, and it is likely to be created through personal relationships, a unique skill set and, in the long run, an understanding of the business. As we know, there are also no laws, regulations or requirements that make it difficult for a consultant to establish himself in one way or another. This makes it easy to start a consultancy business. All this illustrates how the consulting industry is an example of an industry where barriers to entry are low, and to some extent the pressure for change on the players is high.

## Threat of substitutes

The fourth force in the model is the *threat of substitutes*. A substitute is something that a buyer might consider choosing instead of what he usually chooses. The viability of a substitute is usually judged by price in relation to performance: what do I get for the same or less money? If I pay a little more, I am likely to want a little more. If I pay a little less, I'm likely to want about the same, but might be able to imagine something a little worse.

As a private individual, we may have one car, or even two. In tougher economic times, we may not be able to afford it anymore. A substitute may be a bicycle, moped or motorcycle. The choice of a substitute or an existing offer depends, of course, on what the buyer wants. Most people are interested in lowering the price a little and still getting the same quality or function. If it is possible to offer that, then it is likely to be a substitute that is easy for buyers to choose. One conclusion of this reasoning is that the easier it is to choose a substitute, the higher the pressure for change in the industry.

Within the power of the threat of substitutes, we can also usefully add 'non-purchase' of what the industry provides. Keeping what exists, saving money. Instead of buying something new, buyers may also see it as a substitute not to buy. This also affects the industry's pressure to change. If no one or fewer people are buying our stuff, we need to do something different. If we look at public investment, it adds another perspective. Public money can be spent on healthcare, schools or something else. This means that organisations that have a clear link to external political factors and part of their business towards public procurers are likely to benefit from understanding the concept of substitution as something broader. Substitutes then need to include other types of investment or non-investment that affect pressures for change in the sector. Somewhat mischievously, we can conclude that the most important mission of politicians is to get elected, their second most important is to get re-elected, the third most important is to serve the citizens of society. Based on that, we can easily understand that politicians

45

invest in what gives them votes: increased pensions, increased teacher salaries, etc. The more that is invested in the welfare state, the less is left for private actors to provide products and services to public organisations.

In fact, this reasoning is also valid in private organisations. Indeed, the same argument applies to the consumer electronics industry, for example. It is usually easy for a buyer not to spend money on a new TV at a certain time, but to wait for Black Friday or until the TV breaks down. It is also possible that private individuals decide to spend the 600 Euros intended for a home cinema system on a holiday trip to Mallorca instead. Suddenly MediaMarkt and TUI are competitors. This creates a need to broaden one's understanding of what a substitute can be. It also means that we can reflect on what competition is. Does the competition consist of those who do the same things as us or those who my prospective buyers spend their money with instead of me?

In some parts of the industry, where we often need a certain material at a certain time to make the products we are going to sell, this reasoning becomes flawed. This has been painfully evident from 2020 onwards when shortages of certain materials, such as semiconductors, have caused industries to slow down production due to a lack of materials that cannot be substituted. It is therefore a matter of understanding what can and cannot be substituted to gain a deeper understanding of the pressures for change in a particular industry. Understanding this also gives us an idea of what we can and want to do going forward. In conclusion, the easier it is to choose a substitute (including the choice not to buy anything at all), the greater the pressure for change in the industry.

## Industry rivalry

The fifth and final force is the *industry rivalry*. The strength of this force, like the bargaining power of suppliers and buyers, depends on how many and how dominant players there are in the industry, and what their agenda is. If there are one or a few dominant players who have a secure position and are not driving development, this reduces the pressure for change in the industry. We can see this in both the financial and construction sectors. On the other hand, if there is one or a few large leading players who want to grow simultaneously at each other's expense, then there is increased pressure for change. Just think about how HBO, Netflix, Disney+, etc. have developed over the last decade.

In a market where all players are doing much the same thing and it is difficult to distinguish one from the other, we tend to say that there is a low degree of *differentiation* between players. Low differentiation makes it easier for the buyer to choose any operator. Often the price is the deciding factor. This increases the pressure for change in the sector as money is often a scarce resource. Another influencing factor is the *cost structure*. In certain types of business, we need to tie up a lot of capital because of a large amount of fixed costs. For example, it may involve a large production facility. In this case, relatively large production and sales volumes are needed to cover these costs. To sell plenty of units, we sometimes need to reduce prices. Price pressure in an industry means that operators must change to remain profitable, thus creating pressure for change in the industry.

In some sectors, there may also be trends for different types of *strategic initiatives*. Examples may include mergers and acquisitions of organisations or the entry of players from other countries into a regional market to establish themselves. It may also be the case that during a difficult period there are several bankruptcies that affect the composition of the sector.

One example of such a strategic initiative that is prevalent in many manufacturing companies and retailers today is servitisation.[45] Retailers rarely have a unique quality. If we look again at the consumer electronics industry, it is likely that the buyer wants a certain Apple or HP product. It is probably rarer that the buyer wants to buy the product specifically from Dixons Carphone. This can be described as a low degree of differentiation, and it creates a pressure for change on the players in the industry to change. They need to try to find other ways to differentiate themselves and strengthen their position than through their products. What many are doing today is to expand their product portfolio and offer different types of services. Some examples in the consumer electronics sector are insurance and installation services. For travel companies, more experience-based services (e.g. yoga passes, surf training) are similar phenomena. Every travel agency, basically, has trips to Thailand.

One of the reasons for this is that with different services we have an opportunity to differentiate ourselves from our competitors. We don't have that when we are a retailer. Another reason, in addition to differentiation, is that services can provide yet another new and perhaps different stream of revenue (e.g. subscriptions). This in turn increases the need for others in the industry (suppliers and buyers) to maintain their profitability. In this way, the five different forces are also interrelated in many ways: after all, a supplier in one sector is a player in another, and a buyer in a third. We need to understand this kind of reasoning when making decisions on how to change in the future to become more competitive.

Finally, there may also be *barriers to exit* in an industry. Just as the pressure for change increases when new entrants enter the industry, it also increases when there are barriers for existing entrants who wish to leave the industry to do so. If it is difficult or costly to exit an industry, for example because of long-term contracts with suppliers or buyers, fewer will leave. Barriers to exit may be lock-in effects in investments made in technology or other resources, leases on a property, contracts with suppliers or guarantees to buyers. These factors, as we will see later, are common resistances to change. If we are stuck and unable or find it difficult to exit a market, we are likely to do what we can to change and create a better position. If it is difficult for players to exit an industry, this often puts more pressure on most players in the industry to change. We can thus see how high barriers to entry and exit preserve industries. An example is again banks, which are generally not the most change-prone firms.

## Pressures for change and industries

In conclusion, we can say that the five forces influence the pressure for change in an industry. Looking at the consumer electronics industry, we can see that suppliers are large and strong, buyers are certainly quite numerous, but not at all loyal to a particular company. For many buyers, the substitute of not buying is an easy option to choose. It is also relatively easy for a new entrant to set up a business selling consumer electronics and competing with existing players. Anyone can set up a website called buyanewtv.com and sell things that way. There is hardly any investment capital needed. You can act as a broker or an intermediary. That means you don't have to build up a distribution network. There are no direct certification requirements. Nor are there any direct laws that decisively regulate who or how we can trade consumer electronics with, other than standard commercial contracts. Few customers are loyal to NetOnNet simply because NetOnNet is NetOnNet (to take one example). Internal competition in the industry is high and it is difficult to differentiate. No one has any unique products and thus very little 'uniqueness' in quality. Those players who want to exit the industry are often stuck in contracts with both suppliers and guarantees to customers.

What we know relatively well from research is that the greater the pressure for change in an industry, the harder it is to make money in it. In this respect, the consumer electronics industry is a clear example of an industry where it is difficult to make money, even though there is a large and growing demand for the products they offer.

In this book, we can only describe the five forces and give a few examples to clarify how the different forces affect the pressure for change in different sectors. By building the analysis with information, actual data, for example which of the suppliers account for 80% of the costs and what percentage of the total suppliers they represent, or how many buyers account for 80% of sales today and 3 years ago, to take two simple examples, we can create a lot of insights about where we have potential for improvement and therefore changes to realise. A five forces analysis with data provides powerful explanations of the pressures for change in an industry and gives us an understanding of what we can do to be more successful by managing the changes we need to manage.

In addition, if we look at how the factors change over time (e.g. how suppliers have bought each other out, how a number of digital players have started to compete with us), as we did with the PEST factors, we can get a picture of how the pressure for change and its various factors have increased or decreased over time. This gives us a picture of the dynamics of the industry now and in the future. It gives a pretty good description of the different changes that will be important to us.

So, also when we do an industry analysis, we want to understand how the five forces of the industry evolve over time to see the pressure for change as a line in the linear equation.

The questions we need to ask ourselves are:

1.  How strong is each of these five forces and its constituent parts?
2.  How much pressure do they put on us to change?
3.  How have they changed over time (e.g. in the last 3-5 years)? Have they increased or decreased (has the slope become steeper or flatter)?
4.  How do we think they will evolve over time (e.g. 3-5 years)? Will they increase or decrease (will the slope become steeper or flatter)?
5.  How do the different forces interact with each other? Reinforce? Weaken? Cancel each other out?
6.  How do the five forces and the PEST factors interact? Reinforce? Weaken? Cancel each other out?

All models are simplifications and are therefore subject to ongoing questioning. That is how it should be in the name of science. Knowledge is provisional. This also applies to the five-force model. The big challenge when we do a five-force analysis is to set the boundary of the industry we are analysing. In a world where traditionally defined areas merge, it can be difficult to set this boundary. That Deutsche Telekom, Orange and Vodafone are competitors is obvious, but are they also competing with Elon Musk's SpaceX and Starlink, which provides internet via satellite to over 40 countries? Where is the line between telecoms, IT and for that matter defence or space industry? As I mentioned above, TUI and Thomas Cook are competitors with each other, but they are also competitors with the consumer electronics chains. Both industries are competing for private money spent on entertainment (in the broad sense). Sometimes this is even expressed as if we are in a world where this kind of model is outdated. I would argue that this is an exaggeration. The models are still powerful - if used correctly and they highlight how important it becomes to try to define what industry we are actually in. For large organisations that are in multiple industries at the same time, this becomes even more important. A challenge for them then becomes balancing the coordination of business which is the purpose of *corporate strategy* with the individual driving of a business which is the purpose of *business strategy*.

> The important thing about strategy analysis is not to put the right labels or numbers with the right decimal point, but to have a factual dialogue and learn together how to improve over time. Then the dialogues provide input on what changes we need to realise to be more successful.

## Organisations over time

People have always organised themselves. When we can't achieve certain things on our own, we come together to help. We organise ourselves, sometimes to the point of creating a permanent structure: an organisation. These structures change when they no longer serve their purpose (or at least should change).

Paradoxically, the third level (after environment and industry) that exerts pressure on organisations to change, is the organisation itself. In essence, organisations are living organisms. They evolve over time, grow, shrink, etc. They have a life of their own. One micro-decision is reinforced by another micro-decision somewhere else without anyone taking conscious action to drive it. Leading change is partly about identifying and encouraging the kind of behaviours that drive the organisation in the right direction. However, because it is difficult to know in advance what is right, it is also important to encourage change as such - any change.

In a nutshell, we can say that the pressure for change in the world and in the industry is such that we need to respond to it. Sometimes we may be able to pursue an issue proactively, when we are ahead of both the industry and our competitors and may even have a competitive advantage because of this head start. In contrast, the organisation's pressure to change is of a more positive nature. The greater the pressure for change from the organisation, the greater the likelihood of successfully changing and remaining relevant.

As organisations evolve, they go through different phases. These phases are mainly influenced by two factors. Firstly, organisations grow in sheer size: in the number of people who are part of the organisation, the number of stores, the number of countries, etc. Secondly, they evolve as they get older. Just like people, organisations grow both larger and older, and as they do so they try new things, succeed, fail, learn and evolve in different phases.

Conceptually, we can see that different phases of an organisation are replaced by different crises (which may also remind us of people, for that matter). Crises, as we get through them, create opportunities for new growth. In his article *Evolution and revolution as organizations grow*[46], Larry Greiner describes these phases and crises in a vivid way (see Figure 3.3).

Figure 3.3 Five phases of organisational development

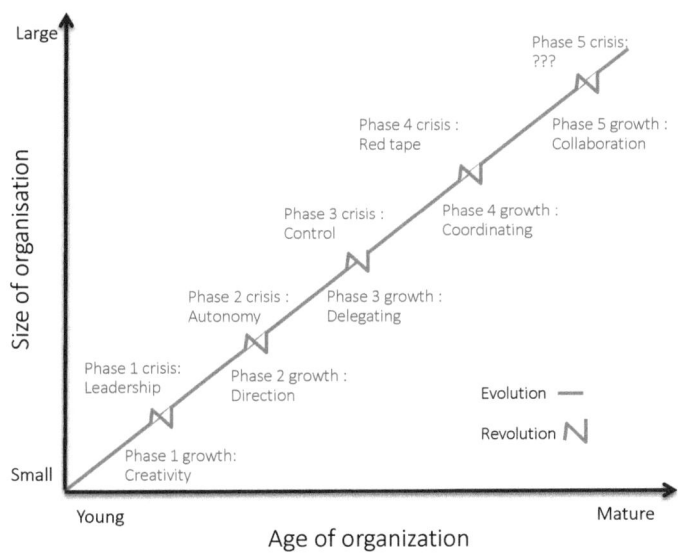

Source: adapted from Greiner (1972)

## Birth of an organisation

In the beginning, at the birth of an organisation, most are small. During this first phase of an organisation's life, it is characterised by growth through *creativity* and *entrepreneurship*. Imagine a start-up. Everyone wants to move forward. Everyone wants to achieve something. Everyone wants to create something new, something unique. Everyone wants to drive the business and build an organisation or company that does something. There is an inherent power in this. That power needs to be directed. If that force is not directed, there is a first phase of crisis that interrupts growth. A crisis of lack of *leadership*. It is natural that when we as an organisation have grown over a period of time, we need to gather strength and create clarity on how to allocate resources in a new and hopefully wiser way to achieve more. Decisions about who decides what become important. A clearer form of

53

organisational structure with accountability is typically required to continue to grow. The structure need *not* be a formal hierarchical structure, but some kind of framework that helps us as an organisation to improve. In other words, the organisation requires a change in the way we work.

In relation to the phases, we can loosely talk about the size of the organisation in absolute terms. The more people, the more complicated structures for employees to work together in a reasonably smooth way. By relying on a number of rules of thumb, we can create an understanding of the challenges and thus change needs an organisation faces as it evolves. There are of course differences between different types of industries and organisations. However, my experience, supported by group research[47] , tells me that the leadership crisis quite often occurs when the organisation reaches about ten people. As long as we are a good handful of people, everyone can be more or less involved in all activities and decisions. Everyone can have access to roughly the same information, and it is easy to reconcile any misunderstandings and reach a common understanding. Then, as we approach or exceed a dozen, the need for clearer leadership arises. Hence the first crisis.

## Growth and the balance between autonomy and coordination

Once we have established leadership, phase two of growth can come to fruition. Then there is a clear *direction* and structure that allows us as an organisation to work forward in a more unified and focused way. This phase of growth is then interrupted by a crisis of *autonomy*. Having been allowed to act, make decisions, drive the business and act largely freely, we have, because of the leadership crisis, established both leadership and direction. This means that individuals, we – the organisation, are not allowed fully to influence our own development to the same extent anymore. We now have to relate to a framework. Then we like to think back to how free we were and how much is now imposed on us.

A second limit in numbers is somewhere around 70 people in the organisation. Up to about that size of group, we can resolve most issues over coffee or lunch. Most people can have a personal relationship with each other and have a reasonable chance of getting to know each other's names and interests. In this way, everyone can develop some kind of personal relationship with everyone. When the number of employees exceeds about 70, we need to build some kind of structure or system that allows us to involve, communicate with and inform all employees without everyone being present at the same time. We need to find other ways of working. We need to change.

Once we have managed to establish a certain autonomy, supported by a structure of communication and information, within a given direction and under a certain leadership, we can grow further through *delegation*. In the best of worlds, this means that we shift power and responsibility from the few at the top of the pyramid (for lack of a better word) to the many employees at the bottom of the pyramid (also for lack of a better word). That way, more people can spend more time doing what they do best. Management, and/or other managers at different levels, do not need to be bottlenecks in communication flows or comment on things they do not have insight into because they are not working on those tasks.

Having a functioning delegation is a big win when we reach the third numerical limit, which is around 150 employees. That threshold is linked to the brain's ability to recognise faces.[48] It has been shown that this is about how many faces we humans can remember in a given context. This means that even if we don't know everyone, we have a reasonable chance of at least recognising most faces. When there are more than 150 of us, this is difficult, and it places new demands on structures and systems for building relationships between employees. When we grow beyond about 150 people, the next crisis arises, which is a sense of lack of *control*. In practical terms, this often means that senior people in the organisation pick up tasks that were

55

previously delegated. This is driven by a sense of not being in control of everything that we have delegated. This in turn creates a series of problems for the organisation in that it creates a passivity and low commitment: 'Am I no longer trusted with what has been delegated to me? Then let them do it themselves', is not an uncommon feeling. Picking up things that have been delegated is not a productive way to develop an organisation, as we are going backwards in our development. That's why we need to change the way we work.

The solution, to the feeling of lack of control and continued growth, is more likely to be found in achieving *coordination*. Coordination enables the next phase of growth. By building structures, processes, agendas and decision trees, we enable coordination. This does not mean centralising decisions, but formalising how decisions are made. Unfortunately, what often results from coordination, when we don't allow people to work reasonably freely, is that we create a lot of forums where different people have to sit and coordinate themselves and others at length and breadth. This easily contributes to what we might call 'meeting sickness', where one meeting follows another, and those sitting in the meeting often have only a vague idea of what the meeting is about or what their specific role in the meeting is. Meeting sickness is a symptom of the crisis that interrupts the growth of coordination. We coordinate ourselves into absurdity. We call this phenomenon *red tape*.

A fourth limit for organisations in their growth I find usually goes at about 500 people. When organisations are that big, it is impossible to see what everyone does, what their names are and what their responsibilities are. In fact, most organisations are not that big or grow that big, either private or public. However, they do exist. There are even those that get bigger, and for them, there is another limit. That limit is also strongly linked to organisational change and occurs somewhere around 3000 people. In practice, this boundary is fluid and really has more to do with the characteristics of the organisation. However, when organisations approach around 3000, they are generally made up of many different types of business units, companies or divisions, often 6-7 hierarchical levels or more, often governance and support functions working in matrices, they operate in different geographies with different types of products and services, and perhaps laws, which make coordination, collaboration and alignment more complicated. In relation to large-scale and strategic change, a fairly large amount of critical mass of change activities is required to reach out to the periphery of the organisation, hierarchically and geographically. This requires something very special. I have met many experienced managers at corporate level in listed companies and in the management of government organisations who are tearing their hair out to understand how to reach all the way out. How we can do that is discussed in Chapter 7. The work of the change manager.

The final growth phase of the model occurs when we as an organisation get into real collaboration in the organisation. The organisations that have achieved this are, in my experience, unfortunately relatively few. Regrettably, I often hear organisations in all sorts of sectors and sizes complain about poor or ineffective collaboration. Far too many organisations are run in ways that privilege individual responsibility over collaboration. Profit responsibility is not at all uncommon, with personal resources carefully guarded, quite low down in the hierarchical structure. It is not clear that collaboration is more important than individual responsibility, but we rarely see organisations where collaboration works well. I have yet to hear any organisation say that they need to start building silos. I hear the opposite almost daily. To me, this means that we need to take the balance between collaboration and individual responsibility more seriously than we seem to do today. The failure to manage that balance means that few organisations create growth precisely through collaboration. This is also a reflection of the balance between corporate and business strategy that I mentioned earlier, and which many organisations are not yet getting nearly right.

Greiner's model shows the evolution of an organisation over time. It does not mean that just because we are past a particular crisis, we are safe. In large organisations we are likely to have been through all the crises and are likely to be in many of them at the same time. Organisations are often made up of business areas, divisions, departments, units, groups, projects, etc. that are continually growing and shrinking, merging and splitting up. As a result, many organisations that are changing their organisational structure are constantly in more or less all phases of growth and crisis at the same time, but in different parts of the organisation. Since all parts of an organisation interact in different ways – employees are part of several groupings – this means that the organisation itself, and the way it operates, is constantly changing.

There is therefore pressure to change as the organisation grows. Organisations are living organisms that are constantly evolving, regardless of whether there is a conscious initiative for change anywhere. Things that happen in the industry or in the business environment provide input to people in organisations who talk to each other. New people meet, new groupings are formed, new sub-groupings are created within them. These groupings and sub-groupings grow and go through phases and crises that give us different ways of talking about things and different ways of behaving. Changing.

## Pressures for change and organisations

When analysing an organisation's development needs, we need to understand what the driving force is. The phases and crises mentioned above give us an idea of that. When we analyse an organisation, we want to create as dynamic a picture as possible, just as we do for the environment and the industry. We want to be able to understand how the changes taking place inside the organisation are also driving the need for change in the organisation itself.

> The more we change as an organisation, the greater the need for new changes. This may sound paradoxical, but it is no different from the way nature evolves. The better we get, the more improvements we see.

We therefore want to be able to draw a line for the organisation and its slope, that is, the pace of change? We want to understand whether the pace of change in the organisation matches that of the outside world and that of the industry. If the gradient in both the business environment and the industry is steeper, if the outside world is changing faster than the organisation, then we know that the change gap and the need for change are constantly increasing. If we don't address this, we risk becoming irrelevant and eventually being sorted out.

The questions we need to ask ourselves to understand the pressures the organisation is putting on itself and which give rise to the need for change are the following:

1. What is driving the change in our organisation?
2. Which phase(s) and/or crisis(es) are we in, in different parts of the organisation?
3. Which of these is/are exerting pressure on us to change today?
4. How have these changed over time (e.g. in the last 3-5 years)? Have they increased or decreased (has the slope become steeper or flatter)?
5. How do we think they will evolve over time (e.g. 3-5 years)? Will they increase or decrease (will the slope become steeper or flatter)?
6. How do the phases/crises interact with each other? Reinforce? Weaken? Cancel each other out?
7. How do the phases/crises interact with the five forces and the PEST factors? Reinforce? Weaken? Cancel each other out?

# People learn

The fourth and final level where we can identify pressures for change is the individual. Through working, talking to friends, colleagues or customers, and just living, we learn new things. Whether or not we make a conscious effort to learn something, we will continually draw conclusions about what works and what does not. This leads us to change the way we behave. We sometimes define learning as the acquisition of new understanding, knowledge or behaviour as a result of interaction with the world around us, leading to a lasting change in capacity.[49] This change in capability can be of different kinds: we can learn to perform a completely new behaviour. We can call this an extension of our existing *behavioural repertoire*. We can learn to refine behaviours that we already perform. We can learn to stop using behaviours that for one reason or another are less functional. So many more options do not exist.

## Four different ways of learning

We humans learn in four different ways.[50] These different ways of learning are often intertwined and run in parallel in the learning process itself.[51] When we do things consciously and unconsciously, we understand what works about what we do. We learn. The four ways are as follows:

*Insight learning* means that the person first thinks about how to behave to achieve a certain result and then performs this behaviour. This is the least common and most demanding way to learn new behaviours. Insight learning is required when I am in a situation and know what I want to achieve but must figure out what behaviour will create that outcome. For example, I may be faced with a unique strategic dilemma that requires a completely new way of solving it. Insight learning requires abstract thinking, that we can solve the problem in our heads. We cannot do that very often.

*Instructional learning* means that rules or instructions of some kind describe how a behaviour should be performed. The instruction is usually verbal or written (text/picture). Based on a given instruction, the goal is to do what the rule tells us to do. This requires intelligence and a language in which we can use abstract terms to describe the behaviour. Or images that we understand. Instructions for use, rules, manuals, orders and strategies are examples of instructions to help us understand what to do.

*Model learning* means that I see, hear or perceive something a role model does and then I imitate the behaviour. We can also imitate the model with a delay in time. We do not have to perform the behaviour at the moment we see it, but can remember what a model did and imitate it a number of days, weeks or even years later. Most social behaviours, conversing and socialising, are learned in this way. We can imitate a model both by consciously imitating and quite unconsciously and unthinkingly imitating. Model learning is often what keeps a culture - what's within the walls - alive.

*Learning by shaping* means that behaviour is learned based on the reinforcing consequences it has had. "Trial-and-error" is when the shaping process occurs randomly. However, it should be called 'trial-and- success' because it is the successful behaviours, which give us reinforcement, that sustain the behaviours. When we learn new behaviours, maintenance is crucial to avoid falling back into old ruts. Shaping is always involved in learning *complex behaviours* and patterns of behaviour. By complex behaviours we refer to behaviours that require many (micro) decisions and activities in rapid succession or simultaneously. Examples of complex behaviours are walking, writing, reading or strategic reasoning. Leading change is very much associated with a large range of complex behaviours. If we want to learn to lead change, we have to be prepared for a lot of shaping.

> The more we learn, the better we can perform tasks. Learning is therefore a force to be harnessed in organisations. The pressure for change that arises from individuals learning is, like the organisation's pressure for change, positive. What organisation wants employees who don't learn?

## Learning and change

Learning is important. It's easy to see and understand. However, it is not so simple that all learning is good for the organisation. Especially not if we are to look at change from a strategist's perspective. Model learning means that we rely on the 'model' to do what is strategically right. It is not always a relatively inexperienced person who learns something from an experienced person who learns 'correctly'.

> Experience is good, but the experience we have gained comes from history and it is not a given that what worked best before is what works best now. Experience is built up over time and may be based on reasoning that is not supported today.

A similar reasoning applies to instructional learning. How do we know that the instruction in our management system, for example, is the one best suited to customer requirements today? As with model learning, this implies that the instruction needs to be updated whenever a smarter way is introduced. Anyone who has worked with management systems knows that changes to them take time. Before we set a new best practice, we want to be sure that it is the best practice (if we think there is one). This means that good ideas are not introduced into the system until some time in the future. In turn, if changes in the world are rapid, this means that instructional learning may involve learning something that should really be officially obsolete. In the long run, this creates a need to unlearn - to stop doing what we are doing - and this is not easy once a complex behaviour has been learned and has become ingrained.

So, we need to be a bit careful with instruction and model learning and rather try to create as many opportunities for insight learning and shaping as possible. Both, especially shaping, are more guided by the function or consequence of behaviours. Not what rule they are based on. In this way, they lead more to a natural selection of effective behaviours, in a way that model learning and instructional learning do not.[52]

This is particularly important when we look at exploratory behaviour, experimentation or questioning. They are often in conflict with existing instructions, rules and the use of existing resources in the here and now. This balancing act - what to question and what to just do - needs to be done on an ongoing basis in a changing environment. When the world moves and we find it messy, a common approach is to define and specify tasks a little more. Then instructions become common. The problem is that by detailing, we limit learning. When we follow a template, we miss opportunities for learning. We miss things that are distant in time and space: far in the future and far away in 'geographical' terms; we also miss the opportunity to learn from our mistakes.[53] When we follow a set path, there is no room for experimentation. When we are not allowed to experiment, we do not learn. When we don't learn, we don't change. So imposing instructions when the rate of change is high, and diversity is high is directly counterproductive.

This means that learning itself must be enabled in organisations. We must learn to learn new things no matter how fuzzy that sounds. Then shaping: testing, evaluating, learning, improving, testing again, etc. is absolutely vital. It is less often about employees learning a unique routine or behaviour as a model shows or an instruction prescribes. That can also be important. However, when we look at pressures for change and how an organisation can become better at adapting to environmental and industry demands, or even driving industry demands for sustainability for example, then we need to look at an overall organisational capacity for learning and change. This is central to long-term success.

The organisational ability to learn and change is seen when there are no barriers in the organisation for employees to try new things and learn from it. A sign of this is when individuals who learn new things and contribute to development ideas are rewarded rather than corrected. Unfortunately, it is not uncommon for new ideas to be met with criticism - often precisely because they are different from what is being done today. Driving learning is thus a strategic issue that increases the pace of change in the organisation (the slope of the organisation's line in the graph). That in itself increases the chances of adaptation and success over time. Those who do not adapt sooner or later will disappear.

> The ability of individuals to learn and to apply new learning to their work is one of the single most important factors in an organisation's ability to adapt to changing circumstances. It enhances the organisation's fit and increases the chances of success over time.

## Pressures for change and people

When we try to understand the pressure for change that individuals exert on the organisation, we need to understand how they learn. The questions we need to ask ourselves to understand how they learn and develop behaviours and what the consequences are for the organisation are as follows:

1.  How do our employees learn? Which method (e.g. modelling, shaping) dominates?
2.  In what contexts do they learn new things?
3.  What obstacles (e.g. unclear direction, rules, over-structuring) and enablers (e.g. time for reflection, experimentation) do we see for insight learning and shaping in our organisation?
4.  How have the barriers changed over time (e.g. in the last 3-5 years)? Have they increased or decreased (have they contributed to a steeper or flatter slope)?
5.  How do we think the barriers will evolve over time (e.g. 3-5 years)? Will they increase or decrease (will they make the slope steeper or flatter)?

6. How does organisational learning interact with the organisation's phases of growth and crisis? Reinforces? Weakens? Cancels each other out?

7. How does the learning capacity of the organisation interact with the five forces and the PEST factors? Reinforces? Weakens? Cancels each other out?

## From the environment to people and behaviour

So, there are drivers for change at (at least) four different levels: the business environment, the industry we are in, the evolution of the organisation over time and in size, and the ability for individuals to learn new things. When we want to lead change and ensure that change and strategy are aligned and that the concrete improvements in performance we want to achieve are realised, we need to understand that these four levels relate to each other in a natural way. The logic and coherence are described in Figure 3.4.

Figure 3.4 Change from the environment to the individual

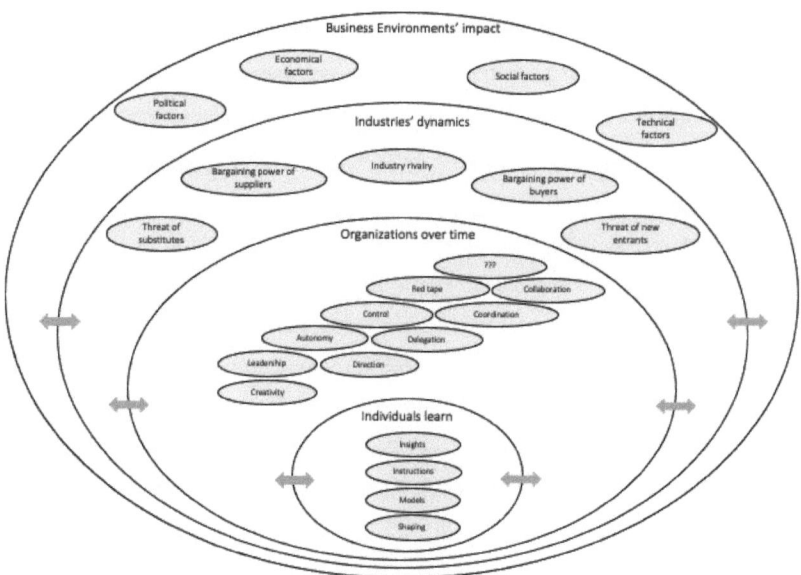

To take one example: we can say with relative confidence that the world is driven by a growing climate focus and a greater emphasis on environmental sustainability (though not enough, many would say). This can be seen as trends in the macro world in the form of policy decisions on laws and restrictions regulating, for example, emissions issues and taxes. It is also visible as social trends such as increased awareness of what we as consumers buy. It also affects industries. We as individuals are both buyers in industries and members of organisations that learn from the consequences of not overusing the earth's resources and thus make demands on those from whom we buy from and those for whom we work.

Organisations in most sectors therefore need to place greater emphasis on sustainability. Twenty years ago, we rarely talked about sustainability; today it is more and more a management and board issue. In several cases, I have seen sustainability managers take on a much more central role in management teams. In some cases, more and more with each passing year, the sustainability manager is the natural right-hand to the CEO as the CFO has been historically. It's not that way everywhere, but it says something about the world we live in and organisations in that world.

To me, it signals that the role many companies want to take today involves a greater responsibility to a wider group of stakeholders than it did just 20 years ago. *Economy* (from Greek word oikonomia) is about the management of scarce resources. Typically, we have seen these resources as financial resources, natural resources, real capital (e.g. real estate, machinery) and human capital. These have usually been within the boundaries of the organisation. *Ecology* (stems from same Greek word, oikos i.e. house) is the interaction between an organism and its environment. Why not think ecologically for an organisation and its industry and environment? A sustainability manager, as an analogy, can then take an ecology perspective and look at the resources also outside the organisation.

Management of limited resources is still the challenge, but the boundary of what resources are included has expanded. Economy is to some extent being replaced by ecology. Two letters, but a crucial difference in how organisations operate.

The ability of an organisation to adapt to this kind of change, over time, and as it grows, is crucial. Processes, structures, objectives, etc. related to sustainability need to be developed. The EU Corporate sustainability reporting directive (CSRD) applies to all organisations with over 250 employees or a net turnover of more than EUR 40 million. So, we need to get a direction on the issue, delegate responsibility for different parts and coordinate around sustainability issues to comply at least with new laws. In some cases (probably many) we may be able to use them to our advantage.

On an individual level, this means that there are many of us who need to learn new things. The governance and production processes that make up management systems today mean that we are meeting the requirements of the law today. This is a good thing. However, they may not be enough to meet customer demands, or the debate in society. Laws, as we have noted, are instructions that take time to develop and are therefore often only a minimum. Relying on instructions or models is therefore not enough to be prepared for future changes. Who knows what demands will be made tomorrow? All we can do is keep our ear to the ground, be out in the market, with customers, in the debate. Only then will we be close to the changes taking place today. The people who are out there listening then need to have an influence on how the work is done. That is, the behaviours that make up the work. They also need to have a say in what they will look like in the future, no matter where they are in the organisation or what their experience is.

It is likely that these people will also have an idea of the organisational outcomes that this type of change can affect. This is vital because we need to define the organisational outcomes we want to influence. If we don't know what we want to impact, and how much, we have no way of evaluating and learning over time.

A common reason why we fail to bring about the changes we want in our organisations, and thus fail to achieve the desired improvements in performance, is that we fail to link organisational change with behavioural change in people. Change from an organisational perspective can be described as a reorganisation, a diversification, a shift in technology, a redesign of a process or a recomposition of a product and/or service portfolio. This is a rather square description, but it clearly explains that it is about change in structures, technology, processes, systems or what we offer to our customers.

Often, when we in organisations try to change something, we make changes in one of these areas. For change to be real and for the benefits of change to be realised, we need to link the organisational change to the behaviours of employees in the organisation. Organisational change must be linked to behavioural change.

Behavioural change from an individual perspective is defined as a new or altered set of a person's behavioural repertoire. Behavioural change thus means that a person needs to do something in a different way. The person needs to do more of something, do less of something, stop doing something or start doing something. There are only these four options. This is also what we need to achieve with organisational change. If we fail to link change at the organisational level: structures, processes, competencies, etc. with change at the behavioural level: how we act, then the change will not lead to the realisation of benefits. After all, moving responsibilities and people within two boxes in an organisational chart is pointless unless people start working differently. New technology, new systems or a new machine in itself will not solve anything. Someone must start using and working with the 'new'.

In other words, if we don't link organisational change, which is only a tool to bring about behavioural change, there will be no real change. Without the kind of change that involves both levels, and which brings in the business environment and industry, we will not have greater adaptation to the demands of the outside world and the market. We don't reduce our change gap; we don't get a better fit with our environment, and we don't increase our chances of success over time.

In terms of **pressure for change,** it is useful to answer the following questions:

1. What are the main reasons why we want to change the organisation?

2. What in the business environment creates pressure for change? What in the industry? What in the organisation? What in the employees?

3. How do these different pressures for change interact?

4. What change do we want to bring about – at the 'headline' level?

# Summary: Pressures for change in large and small

In this chapter, we have discussed pressures for change. The influence of the environment and industries, the evolution of organisations over time and people's learning create pressures for change in organisations. These four levels interact.

### How can we understand changes in business environment and their impact on organisations?

★ Political, economic, social and technological factors affect societies, organisations and people. The stronger and faster the trends, the greater the impact. Different organisations are affected by different trends and forces.

### How can we understand the dynamics of an industry and its impact on industry organisations?

★ Industries have different dynamics, but all are affected by the bargaining power of suppliers and buyers, the threat of new entrants, substitutes and rivalry in the industry. The stronger the forces, the greater the pressure for change.

### How can we understand the evolution and changes of organisations over time?

★ As organisations grow - in size and age - new conditions are created for them to operate. Age creates culture; size drives structure. A critical balance to manage on an ongoing basis is how much individuals and parts of the organisation are allowed to govern themselves versus what should be coordinated with others.

### How can we understand people's learning and the pressures for change it creates?

★ People learn by thinking things out, watching others, taking instruction and by trial and error. Trying things out leads to better adaptation to the outside world than other ways.

### How do pressures for change interact at different levels?

★ Trends in the business environment, industries, organisations and individuals interact. In analysis, these levels are isolated, but they are parts of the same whole. To understand organisations' relations to the world, we must create a synthesis.

### How do change pressures rise the need for change in organisations?

★ All pressures for change create a need for change - in organisations and individuals. An organisation therefore needs to be able to evaluate what has an impact and what does not.

# Reflections: Pressures for change in large and small

# 4. Organisational results and changed behaviour

Once we have an idea of how the world, the industry, the organisation and individuals affect organisations - individually and in interaction - we can learn how performance in organisations is affected by this. We can also think of what behaviours in the organisation to change to affect those outcomes.

In organisations, we are often good at explaining how the world, the industry and the organisation have evolved over time in a comprehensive way. Breadth and history can give us a direction into the future.

I like to understand things in context and go from the whole in the future to the parts here and now; I want to understand what 'embraces' us. But the broad brushstrokes are not more important or more strategic. We must not lose details. Strategy needs a long-term perspective, but if something is important in the long term, we need to start here and now.

This view is excellently reflected by the Scottish historian Thomas Carlyle in his 1829 work *Sign of the Times:*

> Our grand business undoubtedly is, not to see what lies dimly at a distance, but to do what lies clearly at hand.[54]

The performance of all organisations is created by the behaviour of people. If we want to change outcomes over time, we need to act here and now. To do so, we need to learn to define actions, behaviours, so that they become so concrete that we can take action here and now. That's seldom simple.

---

In this chapter, we therefore describe how we can understand how behaviours affect different outcomes in an organisation; how we can link different behaviours to desired outcomes; how we specify behaviours in such a way that it becomes possible to talk about them objectively and then try to influence them; and finally, how behaviours are affected in different situations.

---

# Behaviours and impact on results

In the last chapter, I concluded by saying that it is important to link organisational change to individual change. Why is this so? Well, because the behaviours individuals perform - what we do - in an organisation is what creates all organisational outcomes. Whatever outcome you are looking at and want to improve, customer satisfaction, profitability, legal certainty, quality, productivity, staff turnover, sickness absence, etc., they are the result of employee behaviours. If you want to change an outcome, you ultimately must change behaviours too. There is no other way.

## Organisational results

Organisational results are often formulated as goals. Goals, and therefore organisational results, should be clearly formulated so that employees can understand them. If goals are not understood, they will not influence a change in behaviour. The higher the *instructional value* of a goal - the more clearly described it is and the easier it is to understand - the more likely it is that employees' energy will be directed towards the goal. However, as we will see later, goals are only a prerequisite for following up, analysing performance, learning and developing an organisation. It is in following up that we drive change. If we do not have a desired target, we have no opportunity for evaluation and learning.

> In this book, I define goals as the specific and measurable results we want to achieve in (a certain part of) the organisation at a given time.

Schematically, goals and organisational outcomes can be sorted under four themes: financial, customer and market related, related to internal operations, and related to development.

*Financial* results are those that describe the financial status of an organisation in different ways. They are often different depending on the type of organisation. In private organisations, turnover, profitability, return on investment (not least in listed companies) and costs are often common financial outcomes we are interested in monitoring and changing in different ways. In public organisations, which generally do not have sales (turnover) in the same way, a focus on costs is more natural. This does not mean that cash inflows are unimportant. Public organisations receive money in the form of tax funds and the like. These should also be monitored so that their use has an impact on the customers or beneficiaries (citizens) of the activity. So, whether we are in a private or a public activity, there is a need to monitor financial performance. If we want to improve our financial situation, regardless of the organisation, we need to behave slightly differently in our business. If we do the same, we will get the same results.

One way to influence financial performance is to try to influence *customer and market-related* targets. These types of targets are mainly related to how many of our customers or beneficiaries are and how satisfied they are with what we provide. Objectives of this type can be measured in several ways. In private companies, market share, i.e. the percentage of our sales in a total market, or customer satisfaction, for example how many of our customers return or tell others about us (what we call Net Promoter Score, NPS)[55] are common. However, it can also be about how many customers leave us for a direct competitor. After all, this is a kind of proof that they are *not* (sufficiently) satisfied. In public services, customer and market related targets are relatively rare apart from 'satisfaction'. A common example is how satisfied we as parents are with the treatment or information provided by the staff of nursery schools and schools. If we want to have more satisfied customers, customers who feel that they receive better treatment or information, we need to improve the way we work, our behaviours.

One way to get more and/or happier customers or recipients is to understand and improve how we work in some kind of 'production'. To understand how we work and how to improve production we need to measure and set targets for it. We do this with targets that relate to *internal operations*. Examples of types of targets that we classify under this category are quality of processes, productivity, efficiency, capacity, delivery accuracy. Although these results feel 'machine-like', we have actual production of services as well. In healthcare, we perform operations. That is a form of production, even if the language feels a bit strange. In the same way, an operation can go well or not so well. The 'goodness', that the operation is successful, says something about quality (how well it went) and efficiency, (goal achievement because of the intervention). The goal is likely to be that the operation will go well with a certain amount of resources. The smaller the operation with the goal still achieved, the better the effectiveness. To increase our efficiency or our quality, we need to do something a little better. We need to change our behaviours.

Objectives that relate to improving as an organisation are classified under *the development perspective*. These outcomes relate to innovation, learning, development of the organisation (as such) and employees and their skills. Examples of objectives in this category are personnel and organisational measures: skill level, leadership, number of employees, absenteeism, engagement, health and safety. Other examples are related to change as such: rate of innovation, number of new ideas realised, progress of change projects. These too require behaviours to be realised and new behaviours to be changed.

In summary, we can conclude that the behaviours of employees affect financial performance, customer and market performance, internal business performance and performance related to the development of the organisation and its employees. If we want to influence these results, we must influence behaviours.

Sometimes we may even need to change behaviours and goals in several stages. A development objective (e.g. level of competence of operators) leads to new behaviours. This in turn leads to better quality products (e.g. fewer so-called leaf streaks on the produced carton). The improved quality creates a stronger customer relationship (e.g. more repeat customers) which in turn affects the financial situation (e.g. predictability of sales due to longer contracts). It is therefore important to have a clear understanding of how behaviours and results at different levels and stages are linked to know how to develop them.

However, we need to be careful about which outcomes are linked when we want to make real change. We will rarely be able to prove that one specific behaviour and outcome leads to another, as we do in natural science. That's not the point either. By thinking through how different behaviours and outcomes are plausibly linked, we can try to be a little more 'surgical' in how we use our time and commitment to influence behaviours in our changes. Then we can also learn through our evaluations what works and what doesn't, and thereby improve.

---

In terms of **organisational results**, it is useful to answer the following questions:

5. What concrete results do we want to influence with the change (e.g. profitability, customer satisfaction, productivity, innovation)?

6. Have we covered financial, customer and market, internal and development objectives and understood their relationships?

7. In which direction do we want to influence the results? Increase or decrease? How much? Until when?

---

By being clearer about what improvements in performance we want to achieve, we can also be clearer about the behaviours that drive them. In this way, there is an opportunity to find the link between organisational outcomes and individual behaviours.

## Behaviours and their role in creating results

So how do we link behaviours and outcomes? In fact, they are very similar. They are both measurable, observable and reliable. What separates them is that behaviours are active and outcomes are timed. Another thing that separates them, and which is crucial to understand when we want to drive change in an outcome, is that behaviour 'leads' outcomes, and outcomes 'follow' behaviour as Figure 4.1 describes.

Figure 4.1 Behaviour and its impact on performance

| B | Measurable | | R | Measurable |
|---|---|---|---|---|
| | Observable | | | Observable |
| | Reliable | | | Reliable |
| Behaviour | Active | | Result | Time-related |

Behaviours are therefore measurable, observable, reliable and active.[56] This is what we call *pinpointed* behaviours. If we first look at *measurability*, it means that we can count the frequency of a certain behaviour (the number of times) or the quality of the behaviour (how it is performed - topography). The easiest way to measure frequency is to see that it has occurred. We can count how many times a person thanks for help, as an example. We can also see it. Assuming we are looking. So, it is *observable*. *Reliability* is another for dependability. That something is reliable means that at least two people can observe the behaviour and agree that they have seen the behaviour performed. Two people should be able to agree easily that one person has thanked another for help. As for whether a behaviour is *active,* we can establish that anything a dead person can do is not active enough. We will stress the importance of this later.

For now, we can be content to say that we want to drive activity when developing organisations, not passivity. Reinforcing behaviour, we want to see more of is then both more effective and a more humane starting point than punishing behaviour we do not want to see.

A bit like a litmus test, we can 'approve' behaviours that we can watch and that we can capture on film. We can hear them, see them somehow, perceive them. And those are the ones that influence what our results will be. For example, if we want to influence safety in a workplace, we need to think about which workplace behaviours are safe and which are unsafe behaviours and/or cause accidents. We need to understand which behaviours reduce accidents in the workplace. We also need to understand the people who perform these behaviours. If we want to influence sales, we need to think about which behaviours lead to increased sales and who performs these behaviours. If we want to influence the quality of our products or services, we need to understand which behaviours employees perform that contribute to increased quality - depending on how we define it.

In terms of results, we replace active with *timed*. We do this for two reasons: first, results are not active. They are just results of something. Organisational results are the result of someone in the organisation doing something. Secondly, there should be a time parameter for when a result or a certain level has been achieved. Otherwise, how can we evaluate what we have achieved, analyse why it happened and draw lessons from it?

> In change, we can only be precise when we know what we want to achieve and what outcome we want to improve. Once we know which outcomes we want to affect, we can identify the behaviours that have an impact on those outcomes. We can then build a picture of how those who perform these behaviours can learn and improve their behaviours going forward.

## Precise behaviours

I've been talking since early in the book about behaviours, and that change without change in behaviours is not change. What we need to influence to improve organisational performance is behaviour. The next natural step is to try to understand a little more precisely what behaviours are, what they are not and what they look like in different contexts.

To influence something, we need to know what it is. We should be able to see behaviours being carried out and we should be able to 'catch them on film'. For me, who has been looking at businesses and thinking in terms of behaviour for over two decades, this is perfectly natural. When I look at organisations, I see behaviours that are carried out and that produce results. For others, this is a new way of looking at an organisation and how it works. They may be more used to thinking of a business in terms of roles, processes, systems, people or other things that make up an organisation.

> Whatever approach we take to understanding an organisation, it is employee behaviour that is by far the most central issue. It is employee behaviour that creates results, that is carried out in processes by different roles, that is to be supported by different systems, that makes us happy, that makes us sad, that makes us motivated and engaged, and that makes us take sensible or unwise decisions.

Distinguishing between what is and what is not behaviour is therefore an important issue if we want to bring about change. When we can do that, it is much easier to work with people in change.

## Behaviours and labels

In my experience, quite few are trained to specify behaviours. Often, we use different types of descriptions that are general and describe a mixture of characteristics, personality traits and other things. What we might call *labels*. Label is a collective word for many different characteristics or different behaviours. A major difference between labels or other types of descriptions and behaviours is that labels are often non-specific, subjective and open to interpretation. We often use labels instead of behaviours unless we have trained ourselves to describe behaviour in a precise way. It is natural to do so, but it makes it more difficult to change.

Common labels we use in organisations are social, driven, ambitious, customer-focused, creative and competent. I believe that these characteristics (labels) are important for a successful organisation. However, my interpretation of e.g. competent and someone else's may differ significantly. What I think a 'nice' person does or doesn't do is also very different from the opinion of others. It's not precise. If we are not specific about what competent or nice is, it becomes difficult to know what outcomes it affects. When we can't be precise about behaviours, it makes it difficult to change behaviours, which makes it difficult to influence organisational results.

We should rather look at what is precise. Something a person says or does that can be described in a way that everyone who observes it agrees on it. Behaviours, as I said, are measurable, observable, reliable and active.

What we do when we practice defining behaviours is to set each intended behaviour against the four criteria of measurable, observable, reliable and active. When we do this, we can quite easily judge whether it is a behaviour or whether it is something else (a label).

To give us a chance to practice distinguishing behaviour from labels, I have formulated a few statements describing behaviours and labels in Figure 4.2. Which statements describe behaviours and which describe labels? You can mark the correct options' columns.

Figure 4.2 Behaviours and labels

| Behaviour | Label | |
|---|---|---|
| | | John comes late to our meetings |
| | | We need to work harder to meet customers' demands |
| | | Fatima always asks how I am when we meet |
| | | The atmosphere in the group is bad |
| | | We don't greet each other in the morning |
| | | She spontaneously offered to help me solve my problem |
| | | Sophie shows the right spirit |
| | | Carl isn't safety conscious enough |

If we look at the first statement "being late for meetings", it is a behaviour. As a group, we can measure if someone is late for meetings. We can observe it. There are several of us who can agree that this is the case. It's impossible for a dead person to be late for a meeting, so it's active.

If we look at the second statement, we can see that it is a label. "Work harder" is a general description of several different behaviours that we don't know how to measure or observe. Nor do we automatically agree on what "work harder" means. Likely it should be active but since it falls on the other criteria it is not a behaviour. From a behavioural perspective, this raises a number of questions: what does it mean to "work harder"? Should we measure by more hours worked? Should we measure it by someone hitting harder when typing emails or code? There are simply many different ways to "work harder". The description is subjective, open to interpretation and non-specific. It's a label.

"Fatima always asks how we're doing when we meet." It's measurable, observable and reliable. Asking someone is also active. A dead person cannot ask someone how they are doing. It is a behaviour.

"The atmosphere in the group is bad" is very reminiscent of working harder. We don't obviously have a common picture of how that might show up. We don't know how to measure it or observe it reliably. It's a label. Behaviours that indicate 'bad mood' could include: sighing loudly, interrupting each other, shouting, crying, rolling eyes.

The next statement is a bit special. It illustrates the importance of activity and what we might call *non-behaviour*. This one is a bit harder to wrap our head around. Spontaneously we think this is a behaviour. It's measurable, it's observable and it's reliable. However, it's not active. It's indeed possible for a dead person to not greet someone in the morning. To be honest, if there was a dead person in the room and he greeted me, I would be extremely surprised and frankly quite shaken. Non-behaviours fall for what we call the 'dead man's test'.[57]

Making a distinction between behaviours and non-behaviours is important when working with change. One reason is that when we want to influence behaviours, we want to drive up so-called deficit behaviours. This means behaviours that have a positive impact on the outcomes we want to increase and of which we want to see more. We want to see as much activity as possible that has a positive impact on outcomes. We therefore want to devote our limited time to reinforcing the kind of 'good' behaviours that have a positive impact on a particular outcome.

One reason why non-behaviours are more difficult to work with is because they are not active. It is therefore smarter to rephrase non-behaviours (that we don't want to see) into behaviours (that we do want to see). Instead of commenting when someone is not doing what is expected (for example, using the prescribed safety equipment), we can reinforce what we want to see (using the safety equipment). It makes for a very different working environment, more positive, more driven and over time it affects performance in a very different way. When we talk about reinforcement and weakening later, this will become clearer.

"Offering help spontaneously" is measurable, observable, reliable and active. It is also a behaviour that creates many positive effects and that we like to see a lot of in an organisation. "Showing the right commitment", on the other hand, is far too vague to be classified as a behaviour. However, it is a fairly common formulation and I see it in many organisations' various governance documents. To me, it is unclear what "demonstrate commitment" means. How do we measure commitment? How do we observe it so that we can measure it? If we can't measure or observe it, how can we agree on what it really is? If we can't, we can't work systematically to develop it? The same reasoning applies to "being security conscious".

I really want to stress that commitment, safety awareness, hard work and so on are characteristics that I hold dear. They are important for any organisation. I am absolutely convinced that they are needed. However, when we want to develop them and create a positive impact on the organisation's ability to thrive, we need to understand the behaviours behind these generic labels. Otherwise, we will fail to link behaviours and outcomes and therefore get less out of our change efforts.

---

In terms of **behaviour,** it is useful to answer the following questions:

8. What concrete behaviours do we need to change to influence outcomes?

9. How do these behaviours sound when they are specified, i.e. measurable, observable, reliable and active?

---

## Change of behaviour

How can we change behaviours then? What's so clever about changing behaviours is that whatever behaviours we want to change, they can only be changed in four different ways. We can *start* behaviours, we can *stop* behaviours, we can *do more of* any behaviour and we can *do less* of any behaviour. In practice, and when driving change, combinations of these four are likely to be required. However, as a model for understanding behaviour change, these four ways are quite clarifying. Some employees are likely to need to stop performing certain behaviours. Other employees may need to start performing certain behaviours. Still other employees may need to increase or decrease certain behaviours or perform behaviours in a different way. Some behaviours we want to see more of, others we want to see less of. Behaviours we want to see more of we call *deficit behaviours* and behaviours we want to see less of we call *surplus behaviours*.

If we want to increase sales in a business, there are likely to be several behaviours we want to see more of. I think talking to customers about their needs going forward might be one such behaviour. Sending more quotes on procurements where our expertise is needed might be another. Calling prospective clients and setting up meetings might be another. These are obvious things. It's not that hard to think of behaviours if you're trained in them, but often we're not and instead use labels like 'being more customer focused'.

To determine whether behaviours are in surplus or deficit, we need to put behaviours in their specific situation. To take a banal concrete example: it doesn't really seem sane to shout, 'Let's go, guys!' at a shareholders' meeting just as the chairman is presenting the agenda (even though there may be mainly 'guys' there). Shouting it in a dressing room before a football match is more reasonable.

The specific situation is no less important in more subtle contexts. Criticising someone who comments on a gap in the strategic analysis is something I have seen both now and then. It is definitely a surplus behaviour. Don't shoot the messenger, we say, but unfortunately, we do it quite often. We want to find gaps in our analysis, don't we? How else can the strategy be as good as possible? It may be appropriate to criticise someone, but it should be done in a measured way and in a separate forum. Whether something is a surplus or a deficit therefore depends on the situation.

The rationale for over- and under-performance is illustrated in Figure 4.3.

Figure 4.3 Surplus and deficit behaviour

| | Surplus behaviour "too often, too much" | Deficit behaviour "too seldom, too little" |
|---|---|---|
| Behaviour is … | …unwanted and should not occur at all | …wanted but not occurring |
| Behaviour is … | …wanted but occurring too often and/or too much | …wanted but occurring too seldom and/or too little |
| Behaviour is … | …wanted but occurring in the wrong context or situation | |

Source: adapted from Wadström (2020)[58]

## Behaviour, Personality and Openness to Interpretation

I worked for a period with an experienced academic in psychometrics: developing methods for different types of psychological measurements. Alongside his research, he worked on the selection of executives for management teams and boards, mainly helping clients to appoint management team and board members in listed companies and in government organisations and corporations across Europe.

My contribution was mostly to assess the organisations from a strategy perspective. As his area of expertise was in personnel assessments and appointments, he had a knowledge of the needs of a management team given a situation (the strategy perspective to which I contributed) and the composition of the team. He also had knowledge of how to assess different selection criteria for people, such as intelligence and other characteristics.

Through his research, he had come to be critical of general descriptions that various types of personality tests claim to evaluate. We thus had a common starting point about behaviour as a kind of lowest common denominator. What he therefore did in his work was to find behaviours that illustrated how different traits were expressed. In research, he felt he had support for a number of characteristics that were important for a leader in the role he was evaluating, and he found ways to exemplify these with behaviours that spiked the reasoning.

In personality psychology there is something called the Big Five theory.[59] This theory describes five relatively stable personality traits, sometimes referred to by the acronym OCEAN after the names of the factors: openness, conscientiousness, extraversion, agreeableness and neuroticism. At a general level, these may help us to understand how people act in different situations given some kind of natural tendency. However, to be more precise, and especially if we want to bring about change, these need to be substantially concretised and specific behaviours pinpointed.

My colleague's mission was to give some kind of indication of who was suitable as a leader with a large responsibility in a large organisation. In that respect, he felt that the OCEAN factors were nowhere near providing reliable decision support. It is not uncommon for the scales on which response results are presented to range from 0-100. In simple terms, 0 means nothing and 100 is the full score. Usually, most people land between 70 and 30 because of statistics, no matter what we look at. That was the case in this instance. So, he asked himself, for example: what does 76 say about agreeableness? What behaviours, or types of behaviours can we see then?

He conducted a series of experiments to see how accurate the tests were. After a bit of experimentation, he found that it was indeed possible to identify ranges on the scales. These ranges gave him a higher accuracy in predicting some kind of success for the kind of appointments on which he was working.

What he found was that the single best prediction yielded high *intelligence*. This was already known in research. What he then found was that two other factors, along with intelligence, made even more accurate judgements about who was likely to succeed in their task.

The first factor was to be *agreeableness*. This generally adds kindness, ability to empathise, cooperative, caring and friendly. Here he was able to conclude that the higher the value the better. The same he could conclude about intelligence, but with intelligence there was a caveat. Unless high intelligence were coupled with a relatively high capacity for agreeableness, a kind of willingness to cooperate rather than compete, people with high intelligence could easily be perceived as arrogant and exhibit a range of excess behaviours that are directly detrimental to an organisation's long-term success: interrupting others, making decisions without anchoring or weighing the input of others, overestimating one's own performance and capabilities, etc. In sum, smart is good, but smart, kind and humble is far better.

The second factor was *conscientiousness*. This manifests itself in a need for thoroughness, a desire to plan and control, self-discipline, systematicity and what David Clelland, one of the leading psychological researchers of the 20th century, called the *need for achievement*[60]. Grit, as we mentioned earlier, is thus not so far removed from conscientiousness.

When he looked at conscientiousness, he could see a threshold for when people became too meticulous, too detail-oriented and had an inability to see the big picture. Something that is absolutely critical for someone who is going to be the leader of a large organisation.

Many of the people he met ended up quite high on the 100-degree scale. A 'good' behaviour of a conscientious person is to follow through. So it was not uncommon for people who were considered for the kind of roles he worked with to be executives. He also scored high, so he knew his own.

To exemplify how open to interpretation agreeableness and conscientious are, he concretised them by using behaviours. It also helped him to do a quick screening. This screening he did by asking four questions to prospective candidates. The intelligence he felt he could judge based on how they handled the situation with the questions, which were heavily tapered precisely to elicit a reaction and get beyond clichés like creative, driven and 'go-getter'.

The first two questions were related to agreeableness and were: Are you kind? Do you let homeless people come to your home and have a hot shower and a meal of hot food? He himself had a great social pathos and helped people he met on the street just as he asked for it. He thought that was a kind thing to do, but at the same time he realised that not everyone saw it that way. Based on how those he met reasoned and exemplified behaviours, he was then able to make a judgement.

The next two questions related to conscientiousness and were: Are you thorough? Do you have the spices in alphabetical order? Many people laughed. However, he wasn't joking. In addition to his social commitment, he had a great interest in food and an eye for detail. He had the spices in alphabetical order. He also joked that it was lucky he didn't become a manager himself because he wouldn't be able to let go of details. He realised that he was probably better suited to academia where he could immerse himself in methods of statistical computation and psychological measurement.

It then turned out in his layman's experiments that people who had an accuracy of over circa 88 (out of 100) often had the spices in alphabetical order. Often although they were not interested in cooking. His conclusion was that a person in charge of an organisation with perhaps 10,000 employees in different countries or continents, who is unable to let go of details (e.g. spices) because of his need for control, will find it difficult to create development and space for others to lead and grow.

The conclusion of this is that we need to be careful about the labels we put on people. Labels are unclear and open to interpretation. Thorough, creative, driven, knowledgeable, or even fuzzier 'a good person', are simply not clear enough to work with when we want to change something. Change should lead to improved outcomes or at least changed behaviours that enable us to meet the demands placed on us. Loose labels do not help us to understand how to improve our performance. Another lesson is this: leading a major change is similar to leading a large organisation. This means that intelligence, kindness and conscientiousness are qualities that a change manager benefits from possessing. However, they are too 'fuzzy' to work with. If we want to be good change managers for real, we need to understand what behaviours we need to perform that reflect our intelligence, our kindness and our conscientiousness. We need to be more precise. We will cover some of these laer in the book.

## Context of behaviour

To understand behaviours, we need to understand that they are part of a context. Behaviour depends on something to start it and something to make it last. What starts the behaviour we call *activators* and what perpetuates or 'extinguishes' it, we call *consequences*.

Let's look at a concrete example. I get a headache. It's an activator. It starts a behaviour in me. Examples of behaviours that might be triggered by a headache are taking a painkiller, having a glass of water, having a cup of coffee or going for a walk to get some fresh air.

The expected effect of the behaviour 'take a headache tablet' or 'go for a walk' is in both cases that the headache will go away. The disappearance of the headache is what we call a consequence: what the person performing the behaviour perceives after performing that particular behaviour.

Consequences in this sense are not consequences in the traditional sense of saying, 'This must have consequences!' When we say that, we are equating consequences with punishment, and nothing could be more wrong. Punishments are a very small part of all the types of consequences that exist. Moreover, as we shall see, positive consequences are much more powerful and effective - especially when we want to change something.

Figure 4.4 describes how we can understand the context in which a behaviour takes place.

Figure 4.4 Context of behaviour

| A (activator) leads to... | ...B (behaviour) occurring... | ...that has C (consequences) |
|---|---|---|
| Activators are phenomena in the environment that cause a person to choose a behaviour based on past experience. This could be, for example, training, targets, job descriptions, prompts, reminders or perceived peer pressure | Behaviour is what someone does, says, thinks or feels, for example greeting, talking, smiling, writing, submitting a report, etc. | Consequence is something that follows a behaviour and 'tells' whether the behaviour was meaningful or not. Consequences can be of different kinds: attention, praise, pleasure, complaint, recognition, a feeling that you are capable of something, satisfaction, etc. |

Back to the headache: what do we do if the headache tablets don't help? Do we take another one? Maybe. If that one doesn't help either? Do we take a third one? Probably not. The reason is that the brain learns that some things work, and others don't. We choose a certain behaviour because we have learned that it works. The behaviour has been *reinforced*. The headache tablet is supposed to take away the headache and if it doesn't, then that behaviour hasn't served its purpose. Then the brain tells us to change the behaviour. This kind of feedback is, in my opinion, feedback in its purest form. It is a description of how we learn many of the behaviours we perform.

> Organisations generally spend 80% of their resources on activating, telling us what to do and how. Some examples are goals, strategy, rules, laws and values. Only the remaining 20% is spent on consequences, i.e., feedback of reflections and analyses made. Consequences account for 80% of impact and activators only 20%.[61] So we should work much more on consequences.

Anyone who wants to influence behaviour - and more importantly - anyone who wants to change behaviour, needs to focus on consequences. We need to focus on providing opportunities for people in the organisation to learn what works and what doesn't work, what leads to the desired change and what doesn't lead to the desired change. This is done through *shaping*, as we mentioned in an earlier chapter. Finally, we need to know which changing behaviours lead to which changes on which organisational results. Otherwise, of course, we have no way of leading and driving the change we want to see.

What we get in the organisation if we focus on activators to tell employees what to do without delivering consequences are rules and at best a plan that we have developed for them. There won't be much ownership of such a plan. What we get if we deliver consequences on certain behaviours is learning, new behaviours and in the long run the change we are looking to create.

The above reasoning is illustrated in Figure 4.5.

Figure 4.5 The ABC model

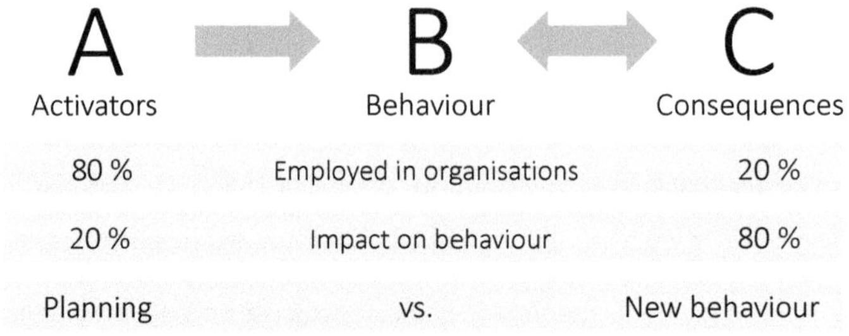

| A | B | C |
|---|---|---|
| Activators | Behaviour | Consequences |
| 80 % | Employed in organisations | 20 % |
| 20 % | Impact on behaviour | 80 % |
| Planning | vs. | New behaviour |

Source: adapted from Wadström (2022)[48]

## Activators start behaviour

Activators provide the answer to this question: What happened before the behaviour? What started the behaviour? The activator is the second component of the context in which the behaviour occurs (activator, behaviour and consequence).

There are different types of activators: instructions, someone asks you something, someone greets you, the telephone rings, the clock strikes noon, the boss enters the room, you get a target document sent to you. All these events come from outside. They happen outside us as human beings. However, behaviours can also be triggered by internal things. Things that happen inside our body. They can be triggered by emotions like anxiety, fear, or joy and by thoughts, ideas and whims that are awakened for whatever reason. They can also be triggered by purely physical things like hunger, thirst, headaches or palpitations.

In every situation we are put in, there are new and different activators. Common intentional activators in organisations are strategies, goals, rules, values, governance documents, job and process descriptions and more. The purpose of these is to help employees prioritise their working day. In addition to these signals that an organisation can control, there are also laws that are beyond the control of organisations that aim to control employee behaviour. In addition, there are direct requests, warnings and orders which are also activators.

There are simply many activators around us, in all situations. Some we are aware of; many we are also unaware of. The email that pops up in the bottom right corner of the screen can be an activator to open it. Someone smiling can be an activator to say hello in the corridor, or on the street. A launch of a project can be an activator for the organisation to focus on a specific issue. A thought that the deadline is approaching can activate someone to work a few extra hours that evening. A target set in an organisation and communicated in terms of customer satisfaction or number of ongoing change projects also serves to activate different behaviours.

Thus, if we want our organisation to achieve certain organisational results, we need to try to deliver activators that are clear, have a high instructional value, and that target the specific behaviour we want to influence.

Based on this insight, we work with goals in many organisations. Properly formulated, they offer just that: instructional value, direction. Goals are by far one of the most common conscious assets organisations have. The purpose of a goal is to guide the organisation's behaviour. The view that goals make employees perform better by making them more motivated to do a good job is widely spread in both strategy and organisational research.[62] Goals seek to influence people to refine their behaviours and thus perform better - however we define performance.

Objectives can be a powerful instrument to help members of an organisation to prioritise. By setting goals, we can communicate what should be prioritised over other things. However, many organisations' goal setting is carried out as an annual formal exercise that is disconnected from both strategy and change. Looking at the previous year's targets and adjusting the budget (this 'blue blanket'), adding a little on income and subtracting a little on costs, to secure a financial outcome does not take strategy and change into account. Goalsetting and strategizing too often involves just this kind of often meaningless revision rather than an exploration of how we need to change to create competitiveness and success over time.

> The purpose of setting targets, which is part of strategy work, is to set a direction and create the conditions for follow-up with analysis, reflection and learning, and thus to be successful. Unfortunately, this perspective is often missing in strategizing and goalsetting.

Activators in an organisation should help us to use our limited resources in the most efficient way possible. We want 'bang for the buck'. This means that the resources we spend, our time, money and commitment, should have a positive impact on what we want to achieve. Whether that's developing a new health app, making sure as much aid money as possible ends up in the field, or building the world's longest suspension bridge. We want what we invest to pay dividends. If we reason that way, we need to take seriously the work that will make that possible. We won't do that if we don't work on strategy and change in a systematic way and strive for continuous improvement.

A natural conclusion here is that more systematics should mean more time for careful analysis and planning. To some extent this is certainly true. Most organisations can get better at doing analysis: real analysis, the kind that answers *why* something is the way it is. Not summaries of the situation that only answer *what* it is. However, we must not be fooled into thinking that analysis and planning are the key to success over time. We don't want to plan too much. A good strategy is one that is implemented. If we plan without pressure-testing our ideas with several stakeholders and letting them question the reasonableness of what we have planned, we risk quickly creating plans that are of no use to anyone.

> Much of what is planned never gets done. All the time we spend planning things that don't get done is a cost with no returns. That is the definition of *waste*. We therefore need to find ways of working that help us to ensure that we plan enough so that we know what we are going to do, but can also adapt on an ongoing basis as things around us change.

Activators influence which behaviours are performed to 20%. We therefore need to devote a lot of time to what accounts for 80% of the impact in our work. This we call consequences. The systematic approach to strategy and change work that I mention above is therefore more about systematic evaluation and feedback than planning.

## Consequences sustain and drive behaviour

Since it is the consequences that determine whether a behaviour will be used in the future, it is important to know how different types of consequences affect behaviours. A behaviour can have four different types of consequences: positive reinforcement, negative reinforcement, punishment and extinction.

These four impacts are visualised in Figure 4.6.

Figure 4.6 Four types of consequences and their impact on behaviour

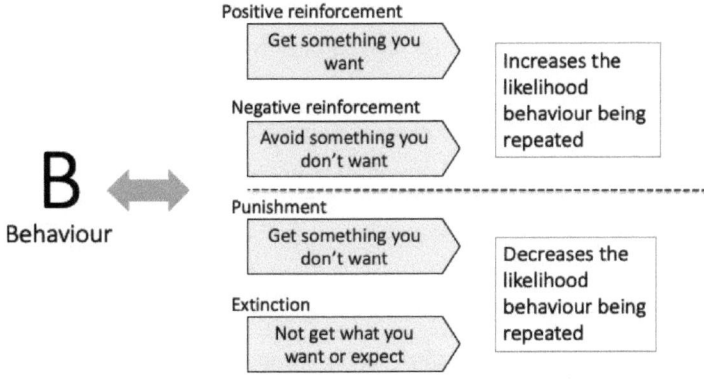

Source: adapted from Daniels (2001)[63] and Skinner (1969)[64]

1. *Positive reinforcement* means that you receive or experience something pleasurable as a consequence of a behaviour. For example, it can be praise, winning a lottery ticket, recognition, access to information, a feeling that you have done something good, a pat on the back, a look, attention, a smile or something else that increases the likelihood that you will perform the behaviour in the future.

2. *Negative reinforcement* means that you are escaping or avoiding something unpleasant as a consequence of a behaviour. It could be avoiding scolding or bad publicity, relieving a headache, avoiding embarrassment, avoiding being part of a change in the organisation you don't want to be part of, or anything else that increases the likelihood of you repeating the same behaviour in the future.

3. *Extinction* means that you don't get what you expected - consciously or unconsciously. You don't get a pay rise or praise for your good ideas. You don't get the appreciation you expected for the effort you put in. Nobody cares. No one asks. No one shows interest. No one 'sees you'. The ineffective headache tablet is another example. The behaviour turns out not to work and is pointless. Extinction will eventually lead to the behaviour ceasing to be used because it does not lead to what we expected.

4. *Punishment* means that you suffer something you don't like - something aversive (perceived negatively) as a direct consequence of a behaviour. You may give away money in the form of a fine, a glare, a derogatory comment, anguish over a decision made or even physical violence as a result of your behaviour.

What we know about consequences is that reinforcement increases the likelihood that a behaviour will be carried out. If we want to see an increase in a deficit behaviour, reinforcement, positive or negative, is the tool we have at our disposal. If we want to see a decrease in excess behaviour, extinction and punishment are the only options because they have a debilitating effect.

In change, we want to increase deficit behaviours and reduce surplus behaviours. Combined, this has the best effect on the outcomes we want to influence.

We can therefore conclude that there are different consequences that work in different ways. The wise change manager learns which ones can or should be used in different contexts to reinforce or weaken behaviours.

Whether consequences reinforce or weaken our behaviours, they can also be differently powerful depending on when they occur and how certain we think they are. Understanding this is the next step in learning the impact of consequences.

## Powerful and less powerful consequences

To understand how powerful, or impactful, a particular consequence is, we can carry out a so-called *consequence analysis*. When we do that, we look at the consequences that follow a specific behaviour. This allows us to assess which consequences have an impact on the behaviour (which in turn affects the organisation's performance).

We are all aware that different consequences are perceived in different ways by different people. One person who receives feedback may feel appreciated, another may feel flattened - even though the feedback was identical. By categorising how different consequences are perceived, we can understand which ones have the greatest impact on our behaviours.

Consequences can be perceived as positive to negative. Some of us get excited by praise. Some of us get a positive feeling in our body when we get to help someone. Some of us get fired up to work harder when we see how much bonus our extra work can bring. These are examples of *positive* consequences. There are many more. Some of us are saddened by a glare, others are very upset. Some feel a real concern about not being able to deliver high quality. These are examples of *negative* consequences. There is no value in positive or negative, it is just an expression that people perceive consequences of their behaviours in different ways, more or less positive and more or less negative.

Consequences can also be perceived as immediate or distant. By *immediate*, we mean that the consequence comes immediately after the behaviour. The feeling of being good at something may come immediately after we have completed a substantial piece of work, such as finishing a report or receiving a signed quotation. We can call this *instant feedback*. By *distant*, we mean that the consequence may come quite a long time after we have performed the behaviour. My increased understanding of strategy due to a training course may occur when I discuss corporate strategy with senior management several years after completing the course.

Finally, consequences can also be perceived as certain or uncertain. By *certain*, we mean that consequences occur every time we perform the specific behaviour. Every time I close my accounts, and everything is in balance, I get a sense of calm or contentment. However, I may feel *uncertain* if I get encouragement when I make suggestions for improvement to my boss (even though the boss has that ambition).

This is illustrated in Figure 4.7.

Figure 4.7 Consequences as PIC/NIC

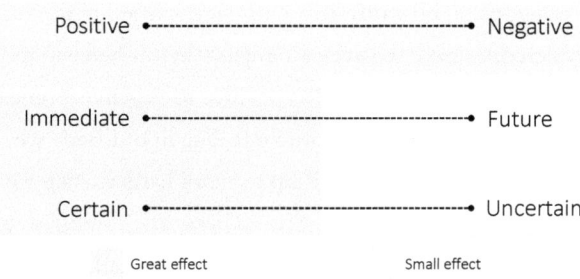

Source: adapted from Wadström (2020)[65] and Daniels (1989)[66]

This means that consequences can be positive, immediate and certain (abbreviated PIC), negative, future and uncertain (NFU), positive, future and certain (PFC) and a range of other combinations. The consequences that have the greatest impact on behaviours, particularly when we learn them (change), are those that are positive, immediate and certain (PIC) and those that are negative, immediate and certain (NIC). Hence, PIC/NIC.

In everyday life, consequences are combined in different ways all the time and we are guided by them daily - consciously and unconsciously. By looking at the example of using prescribed safety equipment, we can learn something about the effect of different consequences and activators.

In activities with safety risks, such as industries, construction sites, mines, power plants, hospitals and ports, we have safety equipment of various kinds to protect ourselves and others. Often the activators (instructions) that tell us what to do are clearly worded. Most (if not all) people working in hazardous businesses know what is required. Yet sometimes we ignore the rules. Activators, as noted earlier, have a limited impact. By understanding that consequences are stronger than activators, and that some consequences (PIC and NIC) are more powerful than others, we can understand a behaviour that is quite strange: going against something that we know is good for our own safety and the safety of others. Why do we do such things?

One positive consequence that is sometimes highlighted is that we finish the job faster if we don't wear safety equipment. Another is that the equipment is uncomfortable or interferes with our work in other ways. These are both perceived as *positive* consequences of doing 'wrong'. The feeling that I will finish faster is also *immediate*. I can start working straight away. In addition, I am quite *sure* (certain) to finish faster if I get going straight away without stopping and putting on safety gear. This means that there are at least two consequences that are positive, immediate and certain (PIC) of going against regulations.

What about the negative consequences of ignoring regulations? Ignoring safety equipment can have several negative consequences. I can hurt myself or others. I can be 'caught' and a safety officer will give me a warning.

Getting caught is not the worst thing that can happen. Of course, hurting yourself or others is much worse, but in both cases the consequence is *negative*. However, the risk of getting caught is relatively low and it's not happening right now. The consequences are simply perceived as *uncertain* if they will affect me. 'It won't happen to me. I've done this so many times'. Because they don't affect me right now. They are more *distant*. This means that these two negative consequences are *distant* and *uncertain*. Given this, it is quite logical to ignore safety equipment, even though it is wrong. The reinforcements on ignoring it are more powerful.

Different people perceive consequences differently, which is also reflected in the fact that some always use the prescribed safety equipment while others do not. One reason for this is our learning history, our experience of similar situations and/or our understanding of why something is important to follow.

To take another example. For people who are unaccustomed to reading comprehensive decision-making documents, it is difficult to start reading a heavy report, even though they realise the long-term benefits of doing so. An experienced reader, on the other hand, has an easier time. The impact of reading a report for an experienced reader is often *positive*, *immediate* and *certain*. As soon as I start reading the report (immediate), I get a better understanding (positive) of the decision I am facing and how I can approach the decision. I know from experience (certain) that each time I have read a decision report I have created a slightly better understanding of the issue.

For the more unaccustomed reader, the consequences may be quite different. I don't understand the report (negative) until I read it a couple of times (distant). I may even have to ask the author to explain and that takes time (negative). Time that I need for other things here and now (immediate). Before I read feel I am convinced (certain) that it will be hard or demanding to read the whole report (negative). If I don't understand, I'm likely to feel stupid (negative). Just thinking about taking up the report feels burdensome (immediate and negative).

In practice, these kinds of judgements are made in our brains without us being particularly aware of it. We can also see that the examples are exaggerated. However, they do help us to understand why some people behave as they do, for example not using the prescribed safety equipment and not reading a decision document. If we want to increase the use of safety equipment, for example, or for managers to read decision documents, we need to find and try to deliver consequences that are positive, immediate and certain.

We can conclude that positive (reinforcing) consequences are used to encourage behaviour that is in deficit. Negative ones we use to weaken behaviours that are in surplus.

For a consequence to have an effect, whether positive or negative, time and certainty are important. Consequences should ideally come immediately on a performed behaviour to have the intended effect. If it comes too late, it is easy to link the consequence to another behaviour performed later. Immediacy, or *timing*, is therefore crucial to ensure that we are reinforcing the right behaviour. For example, if we want to encourage innovation, every new idea, good *or* bad, should be reinforced by praise or a pat on the back just as it is revealed or given when we talk to the innovator about his or her idea. The assessment of the quality of the idea can be done afterwards.

The certainty of a consequence is crucial because if we know that nothing will happen, at all, then this has no impact. It sounds philosophical but let me illustrate. If I know that nothing will happen if I harass someone at work, then there is no risk for me to behave badly. The same goes for the reverse. If I know for sure that if I don't wear a helmet in the mine, I'll get killed. Then you will put the helmet on me. If you know for sure that when you make a suggestion for improvement, you will immediately get a bonus of

10,000 that month. Then you'll most likely come up with suggestions for improvement.

Of course, we can never know that the helmet will help us survive in advance and it is not reasonable that every suggestion for improvement generates extra pay. However, the examples illustrate the importance of whether a consequence is certain or uncertain. It does matter. Few, as far as I know, want consciously to "put on my gasoline boots and walk through hell," to paraphrase Method Man in the Wu Tang Clan classic *Protect Ya Neck*.[67] In many real-world cases, consequences are uncertain.

## Impact of change efforts

The reasoning about different consequences has a direct bearing on changes, and how we can lead them. Changing a business requires more and different efforts than managing a business. We therefore need to be able to focus on some things and put less focus on others. We have limited resources and need to use them wisely: we have already stated that we want activity; we do not want to work on non-behaviours. We want to reinforce deficit behaviours, behaviours we see too little of and which have a positive impact on the outcomes we want to improve in a positive way. That's the most effective. We will now develop this reasoning.

In organisations, we sometimes stereotypically talk about punitive or reinforcing cultures. Since we want to be more precise, we can rather say that organisations with reinforcing cultures are organisations characterised by positive reinforcement. Similarly, organisations with a punitive culture have consequence systems that are essentially characterised by threats of punishment and retaliation that can only be avoided through negatively reinforcing behaviours. We do what we must do to avoid something negative. We know with relative certainty that organisations with mainly positive reinforcement perform better.[68] So one way to prioritise resources is to focus on reinforcing active behaviours that have a positive impact on performance.

In positive reinforcement organisations, employees behave in a certain way because they want to. They feel that their behaviour gives them something: they get something out of it. Their behaviours are positively reinforced. Employees in an organisation characterised by negative reinforcement or punishment rather feel that they must behave in a certain way in order to escape something that is unpleasant. They are negatively reinforced or punished. Organisations characterised by retaliation and the threat of punishment reveal themselves in expressions such as 'If you don't hear anything, everything is fine'.

Organisations are often quite feedback-poor. Specific, positive feedback on employee performance (behaviours and results) is relatively rare. It goes against the way we humans are made. Humans are *herd animals*. We generally want to know how we are performing, for our own sake and in relation to others. Feedback of various kinds therefore drives behaviour. If we want to create an organisation that is high performing and constantly evolving, the right approach is not to act on the 'if you don't hear it, it's okay' thesis. We need to get better at giving concrete positive feedback on deficit behaviours.

This is even more important when we want to change an organisation. All change starts from changing people. We know that many changes fail to achieve the results set out. Achieving real change and thereby realising your strategy, achieving your goals or improving your business is undeniably difficult. One reason for this is that too few organisations are characterised by positive reinforcement. By focusing on positively reinforcing result-driven behaviours rather than, through negative reinforcement or punishment, forcing someone's performance to a 'minimum' level to get away with it, we can achieve much more.

To provide that kind of positive reinforcement, we need to get to know our business and our colleagues. We need to ensure that we understand the business logic and the people whose behaviours create the results. So good advice to anyone who wants to increase performance in an organisation is to get to know their organisation, get to know their staff and colleagues, get to know what positive reinforcement for different people in different departments, units or organisations is. There are many different positive reinforcers to use. These can create an opportunity for employees to enjoy performing, rather than feeling obliged to do so.

To create a culture of positive reinforcement, a good rule of thumb is to give feedback aimed at positively reinforcing behaviours eight times as often as we give feedback aimed at weakening or punishing behaviours. This can be a way to create an organisation where employees perform because they want to perform, not because they have to. People who enjoy their work perform better than those who work to avoid losing their pay. The difference in performance between two employees where one is driven by positive reinforcement and the other by negative reinforcement can be crucial to the success of a company. In Figure 4.8 I have illustrated these arguments.

Figure 4.8 Positive and negative reinforcement effects on behaviour

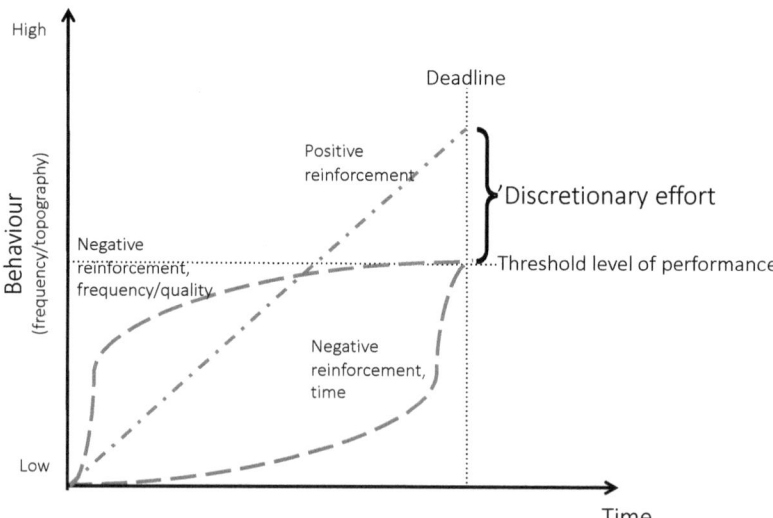

Source: adapted from Abernathy (1996) and Wadström & Ekvall (2013)[69]

In organisations characterised by negative reinforcement, we can see two phenomena that show lower performance than necessary. One is driven by time ("Negative reinforcement, time" in the graph) and the other by quality or frequency ("Negative reinforcement, frequency/quality" in the graph).

When behaviours are negatively reinforced by time, we may see low frequency or low quality of a behaviour well before a deadline. The closer we get to the deadline, the more intense the behaviours become to reach the level required to escape the negative, such as warning, scolding or guilt. Just when we have reached the minimum level required to escape that punishment, we stop performing. We deliver just at the deadline, just the level required. A common example of this is when we are asked at a management team meeting to 'look at something' in which we have no further interest. We don't do anything until we get that we should do, and then we do exactly what is required to make it look like we have done what we said we would.

When a behaviour is driven by the avoidance of unpleasant consequences (often internal, such as anxiety) rather than time, we can see how the behaviour increases rapidly and then decreases. We perform behaviours here and now to avoid discomfort here and now. As we approach a minimum acceptable level and our anxiety subsides, our ambition to perform better also subsides. When anxiety has completely subsided, we do not perform any more behaviours.

What both cases have in common is that we deliver exactly what is required. The focus for us will be to achieve the level of performance required to get away with it. The focus will not be to perform as well as we possibly can. We are driven by negative reinforcement i.e. getting away with something unpleasant (a punishment) rather than being driven to get something we want (positive reinforcement).

If we look at an organisation that is characterised by positive reinforcement, it has a more consistent frequency and quality of behaviour. We do not perform behaviours to deliver a certain result, of a certain quality, at a certain time to get away with it, but because we personally feel we get something out of it. This can be both internal and external: a sense of contribution, of context, of learning, of being noticed or complimented for our good performance. When that kind of positive reinforcement permeates the organisation, we don't stop performing behaviours just because we have reached a certain minimum level. We continue to perform even better even though the target has been reached. If this is an outcome where we would like to see as high a performance as possible, then of course it is grateful to perform better than a minimum level.

The difference between the performance achieved with an essentially negatively reinforced organisation and a positively reinforced organisation we can call *'discretionary effort'*. When we focus on reinforcing what is positive, we get better performance than when we focus on trying to minimise or punish what is negative.

> Reinforcing positive behaviours is more effective than punishing negative ones if we want to create long-term success. We create better performance by reinforcing the positive, the things that drive results, not by spending time weakening behaviours that don't create value.

So, if we want to change an organisation's performance, we need to understand the behaviours that drive that performance and how we can influence those behaviours.

# Summary: Organisational results and changed behaviour

In this chapter we have discussed how we define organisational results, how behaviours affect results, how we can link different behaviours to desired results, how we specify behaviours so that it is possible to work and influence them, and finally how behaviours are affected in different situations.

### How do we define organisational results?

✦ Organisational results (e.g. goals) describe measurable, observable, reliable and timed states we want to achieve with or in an activity. Some examples are profitability (in money or as a %), customer satisfaction (as Net Promoter Score, NPS) or quality (measured as on-time, in full delivery, OTIF).

### How do behaviours affect different results in an organisation?

✦ All results in an organisation arise from the behaviour of employees. If we want to change a result, we must therefore change behaviour.

### How do we link different behaviours to desired results?

✦ Behaviours are leading, results are lagging. Some behaviours have a direct impact on (lead to) certain results. For example, conducting safety rounds is most likely to lead to a reduction in workplace accidents. By focusing on pinpointed behaviours, we can influence concrete outcomes with greater precision.

### How can we pinpoints behaviours in such a way that it is possible to talk about them objectively and then try to influence them?

✦ Behaviours are measurable, observable, reliable and active. They can be captured on film, and they are something a dead person *cannot* do.

### How are behaviours affected in different situations?

✦ Behaviours are mainly influenced by their consequences, i.e. what the performer experiences after the behaviour has been performed. Consequences that are immediate and certain - whether positive or negative - have the strongest impact. Best organisational performance is achieved through positive reinforcement of behaviours that have the 'right' impact on a specific organisational result.

# Reflections: Organisational results and changed behaviour

# 5. Change magnitude and stakeholders

Once we know how behaviours and results are linked, how we specify them and how we influence them in different situations and over time, we can think about which people perform behaviours and influence results.

What we do then is analyse the magnitude and stakeholders of change. Magnitude and stakeholders are interrelated. The larger the magnitude of change, the more stakeholders. The more stakeholders, the more potential supporters who can help drive the change and the more opponents of the change. Magnitude and stakeholders matter, and we need to understand how.

Sergey Brin, one of Google's founders, shares the view on the importance of critical mass of stakeholders and how this mass's collective ownership is crucial for new things to take hold:

> There are things out there that are very simple, and that you never thought would work. ... Wikipedia is one of those things that it would never occur to me that it could work. ... But it does work. ... People who have taken fairly simple ideas ... and after the ideas have got some momentum of their own, they can really take off. It's actually amazing.[70]

In change, we can therefore talk about a *critical mass*. In its original physical sense, critical mass is the mass of a fissile material (e.g. uranium or plutonium) required for a chain reaction to become continuous and self-sustaining. Similarly, a snowball requires a certain weight and speed to start rolling on its own. A change also needs a critical mass: people of a certain quantity with a certain weight behind and/or pushing the change for it to happen for real.

In this chapter we will therefore explain how we can assess the magnitude of a change and what the implications of that magnitude are for the change process, as well as how we can identify and analyse the stakeholders that need to be involved for a change to have a positive intended impact.

## Change magnitude

I hear quite often that one change or another is big. It seems natural in the lingo to talk about almost any change as revolutionary, transformative, disruptive, etc. Many changes seem to be considered as just big or massive. It is probably true that many changes are big, otherwise we might not talk about them. However, there also seems to be a degree of coquetry. It seems that being exposed to or working with big changes is a bit glamorous. If we change (a lot) we are somehow in the game. As you can imagine, I take a sceptical view of this.

Since this book is a book about change in the mind of the strategist, the strategy perspective needs to be highlighted here. From a strategy perspective, i.e. competitiveness, increased performance and success over time, it is by no means certain that major change is either necessary or right. And should it be the case that it is more talk than action, that is also serious. Talking about major transformations because they are considered absolutely crucial and then not allowing the change to permeate the whole way the business works becomes strange for a strategist. It only takes attention away from things that are surely more important.

The most effective changes an organisation can make are those that create a positive impact on some of the organisation's results - whatever they are - without the need to invest significant and targeted resources.

We therefore need to understand how 'big' a change actually is or is not. Assessing the magnitude of a change helps us to dimension resources and change management approaches and is crucial to ensure that the benefits of a change are realised.

> The fact that a change is 'big' does not help us. Big is not a good word. What does big mean? When assessing scale, we need to be more precise about what is going to change and how, so that we can manage the change - not put labels like 'big' or small.

To understand and assess the extent of a change, we can therefore look at two different perspectives. We can look at the *amplitude of change* (depth) and the scope of change (breadth). The magnitude of change is thus a relationship between the depth of change and the breadth of change as shown in Figure 5.1 below.

Figure 5.1 Change Magnitude: amplitude and scope; depth and breadth

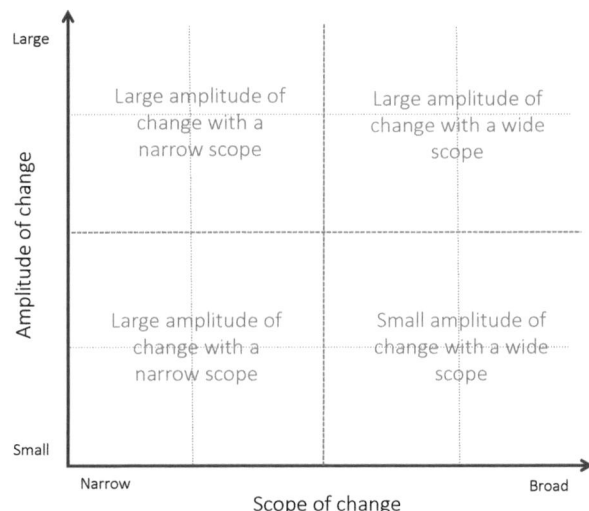

Source: adapted from Wadström et al. (2017)[71]

Breadth and depth are mutually exclusive, which means that one can basically be enormous while the other is almost non-existent; on the other hand, both can also be almost gigantic or minimal at the same time. They are not interdependent. So, when we waffle on about concepts like transformative change and disruption we need to be nuanced. If not before, then at the latest when we try to lead the change and realise the improvements in performance at which it aims.

Depth of change is determined by how different tomorrow's behaviour is from today's. Breadth of change is defined by how much of the organisation and its neighbourhood is affected. How many and how heterogeneous stakeholders the change has. While depth of change is primarily linked to organisational change, breadth of change is linked to the individuals in the organisation who are affected. Here we thus have that relation between organisation and individual change, I mentioned earlier.

## Depth of change

There are several ways to assess the depth of a change. One way is to look at behaviour today and contrast it with behaviour tomorrow. An example of a change with a small depth is employees being required to log in via an app instead of via the browser. That kind of change is shallow. The behaviour of 'logging in' is not that different. When it comes to fundamentally changing the way the organisation operates or completely different ways of working, then the depth increases significantly. Achieving a change where Mandarin is to be introduced as the main language in a e.g. French organisation may be a banal example, but it clearly demonstrates a deep change. Everyone should always speak Mandarin and all documentation should be in Mandarin. There is a lot that needs to change in structures, processes, skills, and so on.

In the innovation literature we make a distinction between modular and architectural innovation.[72] This division can help us to understand the depth of a change. A bit simplified, we can say that *modular innovation* means that we change components or parts of a whole without changing the whole. For example, parts of an organisation – say a few routines – but not how the organisation functions. *Architectural innovation*, on the other hand, is about changing how the whole works and how its constituent parts interact. From this perspective, we can understand that changes in architecture have a greater depth than changes in components. However, what are the components (modules) of the whole (architectures) in this book?

One model that can help us to understand in which areas we need to change and how much, and thus provide an overall picture of the depth of change, is the Star Model (see Figure 5.2) developed by the American researcher J. K. Galbraith.[73]

Figure 5.2 Star Model

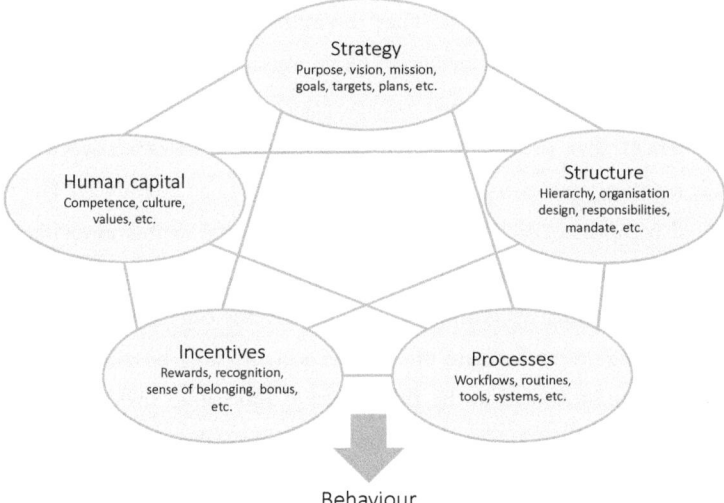

Source: adapted from Galbraith, 2001

The Star Model describes five *organisational* elements (modules) that make up any organisation - regardless of size or type. These five elements are: strategy, structure, process, incentives and human capital.

The first component is *strategy*. Strategy in this context consists of an organisation's purpose, vision, goals and direction: a kind of ambition for the whole organisation, what we want to do and for whom. For this ambition to be realised, it needs to be supported by a structure. *Structure* is the second element. It is relatively closely linked to the organisational structure: hierarchies, responsibilities, powers, positions, roles, information pathways and mandates. The structure can thus typically be considered as what is reasonably hard-coded and described in an organisational chart in the form of boxes, arrows and dashes. The third component is *processes*. Processes are the working methods, procedures, routines, tools and systems (IT systems and others) in an organisation that describe and facilitate how tasks are to be performed and the information in these flows. The fourth component is *incentives*. Incentives are those things that encourage employees to behave in a certain way - in a broad sense. They can be tangible things like promotion, overt recognition, financial incentives like bonuses or more subtle things like a sense of belonging or a sense of learning. Incentives are thus linked to consequences that provide positive reinforcement. In other words, they include anything that encourages employees to act in a certain way. The fifth and final component is *Human capital*. Human capital in this model are the people in the organisation, their behaviour, values and skills. It also consists of what remains after everyone has gone home - the organisational culture.

In trying to understand these components and how they need to change, we are interested in the skills, culture and values that prevail in the organisation in terms of how employees behave, what incentives actually work, what systems, processes and structures actually influence behaviour, and what goals and strategies actually drive behaviour. We are not interested in what is described in some governance or values document. Unfortunately, the things written can differ significantly from what matters.

## Alignment

One of the early and leading strategy researchers, Alfred Chandler, stated that strategy should come before structure and that systems should support structure.[74] It's a good start if after that we also address incentives and human capital. What Chandler pointed out, and what the Star model also makes clear, is that all these components need to be coherently targeted. Like the wheels on a car. All the wheels on a car need to be able to roll in the same direction, otherwise it becomes very energy intensive to move forward. Try to imagine how the car would move with the two rear tires 90° different from the two front wheels. This uniform direction is what we sometimes call *alignment*.[75]

If the different elements are not pointing to the same direction, it will be difficult to bring about behavioural change. We may not need to turn everything in the organisation upside down just because we change one of them. It is rather unlikely. Many organisations have a pretty good alignment. However, the least we need to do is to look at all the elements when there is a change in one of them, to see what the effects are in the others. If we don't do that, we will soon realise that we should have done it. This is true no matter what kind of change we want to bring about. Thus, consistently targeting strategy, structure, processes, incentives and human capital can be seen as a way of 'setting the stage' for a particular behaviour.

One way to assess the depth of change is therefore to use the Star model. Looking at the organisation and its five different elements (strategy, structure, process, incentives and human capital) 'today' and 'tomorrow'. To understand the depth of change, we can therefore try to assess how many of these organisational components need to change and how much they need to change for us to have different behaviours.

If we need to change all five components, the depth of change is likely to be quite large. If any of the five needs to change fundamentally, for example rebuilding the organisational structure from being geographically segmented to becoming customer-oriented, or replacing all the excellence in a particular technology area (e.g. from internal combustion engine manufacturing to battery-powered engines), we can also assume that the change is deep.

An assessment of depth is a step towards a better understanding of what needs to change in the organisation. This, in turn, is a step towards an idea of how to change the organisation and thereby create more value for our customers and for our business.

All five components of the Star model are interrelated. We must change several parts if a change in one element affects others. Often, however, changes have a greater depth in one or more of the organisational elements.

Structure is perhaps the biggest issue given a new strategy. This does not mean that processes can be left untouched, but they may not require as much effort to bring about the desired behaviours. The same reasoning applies to incentives and employees. We need to know in which organisational element(s) the *need for change* is greatest and what it consists of. If we don't know that, it will be difficult to tackle change effectively.

From this perspective, what is sometimes described as a *strategic change* implies a change in the strategy element, i.e. how the organisation should operate in order to be successful. From a strategist's perspective, a change in strategy needs to affect all other components as well - to a greater or lesser extent. If we do not ensure that structure supports strategy, that processes support structure, that incentives drive behaviours that are aligned with strategy or that we have the skills required to realise a strategy, then these need to change. Strategic change is thus almost by definition comprehensive - both broad and deep.

If the strategy says one thing and the structure pulls in a different direction, it will be difficult to achieve what we want to achieve with the strategy. If the processes tell us to work in a certain way, but the people don't have the skills to do so, it will be difficult to achieve what we want. If we set targets for a particular outcome but do not have an incentive structure: bonuses, rewards or promotion on working on that issue, we will find it difficult to achieve what we want. The whole organisation and its elements are interconnected.

## Practical consequences of lack of alignment

To concretise and exemplify, I sometimes describe a change in terms of the introduction of an ERP-system in an organisation. In some ways it is just an IT system. It is just the process element. However, we know today that ERP systems (and many other IT systems) have a much bigger impact than that. For them to be used in a way that delivers benefits to the organisation and/or customers, employees often need to develop skills in using the system.

Employees need to change. It may also be the case that the system itself is so heavy-handed that the organisational structure needs to change. Perhaps the system requires us to move from being product-oriented to being process-oriented. If we don't, we may not be able to use data to better manage critical manufacturing processes. Suddenly, we must deal with structure. And as if that weren't enough, given that we're reorganising, we might have to adjust the goals we set in the business because of the changing responsibilities that the new organisation creates. That means updating the strategy element. It's all connected.

Let's look at another example: we want to move the bulk of our production home from China. This can be seen as a strategic change: it affects the way we operate to be successful. Most changes are not of that magnitude. If we have a stated ambition to move home from China, that ambition must first be made measurable. Otherwise, how will we know what 'brought production home' means? We need to define what the performance improvement, i.e. the benefit of the change from manufacturing in China to not manufacturing in China, actually is. So far, we have stuck to the strategy element. However, if this is to become a reality, there need to be people who are empowered and mandated to take action to make it happen. We need to create structure. We need to look at our processes and ways of working to see how this is going to happen. How working practices, routines and systems are affected. Furthermore, we need to ensure that someone receives recognition, encouragement or perhaps even monetary reward for achieving the feat. Finally, we need to have the skills to move home and build something at home. This gives us an idea of change needs and how deep they are.

To drive change, we therefore need to understand, and if possible, anticipate, how different elements relate to each other, and thereby get an idea of how the change might play out over time.

Assessing the depth of change from a behavioural and organisational perspective gives us a good picture of the changes needed in different areas. Often these two perspectives work quite well together. A major change in behaviour often requires many changes in skills, structures, incentives and ways of working (the organisation).

When we do not see this, when a change in the organisation is considered deep and at the same time quite basic for the individual (or vice versa), our analysis is likely to be flawed. This gives us an opportunity to redo the analysis, get it right and gain a better understanding of the depth of change. This, in turn, gives us a better chance of successfully realising the benefits that the change is intended to realise.

## Breadth of change

One way to get an idea of the breadth of change is to conduct a *stakeholder analysis*. A stakeholder analysis is about identifying the groups and people, stakeholders, who are affected in one way or another by, and may affect, the change we want to achieve. It is important to understand that in this case the impact is reciprocal.[76] We as leaders or agents of change influence others. These 'others' also influence our ability and opportunity to realise the change and bring about the improvements in performance we seek. This includes all those affected before, during and after the realisation of the change. So, it's a general description and it needs to be. Especially when it comes to slightly deeper, and more importantly, broader changes.

Stakeholders, the people, and groups who can influence our ability to successfully realise the change and whom we influence, are almost always within the organisation. However, they can also be outside the organisation. Some examples are partners, suppliers, customers or authorities. The more stakeholders, in terms of sheer numbers of people, and the more heterogeneous or dispersed the categories, the broader we tend to say that the change is.

If a change involves moving from traditional management of paper invoices from customers and suppliers to electronic invoice management, the scope is quite wide. All suppliers need to change their behaviour and send invoices via an interface on the computer instead of by post. All employees who send invoices to customers and manage invoices also need to change their behaviour. Quite a lot of people will be affected by this change. However, the depth may not be so great. It is perhaps most visible in processes and systems, and to some extent skills.

To take another example, the fact that a limited specialised group in time planning or financial analysis will start using a new system support mainly affects one group and is therefore a relatively narrow change.

Conducting a stakeholder analysis at an early stage helps us to describe the breadth of a change. This in turn helps us to identify actual stakeholders.[77] In this book, we make a distinction between stakeholders as groups and stakeholders as people within those groups. We group a natural group, such as a department, everyone in a particular position, or all employees in a particular country, and call them *stakeholder groups*. Within these groups, there are likely to be a number of people who we call *key stakeholders*. Key stakeholders are named people who we want to be involved in the change in some way so that they can contribute their skills, experience, networks or similar. The reason we want to make this division is that we need to work with different stakeholders in different ways.

This is often referred to as *stakeholder management* and we will spend some time on it in Chapter 7. The work of the change manager.

In terms of the **magnitude of change,** it is useful to answer the following questions:

10. How big is our change? How broad? How deep?

# Identify and analyse stakeholders

One way to understand the breadth of change is therefore to identify and analyse stakeholders. Stakeholders consist of stakeholder groups and named key stakeholders and their relationships as shown in Figure 5.3 below.

The figure is a general example of how a combination of a sociogram[78] and a power map[79] can help us to identify different stakeholders and the relationships between them and our change.

Figure 5.3 Stakeholder groups and key stakeholders

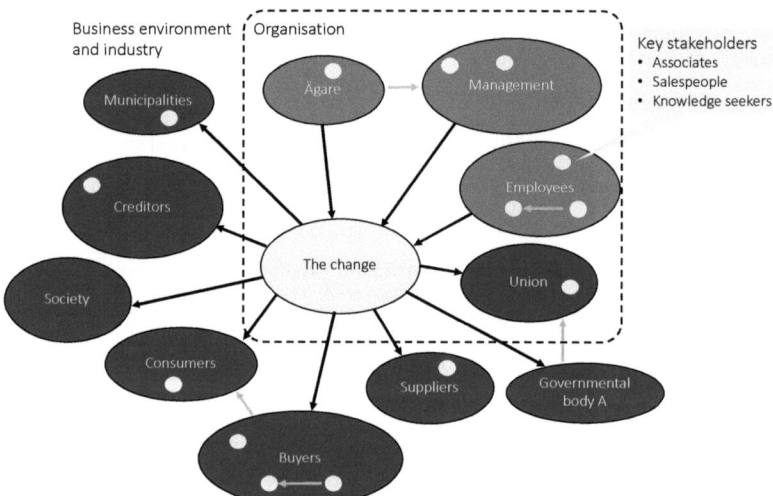

Stakeholder groups make up the larger dark bubbles and key stakeholders the smaller light bubbles (within the darker ones). We can see that the dark bubbles are of different sizes. The size in this case represents the impact. The bigger the bubble the bigger the impact and vice versa. In a large bubble, i.e. stakeholder group, there may then be a point in having several key stakeholders. What we can also see is that the dark bubbles have two different shades. The darker shade means that this group is mainly affected by the change and to a lesser extent influences the change. The arrow, representing the relationship, also indicates this direction. In the bubbles that are not quite

120

so dark, the relationship is the reverse. They mainly have an influencing role and are in turn less affected by the change. It is noteworthy that the influence is reciprocal, so this categorisation is precisely 'mainly'. Another thing we can do to clarify relationships between different stakeholder groups is to draw a line between those stakeholders who are part of the formal organisation and those who are not. Here it is worth pointing out that stakeholder groups outside the organisation may well have greater influence than internal ones. However, one value of making the split is that we can more easily see which stakeholder groups we may be able to influence more easily as we 'own' internal resources to a greater extent.

We can also see that there are relationships between different stakeholder groups and key stakeholders. These are marked on the image by lighter arrows. Which in turn can be both reciprocal and unidirectional and indicate who influences whom.

Through different shades and formats of bubbles and arrows, we can thus understand the main influencing factors in a change. The important thing is not to get an accurate or true picture. It probably doesn't exist. The goal is to create a clear and visually educational description that can help us to allocate change resources wisely.

When we want to make broad changes and must deal with many stakeholders, we need to do it in a few different ways. The stakeholders that affect our ability to succeed need to be brought on board in a completely different way. And in some cases, we may be able to influence one group that in itself has a big impact on another. Hence the importance of difference.

By conducting a stakeholder analysis, we can understand not only the breadth of the change, but also the importance of including more stakeholder groups and more key stakeholders in the change process. As I mentioned earlier, pushing through major change is exhausting. Having the help and support of others to drive it, preferably many others, can be the difference between success and failure.

## Key stakeholders and critical mass

When identifying our stakeholders, it is useful to think about which stakeholders might be considered important to include at an early stage. We then want to understand why and how a particular stakeholder group or key stakeholder might affect the change, what their motivations and drivers might be, and how we can work with them to ensure they are supportive of the change.

A rule of thumb derived from research is to involve key stakeholders from different stakeholder groups, different hierarchical levels and different organisational units (including external units if necessary). This is particularly important if the change we want to realise is broad and deep.[80] We then want to bring as many different perspectives to the change as possible. Different people see things in different ways. Bringing different perspectives into the final solution means a stronger and better solution and greater ownership of the change in the business. The latter is, of course, crucial, as it is the behaviour of employees that needs to change for real behavioural change to take place.

Key stakeholders are named people who are in some stakeholder group and who we have a distinct idea of how they can support our change. A concrete way to identify key stakeholders is to ask yourself the following questions:

* Which people work in the 'area' (e.g. organisation, country, division, function, process) where the change is taking place?
* Who has the most to gain and the most to lose from the change?
* Is there a feasibility study, a previous investigation or change initiative carried out in the area? Who has been involved in it?
* Is there someone you know and with whom you have been in contact in the past who you think can tell you something about the current change or a similar one?

* Are there any people you know who have been with the organisation for a long time and who have had many different roles in different parts of the organisation and know many people? Who are they?

* Are there any people in organisations that you know of who have been involved in pushing through other types of change? Who are they?

The more named key stakeholders, the easier it is to get broad support for the change. It gives us more people to talk to and spreads the message of change to a wider part of the organisation. The wider the organisational spread (and possibly beyond) the better.

> In addition to key stakeholders, achieving change requires that we reach a critical mass that supports and 'lives' the change. As a rule of thumb, we need to have about 15-25% of the population to be changed on board.[81]

For example, if we have 100 District Managers in an operation who need to change their behaviours to achieve the desired improvement in performance, we need to have at least 15 of them with us. To get them on board, we probably need to involve them early on and let them influence both how we work on the change and what the end goal should be.

If we are to have as few as 15%, we also need to ensure that they have certain characteristics. We can talk about three categories of key stakeholders that we want to have on board for change: mavens, connectors and persuaders.[82]

*Mavens* are people who have a lot of knowledge and want to understand things in depth. They often have knowledge about the conditions for the change we want to make, about the organisation in general, what has been done and not done in the past. With their knowledge and insight into different issues, processes, systems, legacies and culture, these people can explain the details, the fine print, the things that cannot be read. They can

123

thus help us by pointing out mistakes that have been made in the past or that could be made if we consider the factors they know about. Often, they can also help change managers to describe why things went the way they did last time, and so provide an idea of why they might succeed this time.

In various changes that I have been responsible for over the years, the mavens have initially been a bit resistant to the change. This is of course natural given the extensive knowledge they have of the history of the organisation. For this very reason, it has often been a success factor for me to initially spend time with maven resisters to understand the resistance and thus be able to get them to contribute to developing a solution that is better than the one I could have arrived at without them.

*Connectors* are people who know people everywhere in the organisation (and outside). They sit on different steering committees; they sit on different networks external and internal. They have worked on the line, on staff and in different geographies. They know people in different parts of the organisation and in different activities. They have often worked with many different people and have a great knowledge of who sits where in the organisation, where they come from, who was whose boss in what situation and how things have changed over time regarding organisations and employees. Through their developed network, they can help spread knowledge and the message of change, creating awareness across different parts of the organisation. This *diffusion*[83] of change is critical for more people to know about change and to be able to contribute to the realisation of its benefits. Connectors can also help identify other key stakeholders. Connectors are absolutely crucial when dealing with broad change. Similarly, Mavens are particularly important when we are dealing with deep change.

*Persuaders* are needed in both deep and broad changes. They are typically those who can sell ice to an Eskimo, to use a worn-out expression. They are good at selling an idea. They are listened to by many inside the organisation and outside. When it comes to change, the future outcome of the change is an idea that we need to sell. If we can get on the arm of persuaders, they can help us get others to understand why the change is good and/or important. When persuaders understand something and once they are passionate about it, they are a tremendous force to have in change efforts.

In the initial stages of change, we therefore need to identify these key stakeholders and try to describe what roles they might have in the change and get them to want to participate and contribute. Some of them may be able to participate in workshops, join reference groups, contribute to communication or advocacy work, or be involved in designing the plans or content of information or skills development activities of various kinds. Whatever we do, we can be reasonably sure that the more we can draw on key stakeholders, the more likely we are to succeed in the change we face.

It is not uncommon for those who are mavens to also be persuaders, for persuaders to also be connectors, or for that matter for all three types to be found within the same person. If we manage to identify individuals with several or all these qualities, then we should do everything we can to bring them into the change as quickly and as much as we can.

## Managing different stakeholders in different ways

Once we've identified our stakeholder groups and our key people, we can sort them based on the impact they have. We already have a rough idea of this based on the size of the bubble that represents that particular stakeholder group (as in Figure 5.3). We also need to sort the stakeholders based on their interest in the change. This sorting helps us understand how to deal with different stakeholder groups and key stakeholders.

To understand this, we can place them in a matrix. On the Y-axis of the matrix, we have the interest in the change and on the X-axis we have the impact on the change. Both interest and impact can be high or low, giving us four quadrants as Figure 5.4 shows.

Figure 5.4 Stakeholder analysis and how we deal with stakeholders

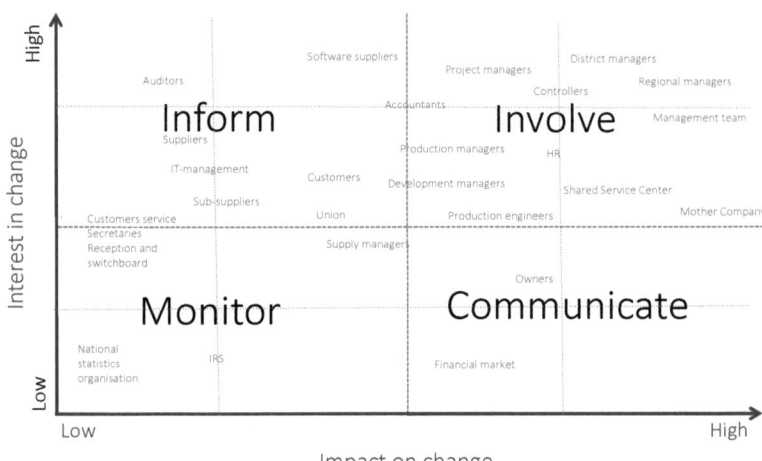

Source: adapted from Mendelow (1991)[84]

If we start in the lower left corner, we have the category of stakeholders we only want to *monitor*. These are stakeholders who have no vested interest in the change we intend to make, nor any influence over whether we will succeed or fail. This category includes various roles within the organisation, with suppliers and with government agencies that we do not believe will be directly or significantly affected. However, we may still want to keep an eye on these in case something happens that affects them.

In change, especially if it is broad or deep, there is often a fairly large group of employees who are interested in what the change will mean but who have little influence. In fact, most employees in an organisation are not able to alone influence major changes that are realised – right or wrong. The category of stakeholders who have a high interest and a low impact, we therefore mainly spend time *informing*. Informing in this sense means one-way communication. We tell them what is happening, when things will happen, how it will affect them and why it is happening. The aim is not to ask for input but to tell what we can tell.

126

A usually smaller category of employees are managers and other people within the organisation who have an actual and perhaps large impact on whether we can succeed with the change. This does not mean that they have a strong interest in it. Stakeholders with high impact and low interest are found in the lower right quadrant. In addition to managers, who are sitting on the resources, they may be owners, informal leaders, key partners or suppliers, or parts of the financial and stock markets for those types of companies that are listed on the stock exchange. We are happy to *communicate* with this group. Communication here is different from information. Communication is a two-way process where information is exchanged between two or more parties: as change agents, we ask questions, ask for input and try to get answers to the questions to gain as much knowledge, experience, support, etc. as possible.

The last group is found in the upper right quadrant. There we have stakeholders with high interest *and* high impact. These are the stakeholders we want to *involve* in the change. Involve in this context means that we want to use them in different types of meetings, workshops and discussions because of their knowledge, network, experience etc. The reason for this is that we believe that these people can contribute in a good way to the change. This is the group in which we generally want to see our key stakeholders: named individuals with a high level of influence, formal or informal, a strong interest in the success of the change and preferably a maven, connector or persuader. In some cases, organisations call these people sponsors or ambassadors, but most often they are 'used' properly. If we are running the change as a project, we would like to see these types of people as involved project owners and/or steering committee members.

The reason we divide stakeholders into four different categories of monitoring, informing, communicating and involving is that change management is really resource-intensive. To successfully realise a change, we need to spend a lot of time talking to people, pushing people, informing,

127

communicating, discussing, etc. By making this distinction, we can allocate our time more effectively. I realise that sounds crass, but the fact is that we need to spend as much time as possible on the people who have as much interest as possible and as much impact as possible. That is the opportunity to create momentum and drive for change. It may even sound self-serving, but if we want to ensure that improvements in performance are realised, then we need to use our change management resources effectively. Involving and communicating with key stakeholders is crucial.

The importance of anchoring cannot be understated when a change goes against the grain of conventional wisdom, history or culture.

A basic rule for how we should work with stakeholders is that: the broader and the deeper the change, the more resources you need to put into interacting with key stakeholders, i.e. involving and communicating.

In terms of **stakeholders**, it is useful to answer the following:

11. Who are our stakeholder groups and named key stakeholders?

12. Which of these stakeholders affect our ability to realise the change? Which of these stakeholders do we need to influence to realise the change?

13. Which stakeholders do we need to involve in the work? Communicate with? Inform? Monitor on an ongoing basis?

# Summary: Change magnitude and stakeholders

In this chapter, we have discussed how to assess the magnitude of a change, the implications for the change process, and how to identify and analyse the stakeholders that need to be involved for a change to have the intended impact.

### How can we assess the magnitude of a change?

★ The extent of a change can be assessed by width (scope) and depth (amplitude). The more numerous and the more heterogeneous the stakeholder groups (e.g. business units, divisions, customers), the greater the breadth. The more different parts of the organisation are changed (e.g. strategy, structure, processes) and the more they change, the deeper the change.

### What are the implications of the magnitude of change for the change process?

★ The more extensive the change, the greater the need for systematic and structured change work (e.g. involvement, communication and information efforts, skills development, monitoring of benefits).

### How can we identify and analyse the stakeholders that need to be involved for a change to have the positive intended effect?

★ Stakeholders include stakeholder groups and key stakeholders. Stakeholder groups are the groups that we influence in the change and that affect our ability to succeed in the change. Within these stakeholder groups are formal and informal leaders, named individuals, who are particularly critical to include. We call these key stakeholders, often they are mavens, connectors or persuaders.

# Reflections: Change magnitude and stakeholders

# 6. Tackling change

Once we have an idea of the scope of a change, its impact and how stakeholders can be involved, communicated with, informed and monitored, the next step is to find appropriate ways to approach the change. All changes are unique. Organisations operate in different countries, sectors and have different circumstances. This means that the approach needs to be adapted.

John Dewey, American philosopher, psychologist and educator, and father of what we call active learning (learning by doing and trial and error), explains in his classic 1916 work *Democracy and Education* his view of the lack of adaptation to unique circumstances.

> Imposing an alleged uniform general method upon everybody breeds mediocrity in all but the very exceptional. And measuring originality by deviation from the mass breeds eccentricity in them.[85]

We know that adapting to unique conditions and circumstances is a requirement for creating good conditions for development. We also know that learning is a requirement for change. However, there is no one-size-fits-all solution to learning. We do know, however, that there are questions that research considers important to address. So, we can create general questions that help us find unique answers. We have previously addressed questions about the purpose of change, pressures for change, and the magnitude of change. There are also a few known questions that we need to answer when making an assessment about how change can or should be tackled. These we are now ready to explore.

In this chapter, we will therefore try to answer how we can approach different changes; what revolutionary and evolutionary change are; how they need to complement each other; and how these approaches affect the pace: speed and timing of change in terms of how we can manage change to realise the intended benefits.

# Revolutionary and evolutionary change

Academics like to paint contrasts because it puts things on edge and forces us to think. In fact, theorists and practitioners alike are in most cases aware that nothing is just black or white, but shades of grey.

In the strategy literature, we talk about planned and emergent strategy.[86] *Planned strategy* is based on a formal, often annual, strategy formulation process where goals are set and often plans are developed to achieve these goals. *Emergent strategy* is more based on how an organisation's behavioural patterns evolve as its members adapt to how the world changes - regardless of what the organisation's goals are.

In behavioural psychology there is a similar logic. The concepts we use here are *rule-governance* and *contingency shaping*.[87] Rule-governed behaviours are those that are triggered by an instruction, law, expressed wish (someone else's or our own) or the like. In organisations, such 'rules' often consist of goals, strategies and plans of various kinds. They tell us what applies. There is thus a clear link between planned strategy and an ambition to use activators to influence behaviour in an organisation. Contingency shaped behaviours are those that are caused by the consequences of these and similar behaviours in previous situations rather than by rules. They evolve as we learn what works and what does not. They are thus closer to emergent strategy.

In research, when we talk about managing change, we are also talking about two opposing perspectives, approaches, or even *change strategies*.[88] We call these revolutionary and evolutionary change[89]. As we shall see, these two approaches are related to planned and emergent strategies and to rule-governed and contingency shaped behaviours.

## Revolutionary Change

*Revolutionary change*, somewhat paradoxically in relation to our general understanding of revolutions, is driven from the top down. The name is thus linked to the fact that the change is revolutionary or abrupt. This is traditionally the kind of change that we call *top-down* in the language of 'corporate BS'. Revolutionary change is typically supposed to break the existing, the assumed, for example structures or values.[90] Revolutionary change is often planned, centrally controlled or at least centrally sanctioned. They are often tangible or purely physical things that change. Relating this to the Star model, it is easy to think in terms of structures, processes, methods, tools or systems. In practice, this may involve an organisational structure or the introduction of different types of (IT) systems in one or more parts of the business. However, it can also be a fundamental change in the idea on which the organisation rests, such as member-ownership or decentralised decision-making.

Proponents of revolutionary change lean towards the view that people are generally a bit lazy. That there is a natural inertia in organisations.[91] We get stuck in the same rut and find it hard to think in new ways. We humans do things the way we are used to doing them and habit exerts a strong power. There is of course some truth in this.

> Habit is the same as negative reinforcement of existing behaviours: we do what we do to avoid inventing new ways. We humans don't always have the ability, skills, time or energy to think in new ways, so we use our habitual ways of working and behaviour. And the same way of doing things does not lead to new ideas, new products, new services or new values.

For this reason, advocates of revolutionary change believe that change should be tackled mainly from the top down.

In engineering (mainly mechanics) there is a concept called *Yield point*. It means the point that indicates the limit at which a substance goes from being elastic to becoming plastic due to pressure. If we apply more pressure, breaking harder than this point allows, a break occurs in the material. We have broken it.

If we apply this reasoning to an ordinary twig on a tree, we can see that we can bend a twig a certain amount before it snaps. Then we haven't gone beyond the point and if the twig doesn't break completely, it goes back to its original shape. However, if we break even harder, sooner or later the twig will break completely. Then it cannot return to its former shape. We have gone beyond the yield point. Part of the logic of revolutionary change is that we want to break something so fundamental, so revolutionary, that it is not possible to go back to the old way of functioning. That's what makes change possible.

## Evolutionary change

Opponents of revolutionary change rather advocate *evolutionary change*.[92] Advocates of evolutionary change say that no matter how hard we break structures, how clear decisions are from the top, and how centrally directed and sanctioned change initiatives are, employees will not change their behaviours just because someone centrally or higher up the hierarchy says so.

If revolutionary change in many cases takes as its starting point in the organisation and what is hard-coded, evolutionary change takes as its starting point in the individual and his or her learning. Learning behaviours is the starting point and a large part of the point of change for an evolutionary change agent. If employees learn new things, the organisation (structure, processes, systems, etc.) in all its important parts will change over time.

Advocates of evolutionary change also believe that central initiatives pushed from the top down have a distinct disadvantage. They easily risk becoming so-called *BOHICAs* (Bend Over Here It Comes Again)[93], i.e. an awkward situation that repeats itself, where the wisest course of action is to pretend that we are doing as we are told. In practice this often means ducking, waiting for the wind to blow over and then getting up and getting on with business as usual. It goes without saying that there will be no change in employee behaviour if this is true.

The logic behind evolutionary change is that if employees are involved in describing their future and the path to it (i.e. the change) and how this understanding of the change might affect their everyday work, they can take ownership and want to contribute to the change. They will embrace it and change their behaviours.

Evolutionary change is therefore emergent rather than planned, like revolutionary change is. It is typically bottom-up. Often it does not start centrally but somewhere further out in the organisation where a concrete need arises because of customer demands or a changing competitive situation. At the periphery of the organisation, we generally do not have the same resources as centrally, so we must find ways to solve the problems. Evolutionary change is not always sanctioned by any form of management. Rather, it is linked to the learning that occurs when people experiment to take responsibility for developing their role, their products, their work and their business.

## General and linear change

In practice, this means that change management needs to consist of both revolution and evolution. The revolutionary perspective needs to ensure an overall well-defined process with different phases describing how we move from the current state to the future state. After all, this is how we define change management: a structured and systematic way of moving an organisation from one stage to another.

One way to describe such a process is to start from general project management models.[94] In these, we typically find a number of phases, each with a number of *decision points*, (DP, or toll gates, TG) to ensure that we move forward in the right direction, with the right priorities and in the right order.

Figure 6.1 illustrates a general picture of the revolutionary part of a change process, which consists of seven phases with ongoing decision points to ensure that we are constantly in tune with the business.

Figure 6.1 Revolutionary process of change

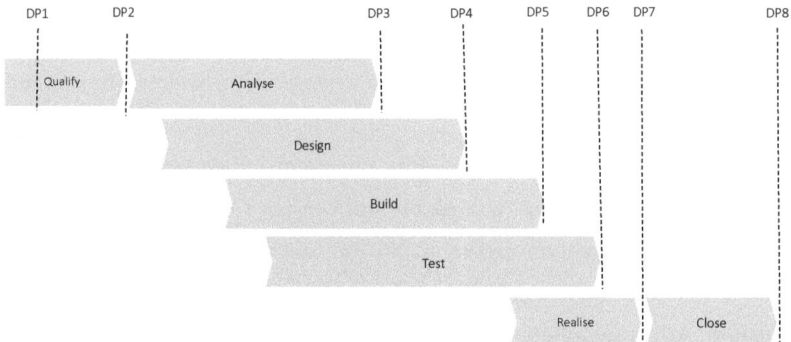

A natural first phase in a change is a *qualification phase* where we think through the change on an overall level. We try to understand the pressures for change, the outcomes we want to improve, the scope and stakeholders, and the approach. Here we also develop a main message of what we want to achieve with the change, and to some extent what we think we need to do. In fact, we often know from the outset several activities we need to undertake. We know that we need to do a goal analysis, describe the benefits and costs of the change, have regular decision and review meetings, communicate and inform. The sooner we can involve key stakeholders in these activities, the better.

These activities need to be described in an overarching *change plan*. However, sitting in one's chambers to analyse and plan this in detail is undone work. It is impossible to think of everything that might affect the change - especially alone. Together with a well-selected group of key stakeholders, however, we stand a good chance of covering most of the critical areas in our analysis and planning, and creating a possible first wave of communication about what is coming. The qualification phase ends with a decision on whether it is worth continuing to work on the change. An important component of the basis for such a decision is a first version of the benefits and costs of the change, what we usually call the *Business case* of the change.

Although we generally call these decisions decision points, we need to remember that decision making is not a point but a process. The point is simply the point in time where we decide what to do here and now based on all analyses, discussions and similar coming up to that point. So again, the systematic processes matter.

The qualification phase is followed by a slightly deeper *analysis phase* where we try to detail what goals we should set for the change and what we need to do in more detail to understand and change the business. Here we analyse different types of change needs in different parts of the business. When we analyse alone, we tend to lean on experience, tried and tested methods and tools, and personal preferences. Involving a larger group in the analysis phase is therefore crucial for a good result. It creates both ownership from those involved and a sharper analysis. The more perspectives that are considered i.e. diversity of ideas, generates more alternative problems that need to be addressed and solutions to these[95] . The analysis phase also ends with a decision on whether it is worth continuing to work on the change, what should be achieved, how it should be done and when it should be evaluated again. As a natural consequence, the business case for the change is updated.

The analysis phase is followed by a *design phase*. By design in this book, I am leaning towards the recipient of the Nobel memorial prize in economic sciences and one of the most influential thinkers of the 20th century, Herbert Simon's description. Designing is "creating approaches that aim to change existing situations into preferred ones".[96] Thus, it is practically the same as change and does not stop at the drawing board.

This means that in the design phase we start to describe what the new solution looks like. The solution could be a new process, a new organisational structure, a new system, a new skill set, a new product, a new strategy or all of these. So here we need to describe what is to change and how. Here we can use the different organisational elements of the Star model: strategy,

137

structure, process, incentives and human capital as a checklist. We know that if the design is to ensure the change of behaviours, all elements must be uniformly targeted. This means that all elements need to be assessed in the design. In the design phase we therefore also develop ideas for skills development interventions. We also start to look at what the eventual support to the business once the change is complete will look like.

It cannot be stressed enough that the design phase is an iterative process with many twists and turns to ensure that the blueprint of the solution has the intended effect on behaviours and result. During the design phase, business involvement is crucial. Those who will benefit from the solution - or a reasonably representative cross-section of them - must have a chance to influence it. We can't leave input to a steering committee or management alone. Multiple key stakeholders from many different organisational units, functions and levels need to be involved in different ways.

The design phase does not actually end when the next phase begins. It continues until we 'close' the whole change. This also applies to the construction phase that follows the design phase. However, we need to make an ongoing decision whether to start building something or to close the change.

By the time we decide to go ahead and build, the proposed solution (or parts of it) should have been drawn and tested on stakeholder groups and key stakeholders. Then we can start building a solution. *The construction phase* begins. During the construction phase, we create the actual solution using the blueprint. So, this phase is about changing the structure of the organisation, improving the process, developing the system, setting the parameters of the rewards programme, creating the training programme or similar.

The construction phase is, as I mentioned, an iterative process. Because we continuously discover things that don't work while we are building them, we sometimes need to go back to the drawing board (the design phase). It is likely that we have not thought of all possible challenges already in the design. Based on how the solution changes, costs and benefits we didn't think of may be added or removed. This means we need to update our business case again.

Conceptually, this means that we jump between the design and construction phases. Ongoing alignment with stakeholders is therefore critical here too. In these check-ins, an important question to ask stakeholders is whether they believe that the solution contributes to the changes in behaviour for which we hope. We also need to ask whether they believe that these changes in behaviour will lead to the realisation of the benefits (improvements in performance) we have identified. Based on the answers we get we then need to update the costs we will incur for the change and the benefits that will come to us through the change. We will then again have an updated business case that will enable us to ensure that we realise the benefits we can realise, rather than starting from a 'hit-or-miss' business case that is long out of line with what we thought we would achieve when we started the change work.

The construction phase is not fully completed before the next phase. It runs in parallel also with the next phase, which is to test our built solution (or part of a solution).

The next phase is thus *the testing phase*. This is when we test the solution we have developed. If the change is extensive in different defined areas, departments, divisions or geographies, we can consider test pilots in these to ensure that the solution built is right. In this case, it is important not to choose the unit where we have the best chance of success. On the contrary. The lessons we can gain from conducting pilots in a unit where it may be particularly difficult can be incredibly valuable for the future and our ability to realise performance improvements across the organisation. However, pilots are not always needed. If it is a minor or urgent change, it is better to avoid pilots, which take time and realise everywhere at once. Then the effects will also come faster. As in all earlier phases, the testing phase must be inclusive and iterative. Stakeholders need to be involved, discuss the pros and cons of the chosen solution, and make suggestions for improvements.

In the testing phase, it is not only the solution that needs to be tested. To the extent that information, communication, skills development and workshop materials, tools, support functions and the like are available in some form, we also need to ensure that they work for stakeholders.

The testing phase runs in parallel with the design and build phase as we are constantly learning what could be even better. When we start to realise the change in the business, it also runs in parallel with the next phase where we are just materialising the change, making sure that the new thing starts to be used or complied with. We call this the realisation phase.

As a first step in *the realisation phase,* the updates resulting from the test phase are made. Changes to the solution, its components and/or the material that will support the functioning of the solution. In practical terms, the realisation involves a formal and gradual handover of the new solution to the business. Change managers need to continue to work on an ongoing basis to inform, communicate, monitor, drive and respond to any resistance to change that may arise. One of the most important functions of rolling out is to ensure that the new solution leads to changes in behaviour and that the new behaviours lead to improvements in performance.

> Intentionally, I don't use the word implement (although it's common here). Implementation to me signals that 'someone' has thought it through and now it's time for everybody else to just go. I don't think such a view on strategy or change can be successful under any circumstances.

Thinking and doing must support each other in the realisation of change. We will always come across something that makes us re-evaluate what and how we do. We will always be learning more, and all these lessons will of course be woven into the final product. For that reason, I use realise. It better reflects the nature of combined thinking and doing that characterises change and the ongoing adjustments we need to be ready for. It is when the roll out phase is underway that the change manager needs to really scuff the floor.

Once the realisation phase has been going on for a period of time, either as decided, or when the improvements in performance start to approach set targets (i.e. the benefits have actually been realised), the change can then slowly start to be completed. The realisation phase therefore ends when we no longer consider it necessary to have people actively working on the change. One reason may be that we do not believe that more resources bring more benefits. Another may be that other more pressing changes need to be addressed or that we feel we have finished with the change. When we close the realisation phase, we also close the design, build and test phases, and enter the closure phase. This is started by making an active and conscious decision to start closing the change process. No change should be self-destructed. When some are allowed to self-destruct, we easily let all self-destruct. Even the most important changes.

*The closure phase* ensures that the change is completed in a way that ensures that further improvements in performance are monitored. In major changes, it is often difficult to see results in the shorter term than six months. It is also difficult to maintain focus on a specific change for longer than a year. We lose focus, patience and other things take our attention. This is true almost regardless of the magnitude of a change. So, when we close the change (or a major part of a change), rarely have all the benefits been realised. A final step before we close a change is therefore to deliver an updated business case describing what benefits have been realised, what remains to be realised, when they will be realised and what is required to realise them (including costs going forward). The handover needs to be to the person who will be responsible for monitoring continued performance improvements. Where there is a controller, or similar, who is already responsible for monitoring and metrics in an operation, this is likely to be a good person to hand over the benefits to. In other cases, line managers are a natural counterpart. More on handover later in the book. Once we have handed over all this, we can make the decision to close the change officially: end the closure phase.

## Specific and circular change

If the general and relatively linear sequential process with its different phases is allowed to symbolise the revolutionary approach to leading change, we should also consider how the evolutionary approach can be used in practical change management. As I mentioned earlier, we need both.

In summary, we can say that the evolutionary change process consists of seven steps that should contribute to learning, changing behaviours and thus developing the organisation and improving desired outcomes. The revolutionary approach is relatively linear. In fact, several of the phases run into each other. The different phases have fairly clear starts and ends determined by decisions, iterations occur mainly when we design, build and test as well as within each phase. We want to drive a whole – the whole change – forward to some extent.

> In the process of change, things arise that we need to deal with - in our environment, industry, organisation. We can call these things *change challenges* and they represent challenges we need to understand and manage to succeed with the change.

The evolutionary process is one way of addressing these challenges. It is circular and iterative, spinning in multiple feedback loops. Its purpose is to continuously address the challenges that arise. Challenges that are usually relatively specific and can therefore be dealt with at different speeds and for different lengths of time. A crucial key stakeholder starting work at another company is one such challenge. Who will manage the dialogue with a specific customer affected by the change is another. We may be able to resolve these in a few days, or even a few hours. Members of management teams that oppose the proposed solution at a late stage, is another quite common challenge. Especially if there is a lack of involvement. That challenge takes a little longer. Probably at least a couple of weeks or months. Challenges can also involve even bigger things. That in our efforts to develop a whole new product group, we lose one of the new suppliers. This challenge requires a longer period of preparation before a decision can be taken and we can move forward. Often many of the change challenges we face are such that we cannot anticipate them in our analysis or planning phase. They therefore need to be addressed as they arise. To deal with them competently, when they arise, we need a systematic approach.

Figure 6.2 describes seven general steps that can form the basis of such a systematic approach: an evolutionary process of change.

Figure 6.2 Evolutionary change process

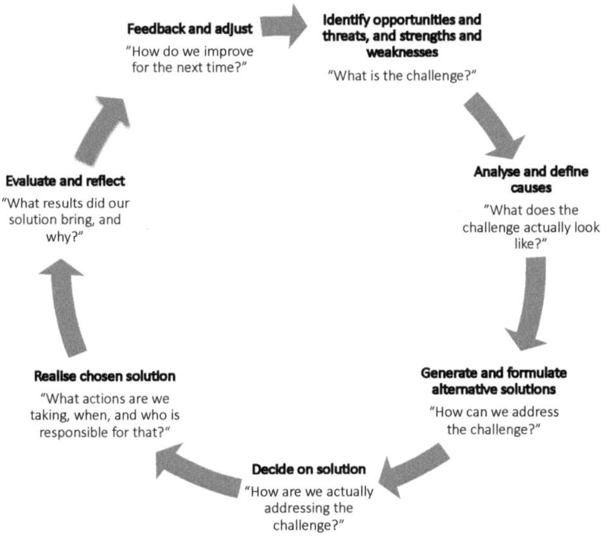

The first step in such a process is to *identify external threats and opportunities and internal strengths and weaknesses*. When a challenge arises, we need to understand what the challenge really is. Threats and opportunities are external factors in the environment and in the industry that can affect the likelihood of behavioural change and the realisation of benefits. So, in this phase we are not just interested in solving problems. In other words, it is not just risk management, which is unfortunately quite common when we work on development projects. To ensure our performance improvements, we need to pay equal attention to exploiting the potential opportunities and strengths we see. This requires us to describe them as well.

The second step is to *analyse and define the causes* of e.g. the opportunity or threat. The reason for this analysis is to ensure that we are not curing a symptom but understanding the threat we need to address or the opportunity we want to exploit. We then need to ask ourselves what the challenge really looks like. Where does the challenge come from? If we have a good analysis of the business environment, we might find some of the answers there. If we have done a thorough analysis of the pressures for change in the industry, we may find information there. Do we have a sufficient understanding of our organisation's strengths and weaknesses relative to our environment's and industry's expectations and demands on us, our ability to deliver on those expectations? Or strategic fit. Strengths and weaknesses in this case are therefore seen as internal factors within the organisation and its individuals that can be used to meet the challenge.

Once we have carried out these analyses or gone back to the ones we have done before and thought them through in relation to the challenge, we are likely to know what the challenge is and where it comes from. Then we can move forward.

The third step is to *generate and formulate alternative solutions*. Once we understand what the challenge (threats and opportunities) looks like, we can try to understand how we can address it (with our organisation's strengths and weaknesses). This work must initially be a 'yes/and' exercise. This means that when we generate alternative proposals, we do not prioritise. We would like to see many alternative proposals. All reasonably relevant alternatives are welcome. The prioritisation - the 'no/but exercise' - is saved until we have a few different relevant options that can be put against each other. That is the next step.

Once we have generated and formulated a number of possible options, the next step is to *decide on a solution* to address the challenge. This is the fourth step. No decision we make at this stage will be right or wrong. There is no right or wrong until after the fact. We can never know in advance what the consequences of a particular decision will be. We cannot see into the future and every decision we make here has pros and cons. All we can do is to try to understand to the best of our ability what the best way forward is, to make a decision about it and then move in that direction as quickly as possible.

Just this, *realise the solution,* is the fifth step. This step is about deciding what specific actions should be taken by whom and when. It also involves performing them or ensuring that the actions have been carried out.

So far, the evolutionary learning process resembles a traditional waterfall model, as does the revolutionary approach. In a clear order: identify, analyse, formulate, decide and realise. The big difference so far is that the revolutionary change focuses overall, the entire change, while the evolutionary focuses on a specific challenge. Reflecting on a smaller challenge makes it easier to isolate events, draw conclusions and learn lessons. It can be difficult to see connections and how different things are connected in the big picture. The focus of the evolutionary process on the specific challenges, together with the next two steps in the process, is what creates the conditions for learning for individuals in the organisation.

The sixth step is to *evaluate and reflect on the solution* and its effects. Evaluation and reflection are about analysing in a systematic way the results of the chosen options. We want to focus on the benefits, the improvements in results, so it is not enough to look only at how the challenge was addressed. We also need to look at what impact, if any, we see on the results we wanted to improve. What we are looking for in our evaluation and reflection is evidence, data, that shows in as clear a way as possible the positive or negative relationships between the actions we took and their impact on employee behaviours and organisational performance.

It is not possible to isolate events completely. Most things in an organisation and the world around it are interconnected. However, if we are to draw conclusions about what is working and what is not, having an impact or not having an impact, we need in our analysis to try to understand why something has worked and something else has not worked. Strategy is about achieving a goal or purpose with limited resources. We then need to be able to prioritise in our change the actions that have the most impact for the least use of resources. We learn how to set these priorities on an ongoing basis through evaluation, analysis and reflection. There is no other way.

The seventh and final step therefore involves *feedback and adjustment.* This step involves providing feedback based on the lessons learned from the evaluation and communicating these back to the organisation at large. Given that we have learned what works, we can express any changes in expectations and goals to different parts of the organisation. Adjustment also means correcting activities we realised based on the impact they had on selected behaviours and outcomes. The question we want to answer is: how will we do even better next time? The answer to that question is partly about specific actions in the change we want to add, remove or refine. It is also about how we will get better at driving the evolutionary change process. To do that, we need to ask ourselves: what in our process do we need to change? Was identification good? The analysis? The generation of alternatives? The decisions? The realisation? The evaluation? Feedback? Where in these steps can we get even better and thus create even greater improvements in performance?

Another major difference between the revolutionary and evolutionary approaches, and which we talked about earlier, is the breadth of stakeholders. This has implications for involvement. In the revolutionary, we typically identify key stakeholders in advance of the change at large. These are critical.

In the evolutionary, we can select the people who have the most knowledge about a challenge (e.g. issue, domain, system, country) and thus more easily create a 'dream team' to address a particular challenge. Thus, in the revolutionary initial change effort, developing a core team of key stakeholders and then in the evolutionary selecting and picking unique mavens, connectors or persuaders is a way of combining involvement in both approaches.

Another difference between the revolutionary and the evolutionary approach is time. In the revolutionary approach, there is a relatively clearly defined timeline where phases are divided by decision points. This is necessary to drive the whole of a major change forward in a structured and systematic way. However, this can create problems with the complexity of large-scale and strategic change. When the practical consequences of this complexity strikes, it is easy to be paralysed by a sense that everything is connected to everything else. Where do we start? Set decision points then helps us to prioritise up to a certain point in time. That's a good thing. The weakness of such an approach, on the other hand, is that things happen all the time and much of the planning is undone. If conditions change, we must replan, but we never get back the time we spent planning. In a profit and loss account, these sunk costs are merely costs we have incurred without any benefit at all.

In the evolutionary, we manage time based on the scale or complexity of the challenge. If it is the case that we need two weeks to go through all seven steps, then we solve the challenge in two weeks. If we need six months, we take six months. If we need one day, we take one day, etc. The evolutionary approach is thus more flexible in terms of time and linked to the nature and complexity of the challenge rather than to the planning of the change.

Combining these two approaches, then, puts us in a good position to manage change, even of a major and strategic nature, in the most effective way possible.

## Revolution and evolution as complements

In theory, these two approaches are called Theory E and Theory O.[97] *Theory E* is then revolutionary, centrally controlled and sanctioned from above, emphasis on structural change, linear, sequentially implemented and with clearly stated economic benefits. It is also economic value that the E symbolises. This, to some extent, 'hard' approach is probably the most common for driving change in organisations. Not least in large organisations and/or organisations with a clear economic agenda. Listed companies need to show results every month or quarter. Or they need to demonstrate action to try to convince the stock market that they have control over future financial performance.

*Theory O* is the opposite. It is evolutionary change, initiated from the bottom up without clear sanction from any management, emphasis on learning and inclusion, circular and iterative, and focus on the organisation and its people. The O, in this slightly 'softer' approach, symbolises the organisation and its ability to learn and evolve. This is not a very common approach to change in organisations. It occurs in many organisations, but not so often as part of a structured approach to leading (a) change. Not infrequently, management's need for control and fear stand in the way of this approach. It takes considerably more courage from management to open up to participation than to command.

Another reason why revolutionary change is more common is a perception that it is a faster route to change. As we shall see, this is not a given. Yet another is that when we talk about learning and 'less managed' change, it immediately seems abstract to many. But that evolutionary change is abstract is not a given either.

What we know from research, and what I am increasingly convinced of in my work, is that those organisations that are able to combine these two approaches are more successful in implementing change and achieving targeted improvements in performance.[98] Of course, it is not the case that the change manager who drives revolutionary change will be more successful, or vice versa. Rather, the change manager who learns to approach different changes or different parts of the same change in different ways will be successful. As change managers, we need to understand what can and should be driven from the top down, requiring for example structural changes, and what can and should be driven from the bottom up, requiring for example routines for conversations with customers where the learning occurs. In strategic and/or large-scale change, I am convinced that the two approaches need to complement each other.

Moreover, if we look at the different components of an organisation (strategy, structure, process, incentives and human capital), we can fairly quickly conclude that strategy, structure and processes may need a revolutionary start. To some extent, ideas about strategy and direction need to be set by a management or someone who is responsible for the development of the organisation over time. To some extent, decisions on whether structures with positions and mandates should be reviewed and possibly replaced given a new strategy also need to be made. Similarly, a decision needs to be made by management that processes should be reviewed to support the new structure that will in turn facilitate the realisation of the strategy. These may thus initially have a revolutionary approach. Not always, but fairly often.

Someone sometimes needs to decide that we should do something that is aimed at something. Not everyone can give up that leadership. However, the decision that we should do something does not always come from a leader. It's not logical to think that changing employee skills is always top-down. You can lead a horse to water, but you can't make it drink, is a good saying. We can't force learning on anyone. Changes in different organisational elements are therefore likely to need different approaches. For skills and incentives, an evolutionary approach may make more sense. For strategy, structure and processes, a revolutionary one might possibly make more sense – at least initially.

What we need to bear in mind here is again that it is not a question of one or the other approach, but of variants of both. However, we should not underestimate that there is a logic based on what in the organisation we want to change in the main and what results we want to improve.

Another logic, similar to this one, is to divide the change into the decision to change and the realisation of change. Deciding on a change and realising it are in some cases two different things. If something must change, it should be impossible for a management to abdicate that responsibility. That something should be done, and perhaps to some extent what, sometimes needs to be decided revolutionarily, at least at an overall level. Then, when we get down to the detail of what that means, what the new ways of working, systems, responsibilities and roles in the structure or new skills will look like, then we need to involve employees and move from a mainly revolutionary approach to a more evolutionary one for the change to become a real change.

This is sometimes seen as a variation on the adage 'management should say what, but not how'. There is a point in re-evaluating that statement. Management does not always know best 'what' needs to be done. Those working on the issues do. Management may need to say *that* something needs to be done, or even should be done, and at the same time justify why. Describe the reason (pressure for change) and the purpose of the change, why it is important.

I personally like to get the 'what' and 'how' from the organisation's knowledgeable staff to sort it out. I'd much rather ask: 'What do you think we need to change to double customer satisfaction, profitability or turnover, or survive, and how are we going to do it together'? Then we create ownership.

Organisations and individuals who become good at driving change learn to understand how to use revolutionary, structural, centrally sanctioned change management from the top down, while driving from the bottom up by including employees to benefit from their knowledge, commitment and learning.

In conclusion, we can say that good change management combines revolutionary and evolutionary approaches. In the big picture, we need a well-defined process that ensures that we have momentum in the change. If behaviours do not change, no benefits will accrue. In the small, day-to-day work, we therefore need several evolutionary processes where selected employees with insight, understanding and knowledge of a specific challenge are involved to address that particular type of specific challenge.

A schematic of what such a combined change process might look like is described in Figure 6.3.

Figure 6.3 Combined revolutionary and evolutionary change process

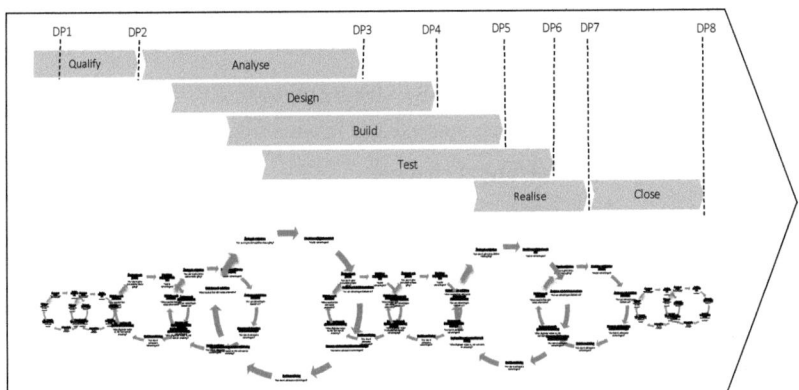

In terms of **change strategy**, it is useful to answer the following questions:

14. How is our change mainly driven through? Revolutionary or evolutionary?

15. What, which parts, stages or elements of the change, need to be driven revolutionarily? Which parts, stages or elements of the change need to be evolutionary?

## Pace of change

Once we have assessed our *change strategy*, the approaches we believe are appropriate to achieve the change in different areas, we are ready to tackle the issue of *pace of change*.[99] At this stage, we should have in mind which parts of the change we want to tackle in a revolutionary way, from the top down: probably some structural and procedural components. We should also think about which parts we want to tackle evolutionarily, from the bottom up, to create as much individual and organisational learning as possible. This is likely to include incentives and human capital and involvement to develop specific solutions that lead to behavioural change.

The pace of change is, just as it sounds, about the pace at which a change should be realised. In turn, pace of change consists of two parts: *timing of change* and *speed of change*. Timing is related to when specific actions or activities are to be performed or realised. If we are launching a new organisation, or starting to use a new system, this needs to be given a specific date. Speed of change is related to how fast we can carry out change activities without exhausting the organisation or ourselves as change managers.

Change is rarely a sprint, it's usually a marathon. Sustaining and working towards a longer-term goal is a must if we want to see tangible improvements in results as a result of changing behaviours.

## Unsteady pace and timing of change

When we lead change, we can distinguish between a unsteady pace and a steady pace. These two beats should be seen as complementary to each other. One pace is not better than the other. Nor is it the case that one is faster, just as we discussed regarding revolutionary and evolutionary change. We do not get further in our change with one pace or the other in a given period of time. On the contrary, the cumulative change that we manage to achieve over a given period may be the same. Again, it is a skilled change manager's knowledge of when to use one or the other pace that enables the amount of impact of the change we get out of a given period of time. A skilled change manager can combine the two wisely to get further in the change in a faster way as Figure 6.4 shows.

Figure 6.4 Pace of change: timing and speed

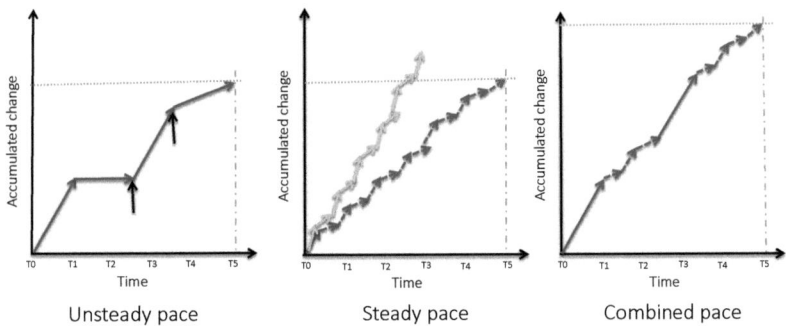

| Unsteady pace | Steady pace | Combined pace |

An *unsteady pace* means that several or a few larger and/or heavier initiatives and activities are implemented in a piecemeal fashion to achieve maximum impact at a given time. In this way, unsteady pace becomes quite naturally linked to revolutionary change and those changes that can, or that we must,

153

realise in a rapid manner or at a given time. An example of this is the launch of a new organisation. If we are going to introduce a new organisation, it needs to take effect on a certain date. If we are introducing a new system, the new system needs to be 'opened' at a given time. If there is an old system to be closed, it needs to be shut down at a certain date. If we do not shut down the old system, we will not be able to reap the benefits, such as cost savings in terms of discontinued licences and management of the system. The same is true if there is a major skills development or brand launch. These also need to be timed. They need to be determined when to start, over what period it will be carried out and possibly for how long it will last.

When we lead change at an unsteady pace, *timing* is critical. Introducing a new finance system over Christmas and New Year when an entire finance department is sitting down to close the year is an example of bad timing. Performing a major skills development initiative at a time of year when the organisation is at its busiest is another example of poor timing. Reorganising an entire warehouse operation in October and November when nearly 60% of annual sales are due to Black Friday and Christmas sales is also bad timing.

However, timing is not only linked to major activities. It's just as important in the small stuff. If we want a high level of participation from the business and a high level of engagement in, for example, a specific workshop, the activity should not be scheduled on a Friday that is almost a bank holiday or the day before Midsummer's Eve.

In fact, it's often easier to find opportunities that involve bad timing than good. Organisations are often busy, and time is a scarce resource. Hence the importance of prioritising activities. It is not uncommon for many managers' calendars in larger organisations to be 70% or more full when the year begins. This can include budget work, forecast reviews, performance reviews, management group meetings, planning meetings, managers' days, annual managers' conferences, steering committee meetings, board meetings and project meetings of various kinds. And so far, I have not even included customer or external work. It is no wonder that it is difficult to get the attention of these people in various changes. If we are to find good opportunities, or at least opportunities that are better than bad ones, we need to be aware of the seasonal variations in different parts of the organisation. We need to know when the pressure is high and when it is calm enough to try to perform change related activities. If we don't find those times, the organisation and our people won't be able to contribute to the change and there will be no improvement in performance.

If we don't know the variations over the year in the activities, it can be difficult to know how to plan our change. I've been in that situation. The lack of knowledge we feel then is a great opportunity to create participation and interest in the change. We can ask those who know something about the year and the people we want to contribute. When we ask them about their annual load, we find out a lot of things that are valuable to us in the change effort and an opportunity to tell them about the change and hopefully influence those we talk to, to contribute. It also increases the chances that they will participate in change activities. This in turn creates a better end solution and increases the likelihood that their behaviour will change, and benefits will be realised. The actual opportunity for employees to participate is crucial. Therefore, timing is crucial.

What we need to keep in mind about timing is that the opportunity to participate can depend both on internal factors such as sales peaks and on external factors, things happening in the outside world or the market. Customers or suppliers may have planned activities that affect our ability to attract employees to participate. New laws or regulations that are introduced and need to be dealt with quickly, such as GDPR have an impact. Or as we have seen in recent years, pandemics, war situations or a tanker blocking the Suez Canal for six days that overturn much of our current ways of working and plans for the near future. Timing is thus dependent on both internal and external factors; things we can anticipate and things impossible to foresee.

## Steady pace and speed of change

In contrast to unsteady pace, we have *steady pace*. Steady pace means that we carry out smaller activities continuously and with a more even frequency than in unsteady pace. This can include various things that create learning and understanding of the change. Examples could be the launch of short films, information material sent out or a seminar that raises awareness of how the change affects different roles in different parts of the organisation. These small things aim to develop and eventually reinforce the behaviours that we believe need to be developed to achieve the desired improvements in performance.

The unsteady pace is essentially about making major introductions to bring about leaps in change with some kind of 'big bang' logic.[100] The steady pace is about continually building change through small things, from the bottom up. Changing by building, requires learning. Learning is a slow process, so change led at a steady pace needs to be carefully calibrated in terms of the *speed*. We need to think about how high a speed of change is possible.

The maximum speed we can have is related to how much an organisation and its members can learn and develop their behaviours over a given period. We can call this *absorbtive capacity*.[101] We all know that there is a limit to how much new we can absorb and apply to our business. Many of us have felt bombarded after a full day of training. There is a limit to how much we as humans can take in, process, learn from and apply to change our behaviour. Beyond that limit, most of what is communicated or that we are trained in will pass without us registering it or enjoying it. Moreover, this type of activity takes us away from our primary responsibilities. It easily affects our clients or users and is not a smart way to manage limited resources.

Setting the right speed of change requires us to understand how quickly we can push for different skills development interventions. So we need to ensure that skills development initiatives - large and small - are delivered at the rights speed so that employees have time to develop their knowledge, learn from it and change their behaviours in the business. All people need a combination of stability and stimulation from new things.[102] We all need to allow ourselves to step back and reflect a bit to apply what we have just learned.

The German-American psychologist and founder of action research Kurt Lewin advocated a process of change where we need to 'unfreeze' the organisation in order to change it and then freeze it again.[103] That should safeguard some kind of stability. The aforementioned Harvard professor John Kotter's 7-step process for change is largely based on Lewin's ideas. Steps 1-3: 1. Create a sense of urgency, 2. Form a strong coalition, and 3. Create a vision. These aim to thaw the organisation. Steps 4-6: 4. Communicate the vision, 5. Encourage action, and 6. Create early wins aim at the actual change. And steps 7 and 8: 7. Continue to build the change and 8. Make the change stick. These aim to stabilise the new situation.[104]

In practice, this means that we cannot have too high a speed. Too high a speed not only results in poorly used resources, in terms of training people who rightly can't be bothered to listen anymore. It also creates frustration among employees because they are not able to absorb or apply the new lessons learned in their daily lives.

Of course, it is not possible to define what the 'right' speed is. However, a first factor to start with is us. We can think about whether we ourselves are used to learning new things and compare that with the employees who now need to develop their skills. Based on what I would be able to cope with, I can then consider what the others might be able to acquire in a given period. In addition to the ability to learn new things, the speed must also be related to the resources we have available in the organisation in the same given period. How much time do we and our people have, how much money do we have to invest in skills development over the period, and how much other resources can we devote to change and learning over that given period of time. Sometimes as an organisation we have a knife to our throat and therefore not the opportunity, or the luxury, to slow down the speed. What we then need to do here and now is to find ways to really prioritise which change activities *must* be realised before others to have an impact of the change. And with that, which ones we can push back a bit in time.

Thus, when assessing the pace of change, we need to consider both timing and speed. Timing becomes particularly important when large, heavy and often concrete activities or actions are performed in a context of unsteady change. Speed becomes crucial in steady change because there are limits to how much we can learn and invest in change collectively in a given period.

Understanding how unsteady and steady change complement each other helps us to achieve the desired change more effectively than if we use only one. Thus, unsteady and steady change are not opposites or substitutes. They are, and should be used, as complements to each other, just like the entire logic of revolutionary and evolutionary change.

---

In terms of the **pace of change**, it is useful to answer the following questions:

16. What, which parts, stages or elements of change are likely to be mainly unsteady? How should we think about the timing of these?

17. What, which parts, stages or elements of the change are likely to be essentially steady? How should we think about the speed of these?

18. How can we combine revolutionary and evolutionary change strategies to make our change and its different parts work in the best possible way?

---

# Summary: Tackling change

In this chapter we have discussed how we can approach different changes, what revolutionary and evolutionary change is, how these approaches affect the pace and timing of change. We have also looked at how the approaches need to complement each other.

### How can we tackle different changes?

★ Change can be approached in revolutionary (top-down) and evolutionary (bottom-up) ways.

### What is revolutionary and evolutionary change?

★ Revolutionary change aims to create a break in the existing e.g. structures. It is often driven or coordinated centrally and from 'the top'. Evolutionary change is built from the bottom up. It not infrequently starts peripherally and is often related to or sprung from learning.

### How do revolutionary and evolutionary change need to complement each other?

★ Revolutionary and evolutionary approaches need to complement each other to ensure that change resources are used effectively and that ownership of the change is created in the business. By combining revolutionary and evolutionary change, we can allow abrupt moments to create 'leaps of change' in hard parts while soft parts can evolve continuously and over time.

### How do pace of change: speed and timing affect change management?

★ Revolutionary change has abrupt and time-bound moments (e.g. a new organisation has to take effect at a certain time). Such a time must be 'timed' with the business. Evolutionary change involves learning. Learning is a slow process; we cannot learn as much as we want as quickly as we want. The speed must be adapted to how much we can learn and how much we can invest in change here and now and still live up to our responsibilities to our stakeholders.

# Reflections: Tackling change

# 7. The work of the change manager

When we know what change and change management is; when we have an idea of the pressures for change that an organisation faces; when we understand the behaviours that affect the results we want to improve, the individuals who need to be involved and how to approach the change, then the next important question becomes: who will manage this change? What responsibilities must change managers take to ensure that the improvements in performance that the change is intended to bring about are also realised? Responsibility is important. Someone needs to be responsible for driving change, particularly large-scale and strategic change.

Responsibility can undoubtedly be seen in different ways. In the satirical masterpiece *The Devil's Dictionary*[105] by Ambrose Pierce, first written in 1911, responsibility is defined as follows:

> RESPONSIBILITY, noun. A detachable burden easily shifted to the shoulders of God, Fate, Fortune, Luck or one's neighbour. In the days of astrology, it was customary to unload it upon a star.

This is, in my opinion, a wonderful description. In fact, when we look at responsibility for major change in organisations, we can wonder if maybe that's exactly how the people in charge saw it. But abdication is not responsibility. If we want to create something real, we obviously can't settle for that. We need to be precise in who is responsible for what and how to ensure progress in, and realisation of, our changes.

---

In this chapter we will not look at the stars or at fate. We will be more precise than that. We will set out the five different responsibilities of a change manager and how we can work practically within these five: realising the benefits; managing stakeholders; developing knowledge and skills; evaluating and driving the change; and handing over to the business.

---

# The five functions of the change manager

In this book, we use the term *change manager* for the person who is primarily responsible for following a change through.[106] Although many people contribute to a change, the individual responsibility for holding the change together and leading it needs to lie with one person. This is especially true if there are major strategic changes. The change manager is therefore also responsible for ensuring that the benefits, the improvements in performance that have been identified, are also realised, as the change is realised. It is therefore the change manager's responsibility to lead the change.

In practical terms, this involves planning, performing and evaluating different types of *change activities*. Although I am not so fond of the term change plan, it is the development, execution, analysis and updating of it that a change manager needs to work on. The change activities that change managers need to carry out, evaluate and improve fall into five functions (responsibilities): 1. Identify, analyse and prioritise benefits; 2. Work with stakeholders; 3. Develop knowledge and skills; 4. Evaluate and drive the change and 5. Hand over the realisation of benefits to the business.

## Identify, analyse and prioritise changes and benefits

The purpose of identifying, analysing and prioritising changes is to try to ensure that the changes we take on have the impact for which we hope. In all major changes, and most minor ones, the initial assessment of performance improvement will not be the actual one. We therefore need to work on an ongoing basis to ensure that the positive impacts we can realise are realised.

Such work involves four different elements: 1. We need to analyse and describe the objectives and benefits of the change in a clear way; 2. We need to make assessments of the opportunity we have to influence different results; 3. We need to assess how likely it is that we will succeed in realising changes and thereby achieve improvements in outcomes; and 4. We need to consider how we prioritise different changes across each other and over time. We will now review these elements.

## Analysis of objectives and quantification of benefits and costs

To know that we have succeeded in a change, we need to know what 'success' means. We need to know what we want to achieve. We need to do a *goal analysis*. It helps us evaluate our success. Here we mean setting goals for our change. To set goals, the change needs to be described in a concrete way at an early stage. A first step that usually helps is to describe the current stage and the future stage in the same sentence. We can think like this: What are we leaving and what are we going to? This helps the brain to concretise the actual changes that need to take place. In a second step, it helps us to identify benefits.

> Benefits are defined as the positive impact on organisational performance that would have been absent if we had not realised the change.

One way to help us define benefits is to use the actual words *Go from... to...* as the example below shows:

*   *Go from* having an organisational structure based on products *to* having an organisation that is has a geographical basis.

*   *Go from* having several different and uncoordinated budgeting, planning and monitoring processes that are decoupled from strategy work *to* having a single, integrated strategy and management process where all governance processes are linked in a logical and as simple way as possible.

Another concrete tip is to avoid terms that are open to interpretation, such as 'better'. What does better really mean? In what way are they better? Faster turnaround time? Better precision in production? The clearer we can be in our benefit descriptions and link them to concrete organisational results that are known in the organisation: economically related, customer and market

163

related, linked to the performance of the business, for example productivity efficiency or indicators of learning and development of the organisation, the easier it will be to quantify benefits and even put a money value on them.

To make predictions, we need to know what something will look like at a given moment. Right now, for example. We need to use these *initial conditions* as input, or starting point, for our future assessment. Then, we do something, try something out. After that, we then follow up and look at the output data to see what happened. Based on that we can make a judgement about how good we were in our prediction, and how well we have succeeded in what we set out to do. In fact, this description is also, in a nutshell, a description of the scientific process since Newton's day, especially in the natural sciences.

So, what does this have to do with benefits? Well, to know what something might lead to (make a prediction) we need to know what the current situation is. We need to define a *baseline*. Baseline is the starting point we compare against when evaluating whether changes have had any, preferably expected or better, effect.

To identify and eventually realise benefits, we therefore need to answer the following questions:

* Which result should be improved?
    o An example might be perceived customer satisfaction with the cleanliness of the rooms in our hotel.
* What is the result today?
    o Today, 76 out of 100 are very satisfied (i.e. answering 5 on a five-point scale).
* How much should it be improved?
    o We think that 90 out of 100 should be able to answer 5.
* When will we have reached this level?
    o If we work on this for a year, we should be able to achieve it.

★ How often should we evaluate and ensure that we are taking action to influence outcomes in the desired direction?

o If we look at and reflect on performance together once a month, we should be able to learn what we can do even better.

Other examples of changes and benefits can be described as follows: increased market share (benefit) by *going from* being a product organisation *to* a customer-oriented organisation (change); more satisfied customers (benefit) by *going from* an internally focused service development process *to* a more customer-inclusive process with open innovation (change); higher profitability (benefit) by *going from* manual ways of working in package management *to* more automated ways of working (change).

## Benefit realisation and different types of benefits

As we noted earlier and as the examples above show, organisational performance can be measured and evaluated over time. This is also true for benefits. And it is the realisation of these benefits that we should strive for when realising change. In our goal analysis, we therefore need to define the benefits of change and how they can be realised from the beginning. The description of which benefits will be realised when, where and how can be called a *benefit realisation plan*.

There are a variety of methods for quantifying benefits. In this book, I use a variant of what is usually called the Peng model.[107] The Peng model is based on the premise that everything in an activity can be converted into money. I know from experience that this is difficult and, more importantly, not always relevant. Nevertheless, it is a good starting point to try as much as possible to define benefits that affect revenue and/or costs. In private companies that want to influence their profitability, this is a must. However, it is also important in other businesses because money is a scarce resource we want to use wisely. So it is also good for public enterprises that are actually mandated to use tax-funded funds as responsibly as possible.

It may sound crude, but in the end money is one of the things that counts - right or wrong. It's also the resource that organisations - regardless of size, type or sector - have the easiest time understanding.

When assessing benefits, we distinguish between four types: green, yellow, red and blue.

*Green benefits* are benefits that generate money directly given a certain change. They do not assume that we need to do anything more in the business than realise that particular (part of the) change for the benefits to be materialised. Green benefits are common when, for example, we buy new machines, computers, etc. that allow us to immediately discard the old ones. The old ones no longer need to be maintained - we avoid a cost. Another option is that we as an organisation carry out new tasks ourselves, thus avoiding the need to buy consultancy services. It could also involve terminating services with one of several suppliers where we can have fewer. On the one hand, we avoid subscription costs from multiple suppliers, and on the other hand, we avoid maintaining multiple contacts. One relationship to maintain is less costly than two. Green benefits are therefore direct cost savings or revenue increases that are realised when the change takes place. Ideally, in these cases, we would like to see an actual reduction or increase in a particular 'account' as soon as possible in time.

*Yellow benefits* are benefits that can be monetised if we perform additional activities as part of the change process. A common example of yellow benefits is time savings. Provided the organisation learns to work differently, with different methods or in smarter systems, we could do the job with fewer staff. The time savings from fewer staff means that we can reduce our staffing costs if we decide in the change process to make staff redundant. If we have accounted for that change at our initial stage, it requires that at some point in the change we also terminate employees because of, for example, the new ways of working.

However, we need to be careful here. We cannot always terminate employees because of a reduction in the workload of a few people. One hour here and one hour there adds up quite quickly to 170 hours a month. In all fairness, that's about one full-time job. However, if the work that makes up the 170 hours is carried out by many different people and roles, in different parts of the organisation, it is difficult (if not impossible) to realise the benefits by dismissing one person. It may then be more intelligent to see how these hours can be used in other parts of the business. In practice, this means that there is no yellow benefit in this case. It means no cost savings in terms of lower wage costs in the long run. However, it can provide other types of benefits, such as red benefits (more below). However, most yellow benefits come from non-value adding activities that are removed or automated through, for example, digitisation and automation in a new process design. Monitoring of yellow benefits can therefore be done by following up that non-value adding activities that were previously performed are not performed, or in cases where they are automated, ensuring that the activities have been automated.

A change can also bring *red benefits*. While green and yellow benefits typically have a savings focus, red benefits have a more optimistic stance. Red benefits are opportunities that we in the organisation believe the change can bring. These are increased or new revenues or cost savings over time based on reasonable assumptions. For example, it may involve winning a reference project that enables more business in a specific area. It may also mean an opportunity to enter a new geographic market or to develop a new product that opens up new revenue streams through sales that did not exist before. A third common category of red benefits is the enabling of other benefits, such as better information for managers through a new decision support system that in turn enables the right information, at the right time, to the right person and thus better decision making. That ought to yield something good.

Finally, we also have *blue benefits*. I sometimes call blue benefits 'qualitative benefits'. This generally means benefits that we cannot quantify so easily, or where it does not feel relevant to quantify. It is important to note that lack of relevance cannot be used as an argument just because we find it difficult or because we do not have the energy to quantify the benefits. Examples of blue benefits could be employee satisfaction, leadership, engagement, learning or reduced staff turnover. I agree that these can be difficult to quantify, but it is by no means impossible. It is possible to calculate the cost of a new recruitment or the cost of a sick leave and based on reasonable assumptions we can conclude that employees who feel better are less likely to leave. They are also less likely to take sick leave. This means that blue, so-called qualitative, benefits can often be easily translated into quantitative benefits, such as cost savings or increased revenues. However, this requires us to think twice and make an extra effort.

> My understanding is that organisations that are good at defining and quantifying benefits also value their employees more highly than those that are not. It's quite logical in all its cynicism. If money is what matters, and we recognise that employees have a big impact on money, then employees become important too. As a next step, it also becomes natural to invest in employees because they are critical to our success. Over time, both organisations and employees benefit from such an approach.

## Distribution between different types of benefits

In most organisations' changes, all four types of benefits are usually present. We are likely to have green, yellow, red and blue benefits. Understanding which benefits exist and of what type gives us an overall picture of how much the organisation, parts of the organisation, and/or customers will benefit from a particular change intervention.

The reason I think it's important to be clear about benefits is that change costs. They cost time, they cost commitment, they cost in lost production and sometimes financial investment. The more extensive the changes in breadth and depth, the more resources are required for the change. This is not surprising at all. The more we need to change, and the more people need to change, the more time, money and commitment we need to invest in business and skills development, communication, information and more. As we need to invest resources in change management to bring about change, we want a return on our investment. We don't want to lose out on it.

Figure 7.1 below shows a visualised business case with costs and the different types of benefits.

Figure 7.1 Costs and benefits of a change in relation to each other

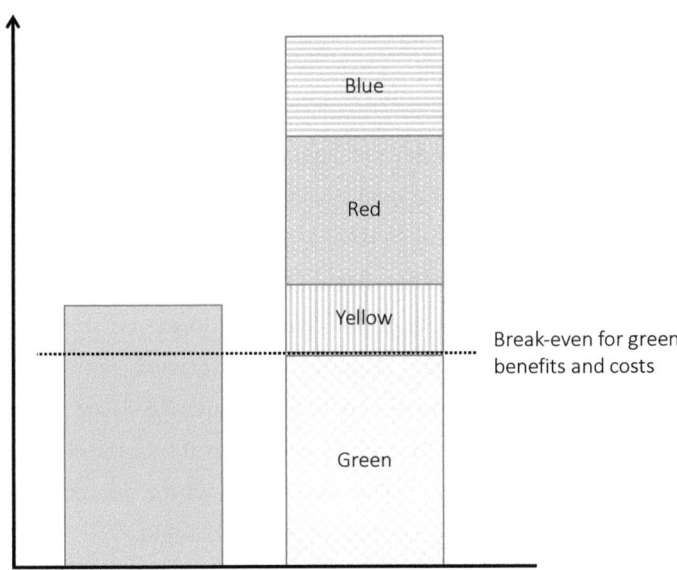

In a nutshell, we want change to pay for itself financially. Even better, of course, we want the change to contribute more than it costs. If a change

doesn't at least break even, it may not be worth investing time, commitment or money in it. Better then to put the energy into something else that will give more back. However, there are exceptions: changes aimed at ensuring compliance with newly introduced laws must be realised and may cost what they cost. There is no choice in these cases. But in many other cases, there is indeed a choice to be made.

By assessing our benefits as discussed above, we have a better chance of understanding whether a change is economically viable. Since the green benefits are the only benefits we know with certainty will be realised, we want to keep track of these. A rule of thumb is to try to design and plan changes, especially those that are voluntary, so that the green benefits cover all the estimated costs of the change.

There are two points to making this assessment. The first is that it means that we do not take on a lot of changes - in the long run and in the short run - that we cannot manage well, and that may have a negative impact on financial results. We become more critical of 'hit-and-miss' changes that have not been thought through. Money and employee commitment and time are limited resources that should be used wisely in all types of activities. There may be other things we can do to have a positive impact on the business rather than pushing for a particular change. Then of course we should do so.

The second is that we reduce the chance of losing out too much in change. Many major strategic changes are associated with risk and opportunity or reward. If we can ensure that the financial risks are reasonably hedged, i.e. that the costs of change are covered, then at least the change need not be an unnecessary financial failure even if not all the potential upsides (yellow and red benefits) are realised as we initially thought.

The clarification of the benefits and costs of a particular change, or set of changes, is what we call the *business case*.

In terms of **benefits**, it is useful to answer the following questions:

19. What measurable benefits - changes in organisational performance - do we see from the change? (Compare with questions 5 and 6 on organisational performance).

20. What and how big are green benefits? Yellow? Red? Blue? What is the distribution between the different types of benefits?

## Impact on results and agency

Typically, change starts with identifying potential for improvement: a risk, a problem or an opportunity that we can do something about or with. Not infrequently, the insight is the result of someone or some people learning something new. Improvement potential often stems from a problem or a question about how something could be. Identifying problems and questions about what we can do instead of what we are doing today is thus a driver for change. Asking these types of questions are therefore also important change-related behaviours in all types of organisations. However, in order to drive through change and ensure improvements in performance, i.e. benefit realisation, we need to have *agency* - not just an idea. We, as change managers, need to have some form of opportunity to own and thus realise the change, for example through decisions on the allocation of resources.

This ownership can be assessed in terms of the different stages of the evolutionary change process as discussed in Chapter 6. Tackling change (Figure 6.2):

*Identification* is a crucial first step. Anyone can identify opportunities. Anyone has power over their own ideas. However, it takes a bit more to make things happen. The first step after we identify something is that we need to *analyse and define* what the change means, what benefits might be realised, what

171

costs it might entail. Then we need to *generate and formulate* different proposals for possible solutions. After that, we *decide* on the solution we believe in, we *realise* it, and we *evaluate and reflect* on how well the solution did what it was intended to do. Finally, we *feed back and make adjustments* to ensure that the lessons we have learnt are applied to the business.

There are many things for which a change manager can be responsible. There is also a big difference linked to the type of change manager a person is. When we as managers of an organisation are change managers and want to drive something through in our own organisation, we typically own the resources required and can prioritise in a way that enables the change. Not always, but often. For a centrally placed change manager, the situation is different. Central development people generally do not - and should not - have decision-making authority over the resources of the business. We will spend more time on this in Chapter 9. Organising Change. What we can already see is that change managers are able to drive change to different extents depending on their roles and positions. This is why we need to sort out the agency.

In most cases, anyone in an organisation can identify, analyse and define challenges (at least initially). Perhaps most can also generate proposals that will bring about changes and improvements in performance. At least that is desirable. The more ideas for improvement, the better. Not always and not everywhere, but continuously and in small ways: we can all contribute in what is close to our daily lives.

After we have generated solutions, if not before, several people in the organisation need to be involved. In some cases, for example when it comes to major changes, it may be the management or even the board, who need to decide on allocating resources to bring about the change or what and how the change needs to be realised. After that, a clear responsibility needs to be assigned to a person (a change manager) to realise, evaluate and reflect as well as feed back and adjust. However, we do it, we need to somehow get through all seven steps of the process for the change to be something serious.

> Regardless of who is in charge, we can say with a fair degree of certainty that no benefits will accrue to the business or customers until something is changed in the business and new or refined behaviours have replaced the previous ones.

What makes this even more complicated is that in major changes, which extend over time, we sometimes don't see the benefits until well into the future. Even if we evaluate and reflect, and feed back and adjust, it is not certain that the change has progressed far enough for us to see improvements in actual results. It may even be that the change is completed before we see the first actual improvements in performance. And then there is no change manager left. Nevertheless, someone must ensure benefit realisation if we want to be serious about our changes.

An important part of ensuring that benefits are realised, therefore, is to understand how far we can take a change and on whom we depend for change and its benefits to be realised.

A question to ask yourself as a change manager, regardless of the type of change, is therefore the following. Do I have *the agency, the power*, i.e. the ability to decide how we will:

* Identify improvement needs that require a change?
* Analyse and define the need for change?
* Generate and formulate a set of solutions to the problems the change will solve?
* Decide to push through the change with all that it requires?
* Lead and drive the realisation of change?
* Evaluate and reflect on the change as it is realised?

* Feed back the results of the change to the business and adjust the elements of the business that need to be adjusted to contribute to better performance?

---

In terms of **agency**, it is useful to answer the following questions:

21. What control do we have over change? How far can we push it without a mandate from others? Identify, analyse and define, generate proposed solutions, decide on the solution, realise, evaluate and reflect, and feed back and adjust?

---

Our understanding of agency, power or mandate in these matters is crucial to ensuring that the changes that need to be made are made. We need to understand this to assess the *realisability of* change.

## Realisability of change

In this book, I define *realisability* as the probability that the change will be realised *and* that it will lead to the improvements in performance we think it will, with the means we have in mind, i.e. within the framework of the business case we have formulated.

I have created and read many business cases in my professional life, and in several different roles. As a consultant, when I wanted to sell in a project, I had a view (fairly inexperienced as I was). As a decision-maker, for example as a project owner, chair of a steering committee, or member of a management team or board, I had (and still have) a different view. We have different perspectives. The ability to switch perspectives is often worth more than intelligence.

It is an important lesson to take away that we see a business case in different ways. A business case is based on principles, and these are very much shaped by the person or persons who set the principles, their will, their appetite for risk, their view of the world, etc.

Nevertheless, we can probably say that costs are quite often accurately described. We often see changes as a cost item. An unnecessary evil. In fewer business cases are benefits described. In even fewer cases are benefits described in a clear way that allows us to understand where the benefits come from or what is required for them to be realised (for example, whether they are green, yellow, red or blue). Often the benefits are put in a single 'bucket' and almost presented in a way that leads the reader to believe that they will be realised automatically. So, there is potential for improvement here. There is also an opportunity for those who procure services where the business case is a natural part of the decision-making process to be more demanding of their suppliers.

In even fewer business cases, in fact almost none in my experience, is the feasibility assessed in a reasonably objective way. Risks are often highlighted. That is part of the feasibility, but the risks are mostly not described in a way that helps us understand what benefits might be lost if a particular risk occurs. That is what we want to know. After all, the purpose of the change is precisely the benefits. The risks are often more related to the change or the project as a whole. That assessment is also sometimes needed. But this assessment is not clearly enough linked to realisability to allow us to make an informed decision on whether we should try to realise the change based on benefits.

There is no benefit realisation if people in the business don't behave in new ways: use new methods, work according to new processes, in new or updated systems, and old behaviours have been abandoned for the new, or refined.

An important part of the early stages of change is therefore to assess the realisability of the change as such. How likely is it that we can do this? Not to make such an assessment is, in my view, as a strategist, irresponsible. We have limited resources. They should be put where they will have an impact. Every minute invested in a change with zero chance of being realised is then to be considered as 'money down the drain'.

However, what is realisability? Realisability depends on different things. Three things have a significant impact. First, there is the magnitude of change: the breadth and depth. The more extensive, the more difficult to realise. Second, the degree of involvement. This means how many and what proportion of stakeholders (both stakeholder groups and key stakeholders) are involved in the change process. The third thing is also about involvement: the support that the change has from management, board, steering committee or similar. The latter is most evident when we as change managers do not own the resources ourselves but act on a mandate from a management or similar body.

In terms of *magnitude*, we have already assessed the breadth and depth of change. We did so in Chapter 5. Magnitude and stakeholders. *Breadth* we concluded was based on the number of people in different parts of the organisation and its vicinity who are affected by the change. Examples might include divisions, departments, districts, units, etc. *Depth* depends on how different the future situation is compared to the current situation. How differently employees need to behave tomorrow compared to today. The greater the magnitude, both in breadth and depth, the more difficult it is to realise a change and secure benefits for the business or for customers.

It goes without saying that if a person needs to log in via an app instead of a browser, the breadth and depth of change is small. It doesn't take much to realise such a change and realise the benefits of it. Instead, if it's about how an entire organisation with all its constituent business areas and geographies should change its strategy and performance review processes, from employee reviews to reporting to the board and financial markets, we see both breadth and depth are great. It is a massive change and leading it, in a way that ensures benefits are realised, is a strategic, structural, process and cultural challenge for the whole organisation. Thus, realisability, the likelihood of benefits being realised, is significantly lower in the latter example. This also helps us understand the point of separating different changes from each other when possible. If we can isolate smaller changes and pursue them separately, we are likely to secure benefits in some cases. And in total, more benefits.

In terms of *involvement*, we assess it in terms of quantity and quality. The *quantitative* assessment is an assessment of the percentage of those who need to change their behaviour who are involved in the change process. We earlier stated that about 15-25% of the population to be changed is a reasonable rule of thumb for what is required as a critical mass. Here our reasoning differs from classical economic theory which suggests that more than half of a population should be involved.[108] We therefore take a round about this.

In a sense, it makes sense that if we see the change as a seesaw, a question of equilibrium, then 51 people are more than 49 (if we have 100 to divide). The problem with the reasoning in organisations (and in societies for that matter) is that one person does not always weigh the same – figuratively and literally. If we can get more heavy adults over on our side of the seesaw and allow many small children to sit on the other side, we don't need to be more than half in number to weigh more.

So, there is a point in thinking about who 'weighs heavily' when we think about quality and involvement. However, that said, the more people who have been involved in the change process, the more people there are who have a chance to take ownership of the change and the greater the chance that the change will be realised, so that benefits are realised.

When we talk about the *qualitative* assessment of the degree of involvement, we lean towards the three categories of key stakeholders:

mavens, connectors and persuaders. We want to include all possible informal leaders who can support, facilitate or drive change. After all, in our view, they should be the people who 'weigh a lot'.

> The more key stakeholders who can help spread the word across the board, quality assure proposed solutions and sell the change to more employees, the better the chance of driving the change through successfully.

In some cases, a change manager can only be responsible for a limited part of the change - especially when they start from a central place in the organisation. Collective responsibility for change in general is a must, but we must also recognise that organisations are in most cases hierarchies where responsibility for resources lies with certain individuals. We may have views on this. I do. There are other ways to lead. However, reality is what it is, and often we must face the fact that senior people sitting with resources have an impact when we want to push through change.

Management teams at different levels, boards, steering committees etc. generally have a responsibility to allocate resources, prioritise and lead different projects and activities. They should be involved in major and/or strategic changes. Having a clear mandate from the people in charge of the resources is then a must to be able to push through such a change.

This *support from management* is therefore the next factor that has a clear impact on the realisability of major changes. Management support can also be divided into a quantitative and a qualitative component. The quantitative component here includes the percentage of the management, board or steering committee that is fully aware of what the change means, even in the fine print.

Few people like surprises when it comes to major changes. This is also true of management that works under changing conditions and where the stakes are high. The more of the 'decision-making body' that is fully aware, the better the chance of pushing through the change as we intended. And therefore, the greater the chance of realising the benefits we set out to realise.

The qualitative assessment of management support can be answered by a question: How likely is management to stand up for the change if the winds of change start blowing hard around it? If it is a major change and if it is of a strategic nature, it will be challenged within the organisation. In that case, leaders must have the courage to stand their ground. As change managers, we can only do 'so much'. Our trust capital only has limited value and we probably need a little more than what we have. The same reasoning applies if the change is perceived as controversial (whether it is or not) or if it is a clear breach of some natural, existing organisational culture. If any of these aggravating circumstances prevail, we need to understand how convinced the decision-makers within the decision-making body are to stand by their decision and realise the change. Perhaps despite extensive and harsh criticism from others. The stronger the conviction of these key stakeholders, the greater the likelihood that the change will be realised.

Howard Aiken, physician and computer pioneer at IBM during the post war era provocatively said something like if your ideas are any original you'll have to ram them down people's throats[109].

If that is true, then support from key stakeholders becomes a crucial issue for anyone driving change. And that support can only come through involvement. Another important factor, at least if this is close to the truth, is that we need to prioritise change. We can't shove just any number of sweeping changes down people's throats. At a certain point, their stomachs are full.

---

In terms of **realisability**, it is useful to answer the following questions:

22. How likely is it that we will succeed in realising the change, i.e. ensuring that the benefits are delivered to customers or the business?

23. What is the realisability of the change based on the magnitude of the change? Breadth and depth? Degree of involvement – the right people and right number? Support from 'management' (if needed)?

---

## Prioritise Changes

Based on the above reasoning about benefits and realisability, we can start to prioritise changes, or parts of changes. We can prioritise based on how much we get back for the time and commitment we invest, and on how likely we are to get back at least as much as we put in.

If we put these arguments in a graph, we can put on the vertical axis the relation between benefit and as relative benefit in relation to cost. In other words, how likely we can expect returns on our investment in the particular change (ROI, return on investment). The higher up the y-axis, the better the investment. This number is not related to money and therefore helps us examine different changes or parts of changes concurrently.

On the horizontal axis we can put the realisability. The further to the right the better the realisability. This means a higher probability that the change will be realised with the desired improvement in results.

This reasoning is illustrated in Figure 7.2.

Figure 7.2 Prioritisation of changes

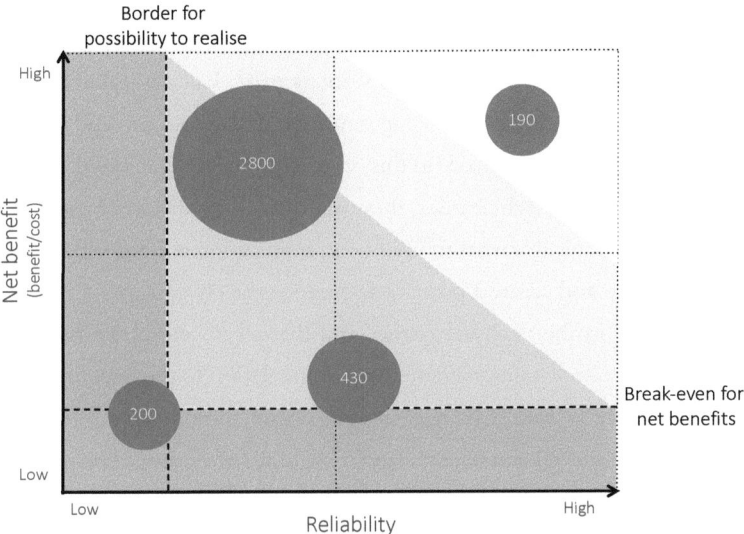

All deliberately led changes have some kind of input that has a cost, at least time. There is therefore a limit to when the benefits exceed the costs. We can call this limit *the net benefit limit*, and it is the breakeven point (BEP) for whether a change is worth implementing (economically) or not.

Similarly, there is a limit to whether it is reasonable to undertake the change based on whether it will be possible to realise it with the desired result. If we can't possibly push through a change, we need to rethink. We may have to narrow the change, pick out certain elements and push them through, or change something that is a blockage first, and then take the real change. No one is served by driving change that will not bring any benefit or use to the business, customers or beneficiaries.

In Figure 7.2 above, I have included four changes from a major change project I ran in an organisation. The size of the full circles represents the total size of the net benefit of the change. That is, actual benefit in money minus the actual costs. In other words, net benefit in any currency. In the example above, these are EUR 2.8 million, 200,000, 430,000 and 190,000. The bigger the ball, the bigger the net benefit.

With this reasoning, the graph can be divided into four areas:

The top right corner is where we want as many balls as possible. This is where we find changes that give a big return on what we put in and that we are likely to push through. Based on this, we can conclude that when we find small balls in the upper right corner, these are often potential *quick wins*. And realising them is tactically smart to use in communication and information to show momentum and create a positive feeling for the change.

If we look in the very left corner and the very bottom, we have the opposite. Here we see changes where the cost in relation to the benefit is high and the feasibility is low. Changes in this sector should be carefully re-evaluated and we should consider if - and if so, how - they should be realised. Perhaps we need to delineate them differently or split them up.

All changes have an opportunity cost, or alternative cost. We have limited resources and could invest them in something else. We therefore need to be a little critical of many of our changes. In some cases, we have to 'murder your darlings', as Arthur Quiller-Couch put it in *On the Art of Writing*[110] already in 1916 (speaking of prioritisation).

We then have a third and a fourth area left in the graph, forming some kind of middle. In fact, this is where we find most changes and parts of major changes. So, if changes are on the right side and above of the lines, it is perfectly fine to push them through. However, what we always should consider is the *speed of change*. How many different change initiatives can an organisation embrace and realise in a way that makes performance improvements follow?

In my opinion, we don't think often enough about how many new initiatives we can keep going at the same time. I am thinking particularly of management teams at different levels. Managers are people too. Not infrequently, these are people with a desire to perform professionally. That is often why they end up there. One thing leaders often do to show activity is to start things, for example change initiatives. This is perfectly understandable. It's a way of showing responsibility and ambition. I've been in that role myself. I've also felt that things are going slowly out there, with safety work, with diversity, with sustainability.

However, when we're not in the business ourselves, it's easy to forget how busy people are. It is by no means certain that a change initiative is the right thing from a strategic perspective. It may well be that the right management behaviour, strategically speaking, is to step back, remove barriers to learning through shaping and thereby enable change evolutionarily. Letting employees do their job, test, fail (once) and learn.

Working like that as a manager is quite different from pushing things from the top. It also creates completely different conditions for the organisation to learn and to change. Unfortunately, this understanding is not very common, and it means that a whole potential arsenal of change resources is not mobilised. That is certainly not strategic. Nor is it how we ensure that performance improvements on the ground is realised.

## Work with stakeholders

Working with stakeholders, what is sometimes referred to as *stakeholder management*, is a crucial task for a change manager. Sooner or later, we have to get people on board and let them be part of the change. Otherwise, there will be no change. The more and the sooner, the better. However, we often don't have the time and opportunity to involve everyone in everything, so stakeholder management is something a change manager needs to be good at. We need to know who, when, how and why to work with different stakeholders.

When we do a stakeholder analysis, as we did in Chapter 5. Magnitude and stakeholders, we create a rough outline of how different stakeholders can be included in the work. *Involving* is about bringing people into the actual work. *Communicating* is about dialogue and exchanging views. *Informing* is about sending information in a direction. *Monitor* is about keeping an eye on things. These are the four overall ways in which we work with stakeholders.

Working with stakeholders gives us an opportunity to demonstrate benefits early in the process. It creates a willingness to contribute. When something doesn't go as expected (as will occur at some point), involvement allows us to create an understanding of the teething problems or challenges that any major change brings.

## Basic prerequisites for behavioural change

In essence, our stakeholder work aims to create and maintain a good dialogue, to build trust and demand for change in the organisation. Stakeholder work really has only one purpose: to ensure that those stakeholders who need to change their behaviour are given the basic prerequisites necessary to enable them to change their behaviour.

We need to ensure, to the best of our ability, that as many key stakeholders and stakeholder groups as possible:

* have clear *expectations* of the changes.
* have the chance to develop the *competence* needed to change their behaviour.
* have the *opportunity* do what is necessary for change.
* receive *reinforcement* when they change their behaviour in a positive way.

All four basic prerequisites for change must be in place for individuals to change their behaviour (see Figure 7.3).

Figure 7.3 Basic prerequisites for behavioural change

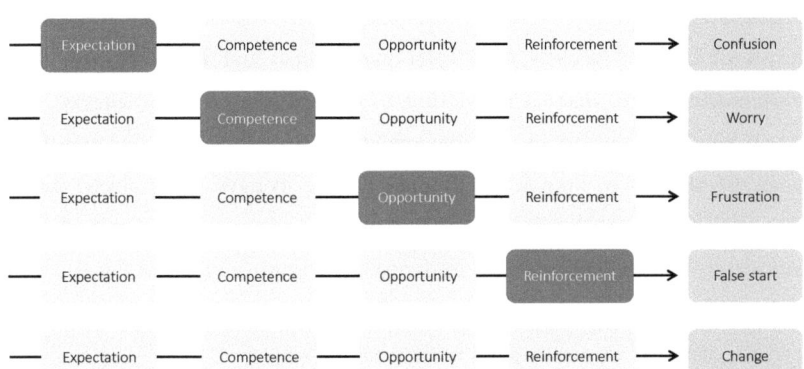

Source: adapted from Wadström (2022)[48]

*Expectation* means that stakeholders who are going to change or refine their behaviours need to understand what behaviours are expected: what they look like (the topography of the behaviour) and how often they should be performed (with what frequency). If the instruction or model to help the stakeholder understand the expectations has low instructional value, it is not easy to change in the 'right' way. If it is unclear what behaviour is being asked for and/or what outcome a behaviour should affect, it is difficult to know how to behave to do the right thing. 'Can you get some new business', has low instructional value. It is difficult to understand what we should do more precisely. It thus provides more ambiguous expectations than the following option: 'Can you analyse the opportunity for us to create growth by offering the packaging solutions we provide to our medical device customers to future food manufacturing customers?' Expectations must provide clear direction.

*Competence* means that stakeholders who are going to perform new or refined behaviours need to know how to do so. It is quite common that employees do not have the necessary knowledge to perform new behaviours. This is even though these are behaviours they are expected to perform. Sometimes we need to develop our skills to do something different. This is particularly common for roles with a leadership responsibility for a large organisation and/or strategic challenges. In these types of roles, responsibilities are unclear, tasks span diverse areas and decisions made will have consequences that are impossible to predict. The change manager role is very similar to this. I have not met any change managers who feel that they have the amount of knowledge they would like to have. They always want more. Therefore, with widespread and ongoing changes in the world and industries, learning has become an increasingly important factor for success in the workplace - not least for work in leadership and strategic roles. Skills need to evolve if we are to work in new ways.

*Opportunity* means that the person who is to perform the behaviour can also do it practically. We must have a certain physical or mental capacity to perform certain tasks. Not everyone is designed or trained to do everything. Becoming a professor of theoretical physics requires a mathematical intellect and a willingness to delve deeply into the abstract that not everyone may be able to develop - regardless of training. To 'dunk' in basketball requires a certain amount of length, which cannot be trained up, and a lot of elasticity (which we can certainly train). Opportunity is also about other practical issues. We may need to have access a certain tool, a method statement or a key/access to a locker or department where information, materials or people we are going to meet are located. A system developer who does not have access to the systems to be developed will not be able to perform the right behaviour despite expectations and competence. Another opportunity that must exist is time. If our calendars are full, they are. If we are to change behaviours, we must ensure that opportunities exist, time is one such prerequisite.

*Reinforcement* means that the people who are going to change or refine behaviours need to have reinforcement on the new behaviours. We have previously discussed how behaviours that are not reinforced - perform an expected function - are extinguished. We therefore need to ensure that there is some form of reinforcement for the person who is going to perform the new or refined behaviour. We need to understand what the person is likely to get out of performing the behaviour. No reinforcement, no behaviours. We need to find ways to systematically reinforce newly learned behaviours for them to be sustained.

> In simple terms, the four basic conditions for behavioural change can be summarised as follows: If I don't have the expectations clear to me, I get confused. If I don't have the skills required, it creates a sense of anxiety. If I don't have the opportunity, I get frustrated. If I don't get reinforcement, the change is just a false start. If all prerequisites are in place, change is possible.

There is no temporal relationship between these basic prerequisites, although this is sometimes claimed. We do not need to have understood the expectations to be reinforced on new behaviours. We don't always need to know why. The 'why' is not magical. We all learn a lot without caring about the why. We might have the opportunity without having the competency. So, we can tone down this temporal sequential stuff; one does not demand a previous one.

However, there is still some kind of connection between them. If I don't understand what is expected of me, it is difficult to assess whether I have the required competence. If I don't know what the expectations are of me, it is also difficult to assess if I have the opportunity, for example the time, for the work in question. Finally, if I don't know what the expectations are, if I don't have the opportunity to do it, or if I don't have the required competence, I will not be able to perform the behaviour. Then, I cannot be reinforced either. We need to be precise with these prerequisites.

In terms of **stakeholders' basic prerequisites**, it is useful to answer the following questions:

24. How well are the basic prerequisites for change in place among stakeholders? How likely are we to succeed in getting these conditions in place in our change work?

## Developing change messages

An early key to successful stakeholder engagement and therefore successful change is to create an understanding of stakeholder expectations. Where are we going? Why is the change needed? What is expected of me? etc. We need to be able to answer these questions. For this to happen, we need a message that is clear, easy to communicate and makes the change feel urgent.

We can ask ourselves four control questions to help us create an effective *change message*:

- ★ Does the message paint a vivid picture of the future situation?
- ★ Can you explain the change message to anyone in the organisation (and outside, if necessary)?
- ★ Does the change message engage most stakeholders?
- ★ Could stakeholders briefly (in 2 minutes maximum) explain the purpose of the change and its consequences?

In the early stages of change, there is great benefit in formulating a consistent message about the change that we can use in the work ahead. The purpose of the change message is to clarify what the change is about, give examples, create an understanding of what the change will mean at different levels and in different parts of the organisation, and what we in the organisation can get out of the change, the benefits.

A change message consists of four components: a change idea; a concrete description of the change; an illustration of the benefits; and a summary description of the change.

*The change idea* should describe the idea behind the change, the reason for the change and create an understanding of why we need to make a change in the first place. Information that can be valuable in formulating a change idea can be found in the environmental scan, the industry analysis, the organisational analysis and the goal analysis. Let's look at an example from a project that aimed to digitise performance evaluation in a large, listed company:

> The change idea is to deliver a system support for the performance review work, streamlining and automating the follow-up work at monthly, quarterly and annual closings. This will also lead to improved quality of the information we use when making decisions.

*The change description* should concretise the change idea, preferably as an *elevator pitch*. The shorter the better, with the caveat that one or two words are not enough to be concrete enough. The term elevator pitch refers to the fact that it should be able to be made in less than 30 seconds. That's the time it takes to ride the elevator up to the management floor (at least that's one of the many stories about the origin of the term). The goal of the change description is understanding, not clichés. If possible, let's formulate the description as one pithy sentence.

The change description should act as an eye-opener, and it should preferably create commitment to the change. To do this, it is helpful if it contains both the problem (or part of the problem) that the change aims to solve and the solution to the problem (or part of the solution). Let's continue with the same example:

> With a sharpened and automated evaluation process, our controllers will be able to free up more time to support the line in their business, and business managers will have better information.

189

*The benefit example* should consist of an illustration of the different benefits that will result from the change. In this example, we cannot describe the different colours (green, yellow, etc.). However, since we are going to exemplify, we need to specify money, numbers or something else that makes the benefits of the change concrete and understandable to the stakeholders. It is not uncommon for us to use terms like 'more efficient'. It is not necessarily wrong, but we need to think about the instructional value, the clarity.

Compare 'We will become more efficient and reduce our costs' with the following: 'Today we spend on average 20% of our working time on administration that tomorrow we will be able to spend on tasks that create value for our customers'. There is a difference in clarity.

The benefit example helps us clarify the importance of the change to stakeholders. In the benefit example, the symbolism of the message is more important than a comprehensive description of the benefits of the change. Let's look at the same example as before one more time:

> 550 full binders - that's how much paper is used annually for the review of the businesses. The binder administration alone takes a total of 64 hours/month for our 20 controllers in our 20 divisions.

Finally, we have *the change summary* which should summarise what the change is about. Here we need to describe what will change, when the change will take effect and broadly how the change will be managed. One last look at our example:

> All operations within the company will start working with Hyperion Planning in the review process from 1 Jan 2014. Division Industry is the first to go.

Together, these four elements make up a combined change message. If we develop this early, we can use it in written information, in communications, in workshops and in other ways. Articulating this early and checking with different stakeholders to make sure it lands well can feel like pointless writing, we are not 'doing' anything. In the long run, however, it saves us quite a lot of unnecessary work. On the one hand, it helps us to think through what we are going to do early on, and on the other hand, it helps us to be consistent in our information and communication. It means there are fewer issues we need to deal with later, so we can focus on leading the change.

Figure 7.4 below shows the example in all its parts.

Figure 7.4 Change message and its components

| Change idea | Change description | Benefits example | Change summary |
|---|---|---|---|
| The change idea is taken from the goal analysis and is the basis for the change message. | The change description should summarise the change idea, in one sentence. The shorter the better.<br><br>The change statement should be an eye-opener and create commitment. Preferably both problem and solution. | The message of change should be exemplified with a benefit example (USD/hrs/no. of, TWh) for selected target groups. | Summarise what needs to change? When will the change start to be realised? Again, it is important to consider the whole change, the roll-out perspective. |
| The idea of the change is to deliver a system support for forecasting work and thus streamline, automate a forecasting work at each monthly / quarterly / annual closure. In addition, the quality of the information. | With a sharpened and automated forecasting process, controllers will be able to free up more time to support the line of business, and business managers will have better information. | 550 full binders - that's how much paper is used annually for forecasting in our regions. File administration takes a total of 34 hours/month for our 25 controllers. | All operations within the company will start working with Hyperion Planning in the forecasting process from 1 Jan 2014. |

In terms of **change message,** it is useful to answer the following questions:

25. What is the message of change and its different parts? The idea of change? The change description? The examples of benefits? The change summary? Do the elements form an understandable and logic whole of the change?

## Tailor stakeholder work

We need to work with different stakeholder groups and different key stakeholders in different ways. We therefore need to use different forms of intervention: meetings, mailings, workshops, etc. Regardless of how we work with stakeholders to involve, communicate or inform, there are a number of things we want to achieve in our work.

We want stakeholders to:

* get the whole picture of the change *and* understand their part of the whole
* feel committed to contribute to the change
* understand that the goal is not so far away in time
* realise that the change affects things that are important to our business
* perceive that the change involves them, perhaps even starts with them
* ensure that management (at the relevant level) has given its full support
* feel prepared to face the change and the consequences of the change in the businesses

A model that can help us determine the type of interventions that may be appropriate for different stakeholder groups and key stakeholders can be seen depicted as a pyramid (as shown in Figure 7.5).

When we want to get a message across, we need to think through three general questions. Firstly, *with whom are we interacting*, who is the counterpart, what stakeholder group or key stakeholders are we meeting? Second, *what is the purpose* of our interaction. Why should we involve, communicate or inform these particular individuals. Thirdly, *how do we reach out in the best way* given who the stakeholders are and what the purpose is? What channels or venues are appropriate?

Figure 7.5 Working with stakeholder groups and key stakeholders

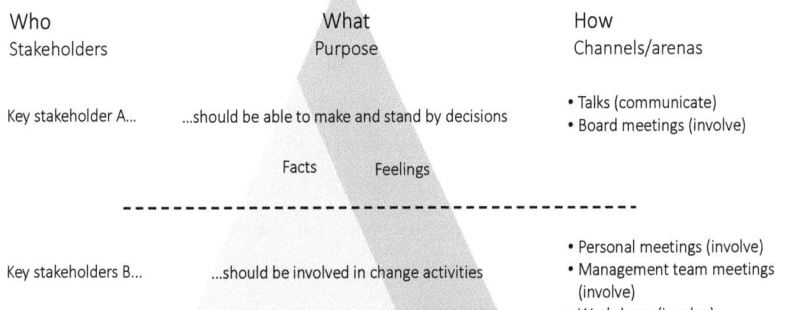

| Who<br>Stakeholders | What<br>Purpose | How<br>Channels/arenas |
|---|---|---|
| Key stakeholder A... | ...should be able to make and stand by decisions | • Talks (communicate)<br>• Board meetings (involve) |
| | Facts   Feelings | |
| Key stakeholders B... | ...should be involved in change activities | • Personal meetings (involve)<br>• Management team meetings (involve)<br>• Workshops (involve)<br>• Individual talks (communicate) |
| | Facts   Feelings | |
| Stakeholder group A...<br>Stakeholder group B...<br>Everyone impacted... | ... should be communicated with (if we want input)<br>...should be informed (if we only want to inform)<br>...should understand the change message | • Intranet<br>• Group meetings (communicate)<br>• Workshops (involve)<br>• Short films (inform)<br>• Manuals/tutorials (inform)<br>• Emails (inform) |
| | Facts   Feelings | |

In terms of recipients or counterparts of our messages, there are three different categories: 1. All stakeholders, 2. The named key stakeholders, and 3. Stakeholder groups of various kinds.

When all stakeholders are the intended recipients, the purpose of our interaction is for them to understand why we are making a change. For the named key stakeholders, the purpose of the interaction is to involve them to get their input into the work and thus create better solutions to the problems at hand. For the different stakeholder groups, they need to be communicated with if part of the purpose is to get input. If we don't want input but only to get the group ready for the changes to come, then information is more appropriate.

In terms of channels or venues to use, when we want all those affected to understand the purpose of change, information such as emails, intranet postings, town hall meetings or short instructional videos explaining the main features of the change are all suitable.

However, these channels are less suitable when we want to involve key stakeholders. Involvement requires more time for dialogue and exchange of ideas. This requires more targeted efforts such as face-to-face meetings, working meetings with an invited group and/or management teams. The purpose of involvement is to work on a specific issue together. A good way is to design workshops that are conducted with a selected group of key stakeholders to address a specific challenge. Just as we discussed in the evolutionary change process. The same goes for the stakeholder groups we want to communicate with and ask for input in different ways. So, in the case of information, regardless of who the counterpart is, we can use intranets for short instructional videos or posts or do mass mailings via email. We can also write manuals or similar when it comes to clear and defined instructions that we want to make public more widely in the organisation.

Regardless of who, what or how we work with stakeholders, we need to think about content. This is one of the purposes of presenting the picture as a pyramid. We may have views on whether organisations are, or should be, seen as pyramids, but the analogy helps us understand something about our stakeholders. In organisations, there are generally fewer people at the top of a traditional hierarchy and more people at the bottom. We typically have just one CEO, but we often have many operators.

This has nothing to do with significance but is merely a matter of numbers. Nor does it mean that all organisations are built like traditional pyramids. However, many organisations have some kind of structure where fewer people are in some leading position and more people are in some 'following' position - hierarchy or not.

Position matters when we want to tailor a good message to the recipient. A message needs to be both factual and emotional. *Facts* typically include concrete information about timetables, benefits, actual changes linked to organisational structures, responsibilities, powers, changes in systems, working methods, tools and processes. *Emotions* rather describe a perception of how it will feel, or what might be possible in the future, and focus more on describing possible threats or opportunities with the change as such.

As the pyramid shows, we need to have the right balance of fact and emotion when interacting with stakeholders. Higher up in the hierarchy, emotion - a vision - can typically form a large part of the message. However, it needs to be complemented by facts. Often these facts should relate to resources and financial impact (the business case). Given that managers higher up the hierarchy have a responsibility for some business, not least financially, it is natural that there is an interest from them to understand how this is affected.

Lower down in the organisation, more facts about concrete consequences are generally needed than a description of a target image to create a feeling. At middle management level, facts about the finances are important, but facts about how their particular organisation's situation will be affected are also important to include. As a middle manager, I probably want to know what scope or opportunity I will have to influence the change here to be able to influence the outcome of the change in the long run.

Further down the organisation, for example with first line managers and employees, the most important question to answer in general terms is how will this affect us in practice? Will I be able to keep my job? Will I have a new manager? What will my working life be like? When will it start? For stakeholder groups of this type, we therefore need to have a lot of facts about how individuals, roles, positions, offices, factories, countries, shops or similar will be affected by the change and when such a change is likely to occur.

What we need to keep in mind when tailoring messages is that the above are simplifications and serve as rules of thumb. People want different insights no matter where they are in an organisation. Organisations also look different. As change managers, we need to make judgements on a case-by-case basis. What the pyramid can help us with, regardless of these factors, is to provide an idea and input that we can use as a starting point when we begin to think about how to work with stakeholders.

## Manage stakeholders in the 'right' order

A next step in our work with stakeholders is to add a time perspective. We now know reasonably well *who*, *what* and *how* the work with stakeholders will be conducted. However, we do not yet know *when* to do what.

In many changes, especially those of great breadth and depth, there are many stakeholders who need to be involved, communicated with, and informed over the lifetime of the change. As many major changes take place over a long period of time, key stakeholders and stakeholder groups are also likely to be replaced. Having an up-to-date stakeholder analysis is therefore important in change management.

We can all agree that change is not driven only from the top down. As I have described in Chapter 6. Tackling change, there are usually elements of change that occur both from the top down and from the bottom up. We have also noted that in an organisation we have both formal leaders and informal leaders, and that change is pursued at both a steady and steady pace. This means that we need to have an idea of the order in which we want to do things. To set an order, we need to know when we want to work with different stakeholders so that it makes sense to those who are involved.

For a change, at least a large-scale one, to succeed, we need a mandate from the leaders who have a major impact on the change because they own the resources. So, in addition to the key stakeholders named, there is a case for thinking about additional groups that need to be involved early on in one way or another. We need to involve some form of management team for the organisation that is to change. In some cases, this group may be a steering committee, board of directors, senior management or other type of management. So, when should we involve whom?

*Key stakeholders*, the named individuals who will be involved in the work, need to be involved early. Key stakeholders should preferably be people with a high level of influence over the change and a strong interest in it. However, it is not always the case that people with high influence also have a high interest. For example, due to time, and other factors, managers with a high level of responsibility (and therefore influence) may have a pressurised schedule which reduces their ability to get involved. They simply can't always set aside the time they want, or that we as change managers think would be worth their time. Nevertheless, they need to be included in the change early. It is then a change mangers responsibility to 'pull them in'.

A next group to be activated at an early stage are various types of responsible managers and specialists who are key players, but who are not part of the management or steering committee and who are not named key stakeholders. Because their business or the processes they work in will change, they will affect the possibility of success in the change. This could be country managers, process owners, system owners, etc.

Once management, key stakeholders, and other responsible managers and specialists are involved or communicated with, we can address other stakeholder groups that are in one way or another important for the change. Finally, we can address the large number of employees who may be less affected and rather need information.

One of the reasons we work with stakeholders in this way is so that senior managers who are responsible for large parts of the business, both in terms of staff and finances, don't have to be worried or taken by surprise when there are major changes in the business. No one appreciates unwelcome surprises in something for which they have a responsibility. The second reason is that it often takes time to build the kind of understanding of a change that is required to communicate it clearly to others. By involving managers and other decision-makers at an early stage, we give them an opportunity to understand the change quickly. They can then help to reach out in their channels, with their credibility and mandate, to wider parts of the organisation. By helping these managers early, we also help ourselves who are responsible for realising the change.

This requires that all stakeholders have understood the *expectations* placed on them in the new change. It also requires that they have the *competence* to perform behaviours in new ways. We also need to confirm that they have the *opportunity* to do what needs to be done and ensure that they receive *reinforcement* on their new behaviours so that they are sustained. This becomes absolutely critical for change managers at an early stage.

Expectations, competence, opportunity and reinforcement evolve over time. We want key stakeholders, such as senior managers, to have all these basic prerequisites in place as early as possible. To do this, we need to start with those people early by tailoring activities to people with high responsibility, high impact and the ability to help us drive change.

I have spent numerous lunches, breakfasts, coffee breaks, walks and car rides from headquarters to another office or to airports with CEOs, VPs, division heads, CFOs and others. It has been a way to escape the constraints on practicality that the calendars of busy people create. If we want to bring about change, as Malcolm X asserted in the foreword, any means are acceptable.

---

When it comes to **stakeholder management**, it is useful to answer the following questions:

26. What specific change activities (e.g. mailings, meetings, training) do we know from the start that we need to carry out? When approximately should they be carried out?

27. Which stakeholders are participants and/or beneficiaries of these specific activities? In what order should they be considered?

---

# Develop competence and ability

In the last section we looked at what change managers can do to reach out to stakeholders. To a large extent, it was about creating clear *expectations*. This section is about helping stakeholders develop the *competence* needed to change their behaviours.

If a person is going to do something in a new way, it sometimes requires the person to learn how to perform the new or evolved behaviour. This newness can be learned through *insight learning, instruction learning, model learning* or through *shaping* (as we discussed in the Chapter 2. Pressure for change in large and small).

In this book, I make a distinction between knowledge and competence. While knowledge is seen as an increased understanding or insight about something, competence needs to be understood as an ability to apply that knowledge in practice. From a strategy perspective, competence should help the organisation to become better at achieving its goals and be successful over time. *Competence* can therefore be linked to the concept of 'competition'. Competence in its purest form, in this context, is about the ability to compete. We can have knowledge without applying it and without it contributing to competitiveness. The right knowledge, used in the right way, can contribute to competitiveness if it is unique, scarce, rare and possible for the organisation to exploit. However, it is difficult to know whether knowledge itself contributes. Knowledge is often socially complex and has unclear causal relationships.[111] In practice, this means that several people need to work together to ensure that the knowledge creates value for the organisation and its customers or clients. But it is difficult to know in advance which knowledge will lead to which effect. It is therefore 'cleaner' to focus on competence and ability. I will therefore use competence and competence development going forward, even if some of the interventions in change management are primarily knowledge enhancing.

When we work on change, we are therefore mainly interested in developing competence. However, to develop competence, we probably need to develop some knowledge. The difference is that the knowledge is not the goal. It is a means to achieve competence. And competence is not really the goal either. The goal is improvements in organisational performance. However, when it comes to various competence and knowledge development activities, we want them to enable as much value as possible.

For knowledge enhancement interventions to be as competence enhancing as possible, we need to ensure that the interventions we perform target one or more behaviours that drive the organisational outcomes we want to improve. They need to be adapted and often tailored. If we are operating in a competitive market, they should also ideally give us an advantage relative to our competitors, a *competitive advantage*.

We can lean towards four principles that we need to follow when developing competence in change management: 1. Analyse the competence gap, 2. Tailor the interventions, 3. Evaluate the interventions, and 4. Disseminate knowledge within the organisation.

## Analysing competence gaps

A first step in tailoring an intervention is to analyse the *competence gap*. We need to understand what the gaps are today. We need to know what we are doing today that we will not be doing tomorrow and what we are not doing today that we will be doing tomorrow. In change and behavioural terms, this means we need to understand what behaviours we want to see more of or see less of, start, or stop. We need to define *excess* and *deficit behaviours*. Based on which behaviours are missing or in abundance, we first create an initial idea of what competencies are missing.

A relatively common mistake is to focus only on employees further out in the organisation and their competence development needs. In the case of major or strategic changes, there is at least as often a need for new knowledge among senior managers and executives. If the change is overall in nature, it will affect the whole company. All those with a symbolic role in the organisation need to set a good example.

To ensure lasting change and do what we can to develop the competence needed for new behaviours, we need to analyse the concrete development needs of different stakeholders. The analysis will help to show what the gaps are for the stakeholders and thus enable the design of appropriate interventions.

## Tailor development initiatives

Different key stakeholders and stakeholder groups have different competence development needs. We know different things; we have different experiences and different competencies. Development efforts must therefore be tailored as much as possible. But we cannot always tailor interventions to each individual, even if it would be desirable. It is too resource-intensive. We therefore need to balance the tailor-made with the standardised. It is often quite a difficult balance, but with the help of different development formats we can succeed.

When we try to tailor to different stakeholders, one thing is to relate to the content of the intervention. The content is driven by the organisational outcomes we want to improve. If it is deficit behaviour that is linked to planning, the intervention needs to be directed at developing the competence needed to plan in a new way. The same applies to workplace safety, to take one of many examples. If the outcome we want to influence is linked to workplace accidents, the effort needs to be directed towards developing competencies that help us to perform behaviours that influence this, such as conducting safety rounds in a careful manner.

Figure 7.6 provides a guide to the different competence development formats that might be appropriate for different types of issues.

Figure 7.6 Skills development format

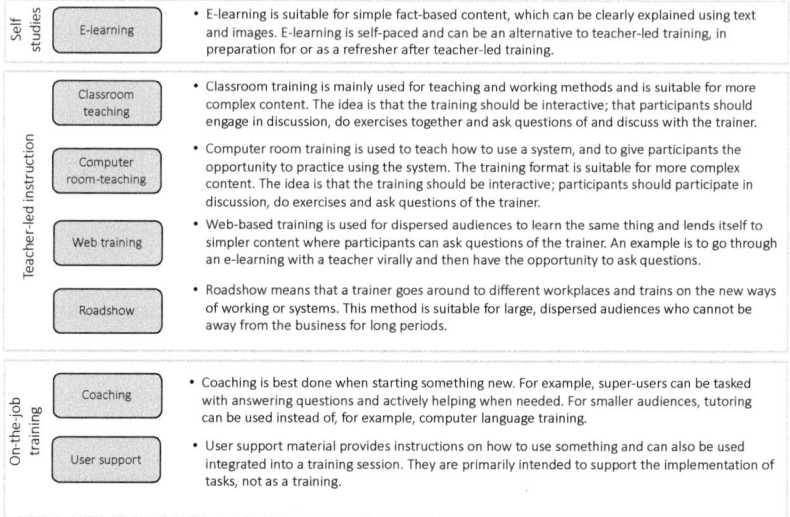

We learn in different ways, which means that different interventions have different effects. It is also the case that a certain type of content, for example learning to work in an IT system, is sometimes better suited to a particular development format, perhaps a webinar. Another example is behaviours linked to competencies needed to understand a particular role.

Let's say we have a person who is new as a transformation manager and needs to understand our company's process for priorities and decisions in the development council where we decide on investments in development projects. In that case, a classroom training or a webinar is nearly pointless. We have to 'live it'. A format that might be appropriate is 'walk alongside' or mentoring, which are two examples of on-the-job training. Competence development is therefore not the same as training. We develop our competencies and abilities much more often than we attend training.

## Evaluate development efforts

To ensure that our targeted development interventions have the intended impact, we need to evaluate them and see what effect they have had. We can do this by monitoring the interventions themselves and by testing the level of knowledge of stakeholders who have undergone a particular intervention. Evaluating development interventions or testing knowledge per se is not evidence that employees are performing their behaviours in new and improved ways. However, it does provide an indication of whether the expectations that are set and the skills that need to be in place are also in place. Evaluating actual behaviours then becomes part of the change follow-up. This will be discussed later.

There is a quantitative and a qualitative part for the evaluation of development interventions. The quantitative part is about monitoring how many people have completed a particular intervention (e.g. training) in relation to the number of people in the stakeholder group: how many of the people who should have completed the intervention have actually completed it? Often there may be a certain number of people in a stakeholder group, for example all quality managers in the organisation, all employees in the stores in a certain region or sales staff in a certain country.

In one organisation I worked with, there were 120 district managers in the country. Based on that, we can assess how many of those 120 need to undergo the training. We can base that figure on the fact that, for example, about 50 of these are likely to need to develop their competencies (based on our gap analysis). We can also assume that 30 of these people need to take it because they represent a critical mass. If we find the right 30 people and they change, then perhaps the rest will follow suit. Regardless of how we make the assessment, we need to set a level, a number, that will allow us to follow up. That way we can at least ensure that the people we want to go through the intervention do.

In the qualitative part of the evaluation, it may be appropriate in some cases to use a standard questionnaire after each completed intervention. This is particularly the case if we think that the change will require a lot of competence development (e.g. if the change is deep).

A suitable selection of questions is as follows:

* Do you understand the expectations this change places on you in your role? What were they?

* Do you think you were able to develop your competence to perform your work in line with these expectations? If not, what is missing?

* Do you know how to change your behaviours in the area addressed by the training (e.g. reviewing sources in a market analysis, giving feedback)? If yes, how? If not, what is missing?

It may also be appropriate to set a level for how many or what proportion of a stakeholder group has undergone the development intervention from which we want responses. We call this the *response rate*. In this way we can ensure a reasonably representative response. The responses we get in such an evaluation are not a perfect way to ensure that employees' behaviours change, but it does give some idea of the impact of the intervention. The responses can help us to improve our interventions. The evaluation also gives us, as change managers, an opportunity to remind our stakeholders of the change, their importance in the change and thus reinforce new and refined behaviours.

As for tests of ability, it is more difficult to give general recommendations on how to conduct them. Depending on the issue we want to address with an intervention, the knowledge or ability can be tested in different ways. It should therefore be the responsibility of the change manager, together with a person skilled in competence development, to assess the type of knowledge test that may be appropriate in different cases. That said, there are a number of pre-determined options for how they might be done.

One option is to take a written test. In this case, we can have participants take an on-site test after completing the training. This is appropriate when the format is a teacher-led intervention, whether physical or digital. Another option is to have participants complete a homework assignment that they will then submit. Yet another way is to do a simpler web-based survey. Finally, oral tests may also be an option. In oral tests, we can have the person in charge of the intervention, or the 'teacher' have an individual or collective conversation with the co-worker or the group to assess what the participants have learned. Another perhaps more resource-efficient way is to ensure that everyone present during the development intervention actively contributes to all discussions by sharing the floor on different issues. In this way, we can get an idea of whether people undergoing the intervention have understood the content and whether they have ideas about how to apply their new-found knowledge to their work. A skills developer or trainer with experience in a field will quickly notice who has understood how things fit together. Based on those insights, we can then add and find new interventions if it is critical that key stakeholders develop their competencies.

Of course, these different ways can also be combined in all possible ways. And as with the quantitative evaluation of interventions, we need to set some level for the testing as well. One example is to assess the percentage of participants who have completed the intervention and who have reached a certain desired level of knowledge (which we need to define).

Assessing the effectiveness of competence enhancing interventions is both difficult and time consuming, so it is important to be smart. Not overdo it, but make sure we get insights about the actual contribution to the change. Frankly it is sometimes reasonable to be a bit hesitant to it. On the other hand, if we must, we must. And if we must, we should it properly.

Later in the book, we will discuss the different roles and responsibilities required in large-scale change. Already now, however, we can conclude that in changes with extensive competence development needs, it is beneficial to have one person responsible for holding together training deliveries and evaluating them. It is also helpful if there is someone who can create opportunities to help spread knowledge, tips and tricks across different organisational units. This also applies to knowledge that is not directly linked to specific competence development activities.

## Spread knowledge within the organisation

Various types of development activities in the form of training and on-the-job training are likely to form a large part of the deliberate competence development undertaken in change management. In addition, it is also important to find ways to disseminate and share knowledge within the organisation across different business areas, countries, divisions, units, functions, groups, project initiatives or other.

For this to be effective, we need to have a clear structure for how we work with different types of knowledge sharing activities, *lessons learned*. There are many ways we can facilitate this type of activity for different stakeholders.

One way is to coordinate structured meetings to exchange experiences. We invite people involved in a particular issue to discuss recent experiences, learn from each other and help each other. Each person attending prepares to discuss the issue at hand, which then typically focuses on what they are involved in changing. Different themes may vary. Examples might be a new system to start using, a new customer group to get more attention, a new tool to support an old process. The theme of the meetings needs to change depending on the issue, but since learning is the focus, the questions that form the structure of the meetings can be general.

One set of questions that I find has worked well in this type of meeting is the following:

* What has happened in your change work since the last time?
* What successes have you had?

* What difficulties have you encountered and how have you managed them?

* What do you think you can improve and how will you do it?

* What lessons have you learned since last time that can help others in their changes?

* What are the concerns of the business (i.e. those affected, stakeholders) right now? How have you responded to these?

My experience tells me that lessons learned meetings should be held at regular intervals. The appropriate frequency depends on the type of issues to be discussed, and who the people are, but there are rules of thumb to follow. If it takes too long between meetings, the initial learning curve will be too long. Too much has simply happened since the last one, or we don't remember how we dealt with the challenges. This limits the value of the meeting. It should also not be too close together. Then we haven't done enough and learned enough to have a meaningful discussion.

One hypothesis to test if you don't have a clue that has often worked in the large-scale or strategic changes I've led, is to hold this type of meeting every four to six weeks.

If the change we want to realise is extensive and takes place in a large organisation, it is valuable to have a structure for lessons learned between change managers and other people who have some kind of responsibility for leading and driving the change. The theme will then be the same from week to week: leading the change

Some opportunities for feedback can also take a looser form, such as a joint breakfast with mingling and/or an inspirational lecture related to the theme. In addition to learning from each other, we also create natural relationships between people who become knowledgeable in a particular area. There is thus an opportunity to create natural networks that we as leaders of change do not need to coordinate. This also leads to the creation of a *common language* within the organisation. Having that for strategy and change issues is something that both I have found to be a strength for organisations.[112] With a common language we don't have to start over every time but can get to what is essential and needs to be addressed more quickly.

Any way of spreading knowledge by creating opportunities for people involved in the change to meet is good. Here, only our imagination sets the limits. One example is to help stakeholders have lunch with someone else who is also involved in the change once a month. Another is to create a list where everyone we want to have a coffee with others involved signs up. This increases exchanges of experience and knowledge sharing. So, in larger change projects this can be set up specifically for change managers. In other cases, it might be key stakeholders from the business, customers or suppliers who we try to ensure we have a good dialogue with.

A final suggestion for spreading knowledge as we lead major change is to create some form of *Q&A*. A kind of material (e.g. film, text, audio file) based on the environmental, industrial and organisational analyses we have carried out and which form the basis for our change message. The material we produce can then be published and disseminated through various channels: email, intranet, social media, printed and displayed in coffee rooms, etc. In addition, if there is a digital platform, we can enable people involved in the change to share experiences and ask questions in a forum, where we can tag different posts to help others find answers to their questions. In such a solution, we can also help those responsible for different changes, parts of changes and/or change projects to find each other's documentation, for example organisational analyses, change plans, communication plans. Accessing other people's material is a way of benefiting from each other's experience and means that I - and everyone else - don't have to reinvent the wheel every times.

This type of intervention and solution can be perceived as costly and is likely better suited to more comprehensive changes. The point is that it helps us to create a first line of support in the change with the aim of informing. By automating parts of the information dissemination, we who are leading the change can spend perhaps our most limited resource, time, on communicating and engaging. This is good because these two are likely to have a greater direct impact on our success in the change than information. As we remember, activators account for 20% of behaviour impact, consequences account for 80%.

Spreading knowledge across the organisation helps us to clarify *expectations* and to develop the *competence* of stakeholders. Since clarifying expectations and developing competencies is crucial for stakeholders to develop their behaviours, this is something we need to manage.

In fact, this type of intervention also *reinforces* behaviours that contribute to change by creating a sense of belonging and learning new things. What we are not getting at with these interventions is the ability of stakeholders to perform new behaviours and to reinforce their behaviours on an ongoing basis. However, by understanding how we follow up and push, we can do just that.

When it comes to **developing competence and ability**, it is useful to answer the following questions:

28. What are the major competence gaps? In which stakeholder groups and key stakeholders do we see these? What are the best formats for competence development to close these gaps?

29. When and how will we evaluate the success of stakeholder competence building activities?

30. How should we create structures and procedures to disseminate knowledge continuously and across the organisation?

# Follow up and drive change

We sometimes call the following up and driving *managing:* managing operations, companies, of projects or, as in this case, managing change. However, managing in different organisations differs significantly. Manging as such has also evolved considerably over time, and different organisations have their own ideas about how managing should work to make the organisation perform. Such basic ideas is what we simply call *management philosophy,* and it is always there - expressed or unspoken. To clarify the practical differences between different management philosophies, we can talk about traditional financial management and modern operational management.

*Traditional financial management* typically starts from the idea that a certain amount of input produces a certain amount of output. The link between cause and effect is considered clear. The information we rely on when making decisions about actions and (re)allocation of resources is mainly financially oriented. The core of *modern operational management* is processes. This means that we focus on how the work is done rather than, as in traditional management, on what the outcome is. This provides an opportunity to detect and manage deviations as they occur and before they have an impact, positive or negative - financial or otherwise. Trying to understand what leads to what, being aware that causality is uncertain, but still continuously monitoring and reflecting to learn is absolutely crucial in change management. Improvements in performance, as mentioned earlier, can come much later than the behavioural changes themselves. And the benefits, especially the yellow and red ones, can also be both unclear and uncertain.

By looking at the work, the process, we can also create more cooperation between departments. It creates a better overall picture of how different businesses in the organisation are connected in a flow. This allows us to better exploit the strengths of the entire organisation. When more people are involved, we create a greater understanding of the change and its effects in different parts of the organisation. This increased understanding contributes to increased motivation among those involved. They are empowered by feeling they can influence their future. The more people who participate, the more they learn and the more they are reinforced to contribute. Such an approach helps to create an environment that values continuous development and learning, making it easier to realise different types of change.

> Managing, follow up and feeding back change work means that we need to evaluate two different elements: the progress of the change and the realisation of the benefits. To do this, we need to have a process-oriented management of change.

## Evaluating the progress of change

We have previously stated that the basic prerequisites for change to occur are that all stakeholders have clear expectations, competencies and opportunities to perform behaviours, and that they are reinforced in the new behaviours. Because benefits are realised by behaviours, there are no benefits until behaviours are changed. For example, we cannot shut down a system if someone is working in it. Behaviours lead and results lag. Behaviours lead to results. As for red benefits (possibilities), for example the possibility of marketing a new product if we change our production process, no benefits are realised until we actually market and sell the new product. That in turn may be years away. Benefits are often not realised here and now, in real time, or even soon. Benefit realisation therefore means that we need to focus on the momentum of change here and now. We then need to monitor whether the basic prerequisites for behavioural change are in place among different stakeholders.

Our responsibility as change managers will be to ensure that all stakeholders in the change have the prerequisites in place: an understanding of the *expectations* set, the *competence* needed to perform the desired behaviours, the *opportunity* to do what is expected and that they receive *reinforcement* for their changed behaviours. One way of monitoring the progress of change, which also gives a picture of how far we have come, is therefore to assess how well these prerequisites are in place for different key stakeholders and stakeholder groups. By continually assessing this, we can begin to understand the progress of the change. At the same time, we can analyse what we need to do going forward to make the change successful.

Figure 7.7 shows an example of such an assessment.

Figure 7.7 Evaluation of stakeholders' prerequisites for change

| Key stakeholders | Expectation | Competence | Opportunity | Reinforcement | Comment to result | Identification of risk |
|---|---|---|---|---|---|---|
| CFO Sweden | 1 | 1 | 1 | 1 | New on the job | Urgent! |
| Business Unit Presidents (7) | 3 | 2 | 1 | 2 | | |
| Controllers at BU X | 2 | 4 | 3 | 2 | | |
| J, Head of accounting | 4 | 4 | 4 | 3 | Involve more | |
| Accounts deliverables staff | 1 | 1 | 1 | 1 | Use SSC-chef | |
| Head of Shared Service Center | 3 | 2 | 1 | 2 | Bring along | |
| M, IT-architect | 2 | 4 | 3 | 2 | | |
| Steering group project Z | 4 | 4 | 4 | 3 | Good! Showcase! | |

The example is taken from a change project that aimed to change the governance processes of a publicly listed group. In this work, all governance and support processes as well as all financial processes (e.g. business planning, forecasting, performance review, reporting, invoice management) and the support systems of these processes (e.g. ERP system, BI system, payroll system) were to be changed.

In a simplified way, we ask ourselves a number of questions to assess whether or not the prerequisites of different stakeholders are in place. Some examples are as follows:

* How clear are stakeholders about the *expectations* that will be placed on them? Do they understand the purpose of the change, what it means? Even the fine print? Do they understand the benefits to the business?

* How well developed are the *competence*, knowledge or abilities required by stakeholders to perform the new behaviours? What competencies do they have to develop to work in the new ways, or in the new systems?

* How well are the actual *opportunities* in place for stakeholders to perform the new behaviours? Are there sufficient resources, such as time? Do they have the mandate to make the necessary decisions? Do they have the access, availability or similar?

* How well developed are our systems and practices to feedback and reinforce stakeholders to behave in evolved and new ways? How willing are stakeholders to drive and contribute to change?

The example in Figure 7.7 above is also 'number and colour coded'. It gives us a visual picture of what it looks like at a particular point in time. When working with this, I generally put green (4) when it is 'fully met', yellow (3) when it is 'partially met', orange (2) when something is 'significantly missing' and red (1) when it is 'completely missing'. The greener, i.e. the more fours, the better the chances that the change will be real, since more prerequisites are in place with more stakeholders. The more red, the less likely it is to succeed and the more reason to think about what the next step should be.

In assessing whether some basic prerequisite is in place, it is certainly not subject to a scientific assessment. We do the assessment to get a sense of what it looks like here and now, how it has evolved over time, and based on that, what we need to do here and now. By doing this on an ongoing basis, for example weekly or monthly depending on the magnitude of the change and the timeframe, we can see trends and tendencies. These are far more important than the snapshot. They help us to identify whether the whole table is becoming greener over time or not. If it is not, then we are doing something wrong and need to think about what we can do differently to lead the change. We can see if there is any key stakeholder or stakeholder group that continues to be red or orange despite multiple efforts. We then need to change our efforts.

In summary, this approach helps us to understand how different stakeholders develop an understanding of the expectations, their competencies and their opportunity to change and feel they are reinforced to contribute (i.e. feel motivated).

## Evaluation and planning of change activities

Evaluating the progress of change is a way of generating ideas about what activities are appropriate going forward. In the example above, we can see that the CFO of the Sweden company was a one (1, i.e. red). He did not have any of the prerequisites in place. As the change in the example was about different management and governance processes such as forecasting and business planning, it was crucial that he was in the know. In this case, he was completely new to his role and could not possibly have had an idea of what the change entailed. Moreover, it was the former CFO (who now became Group CFO) who initiated the change. I could not possibly make a judgement as to whether the new CFO of the Swedish company had the competence he needed to contribute to the change or whether he had the opportunity to do what was required. The same applies to the extent to which he would be reinforced.

Through this simple assessment, I was able to conclude that I need to communicate with him as soon as possible to try to explain what the change is all about in a big way and in a small way. It became by far the most important activity now. Another important insight from the assessment was that not all the people in the accounts payable department were on board with the change. Electronic invoice processing of supplier invoices was part of streamlining financial flows, so they were an important stakeholder group to communicate with and involve in the work. And because the head of the Shared Service Center, was boss over the accounts payable teams, was well aware of the expectations, our change managers were able to join forces with her to reach out to employees. It was also a concrete activity.

For each key stakeholder and stakeholder group, we can also comment on why we have made a particular assessment and whether there are particular risks to consider in the change work with a particular key stakeholder or stakeholder group. This then gives us an understanding of what we need to do next. These insights are reflected in the activities that were generated from the follow-up session I described above.

A few of activities that were generated can be seen in Figure 7.8.

Figure 7.8 Change activities based on evaluation

| Change activities | w.37 | w.38 | w.39 | w.40 | w.41 |
|---|---|---|---|---|---|
| Book and hold meeting with new CFO Sweden | | OK | | | |
| Check updated change message with top management team | | | LATE | LATE | OK |
| Book information meeting with Accounts deliverables staff | | | | LATE | OK |

This way of generating activities is part of the evolutionary learning process and a must to prioritise what is important in the here and now.

However, as we have also noted before, some activities are predetermined. They are compulsory in any change. My view is that the greater the magnitude of change, the more activities are given in advance. By more, I mean in absolute numbers, not in relation to activities that we develop on an ongoing basis. I think the distribution between planned and emergent is the same regardless of the magnitude of change. My guess - what I use as a rule of thumb - is that the planned activities make up a relatively small proportion, 30% at most. However, having said that, activities we have to carry out (ongoing stakeholder consultations, developing a business case, etc.) are part of the revolutionary process and once we know about them, it's just as well to plan for them.

In Figure 7.9 shows a number of mandatory change activities, sorted by phases, in a change of an organisational structure for which I was responsible. This can work as a starting for many changes.

Figure 7.9 General and/or mandatory change activities

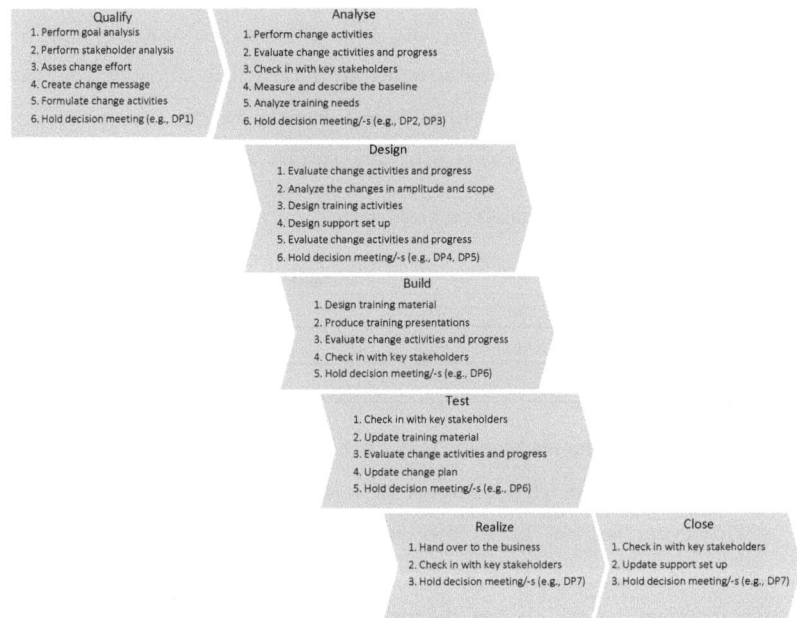

In the initial qualification phase, we always need to do a goal analysis, stakeholder analysis, an initial assessment of benefits and costs. We should also hold a decision meeting to decide what to do. Both the analysis and the meeting can be larger or smaller in scope, but the job must be done. In the analysis phase, the design phase, the testing phase and the construction phase, we need to continuously develop solutions, agree them with stakeholders, update benefits and costs based on the solutions, and prepare for competence development, support and handover to the business. We also know this before we start. Realisation is about talking to stakeholders and helping them to 'embrace' and start working with and in new solutions (e.g. new system, new tools, new organisational structure). To ensure involvement, we need to hold ongoing decision and reconciliation meetings across these phases to drive the process forward. It is also a final decision that starts the closure phase, which in turn ensures the closure of the change.

These activities also follow a natural timeline. Some things must be done before others. However, they do not have to be tied to a certain point in time. Rather, the activities should be linked to how far we have come in the change process. For example, how much of the benefits have been realised, or how well the basic prerequisites for change are in place with stakeholders.

Although many activities are general, there are unique circumstances. In the figure above, the general change activities come from a project where the organisation was to move from a geographical design with country organisations to a process-oriented one, with processes that would instead be global. In such a broad organisational change, at some point there will be a need to coordinate those who are driving the change. Some way into the change, we need to conduct competence development sessions to develop those who are driving the change.

In this case, for me, it involved several activities aimed at coordinating the 8 change projects that were part of the change as a whole and creating cross-functional learning between different change managers, business development managers, transformation officers and project managers working on the change in different countries.

Another critical task was to communicate with all the country directors who would now no longer be country directors. Some of these would be given process-based leadership responsibilities, such as global research and development manager, global sales manager, global production manager, etc. Some of them would have other roles. However, because these were key stakeholders - they had both a major interest and a major impact - they were important to involve at an early stage.

Although this change was large and quite specific, we can see that many of the general activities work for relatively many changes. As we gain more experience and knowledge about change, we also learn to identify these types of change activities early. In this way we avoid the problems that can sometimes arise from too little involvement of senior people.

Once we have an idea of the change activities we need to carry out to help a particular stakeholder group or key stakeholder get a particular prerequisite in place - whether the activities are generated revolutionarily or evolutionarily - we can classify the activity based on what prerequisite it is to set the stage for. In practice, we can relate each activity to the five functions of a change manager.

There are then five types of change management activities: activities for benefit realisation, stakeholder management, competence development, follow-up and handover.

By classifying the activities, it is easier to evaluate whether the activities we have carried out have had the effect we intended in the way we intended. It also helps us to see if there is a type of activity that we are not working on enough.

To illustrate: Devoting time only to stakeholder management and competence development will mean that benefit realisation activities will suffer. We will not get as far as we could. We probably need a reasonable balance between all types of activities if we are to ensure that all the prerequisites are in place.

Another benefit is that the classification makes it easier for those of us involved in the change to see where we can turn if we need support. We can take help from a manager to reach out in their business. We saw this in the example where we enlisted the help of the head of a Shared Service Centre to reach out to the staff working on invoice management. We can rarely have too much of that particular support when we're working on major changes.

So, we need to find ways to get different types of support from individuals doing the actual work.

In most organisations, there is often someone with knowledge of information and communication. In large organisations, there is often a whole staff of specialists. In cases where we need support in stakeholder management activities (i.e. involving, communicating, informing) we can turn to a 'communications officer' e.g. communications manager. When it comes to competence development activities, it is advisable to turn to a training unit, if there is one, or to an HR manager, HR officer or other person with competence development skills. As far as benefits and follow-up processes are concerned, I usually find support from a controller close to the business. Help is often available if we ask. And if we know the type of activity e.g. competence development activity, it is easier to know where the help can be found.

## The change plan and its activities

The different types of activities that we generate on an ongoing basis, targeting different stakeholder groups and key stakeholders, together with pre-defined activities, form a kind of *change plan* for the coming period. Or the next 'sprint' if we use agile models and concepts. By working with a basic plan and continuously generating new activities based on the follow-up, we combine the revolutionary and evolutionary approaches. We create a 'living' and continuously updated change plan.

In our description, we also clarify whether it is a one-off activity or whether it will be carried out several times. If it is repeated, we need to assess how many times and how often. For both one-off and recurring activities, we need to describe how it will be perfromed in practical terms and in what location or through what forum or channel. Then we need to assess the type and amount of resources involved. Finally, we decide who is responsible for the activity. In Chapter 8. Organisation we will dive deeper into responsibility.

Generating activities is an important task. Prioritising is even more important. When resources are tight, we must set priorities. These priorities must be set on a case-by-case basis. A rule of thumb is to carry out the activities that affect the key stakeholders we believe are most critical to engage first, or here and now. So, it relates to our evaluation of key stakeholders and whether their prerequisites are in place. Once the prioritisation is done, we can put the activities into the plan based on when they will be realised.

Figure 7.10 shows an example of what a template for descriptions of this type of activity might look like.

Figure 7.10 Detailed change activities

| Change activities | Frequency | Type of activity | Location | Responsible | Accountable |
|---|---|---|---|---|---|
| Send out information mail | Monthly | Stakeholder management | Stockholm | Communication manager | Change manager |
| Perform workshop with BU management | 2-4 times | Stakeholder management | Berlin | Change manager | Program manager |
| Meet VP and deputy CEO | One time | Stakeholder management | Stockholm | Change manager | Program manager |
| Present Business Case to top management team | Quarterly | Business case management | London | Change manager | Program manager |
| Train controllers western Europe | 2 times | Training | Dublin | Training manager | Change manager |
| Evaluate change progress | Monthly | Evaluation | Stockholm | Change controller | Change manager |

At the next follow-up, it will then be possible to assess which activities have been carried out, which have not, and which have led to a better understanding of the expectations, competencies, opportunities or reinforcement of stakeholders. In this way, we build learning into the follow-up and can prioritise the type of activity that we judge has worked. We can then also prioritise out those that have worked less well. Evaluation then helps us, in addition to planning, to be more effective in our change work by better understanding where to spend time and resources to maximise the impact of activities.

Given that we want to evluate both progress and realisation of benefits, this can help us to create an agenda for our follow-up meetings. This type of meeting can look different in different industries and organisations. They may even look different in different parts of the same organisation. However, there are general questions that we need to answer when following up on our change. We need to ensure that all the change activities that should have been performed have been performed. We need to see what effect these have on the prerequisites of our stakeholders. We also need to ensure that the benefits that the change is supposed to realise are in fact realised.

This follow-up, together with performing the activities decided upon, is, in my opinion, the most important task of the change manager.

An example of an agenda that I think works as a starting point for such follow-up meetings is as follows:

1. Frame the meeting
   * What are the two or three most important issues for change right now?
   * What, beyond our forward momentum, do we need to focus on during today's meeting? These two or three questions and/or something else?

2. Review and analyse activities and impact
   * What change activities have we carried out since the last time?
   * Are these according to what we planned? If not, why not?
   * How have our stakeholders' prerequisites changed? Why? Why not?
   * What impact on organisational performance (benefits) can/do we see now (if any)?

3. Decide on the next period
   * Based on the information we now have, what should we do next? What activities? Which stakeholders? What prerequisites should we influence?
   * What improvements of prerequisites do we think this could lead to?
   * What improvements in results (benefits) do we think this could lead to?

In addition to ongoing evaluation, where we mainly look at key stakeholders and selected stakeholder groups, in major changes in larger organisations, there may be a case for complementing monthly evaluation with evaluation that measures trends in the organisation more broadly. In many cases, I have used biannual change surveys to get a sense of what is happening in the organisation.

The purpose of this is to gauge the businesses' awareness of, and possible commitment to, the change, as well as the perception of information and communication from the change management. In our sample, we then need to identify representatives within the organisation's various divisions, companies, departments, support functions, countries, etc. to get an idea of their perception.

In order not to tire the people in organisations (surveys tend to come be common), I limit myself to two questions:

1. Where in the organisation are you located (e.g. division, HR, IT)?
2. What is your general opinion of the change (e.g. on a scale from 1, inept, to 5, superb)?

The responses to the survey act as a temperature gauge and help us to understand how the change is perceived and realised in different parts of the organisation. It also helps us to understand what we can do going forward in the change to get the most out of our efforts. Which parts of the organisation are involved? Which are not? Where should we focus our efforts? Where do we not need to spend time right now? These are questions that help us prioritise our limited resources on change management.

Working on evaluation of progress helps us drive change forward by prioritising activities to identify and analyse benefits, work with stakeholders, develop competence and eventually hand over to the business.

Evaluation helps us to ensure that stakeholders' basic prerequisites for behavioural change are in place, and remain in place. Stakeholders need understand our expectations, competence to act differently, opportunities to act differently and get reinforcement on behaving in new ways. Otherwise, their behaviour will not evolve, and change will not happen.

## Evaluating result improvements over time

Change is ultimately about improving organisational results, create benefits. We must therefore evaluate that our actions ensure that improvements in results are realised. We need to ensure that the benefits reach the business - or better still - the customers.

As we have mentioned, many benefits are often realised after a change is officially completed. On the other hand, the costs of change, such as information, communication, competence development and lost production, are incurred immediately. As soon as we start talking about the change, we spend resources (time) on it. By definition, this means that a change always loses out initially.

This has implications for change. The change in organisation and behaviour itself is often only the first step in improving performance. This is an important lesson to take away; it creates the conditions for some extra 'grit'. It helps us to sustain the change. Those who are not aware of this relationship can easily give up on change too soon.

The relationship between costs and benefits in a strategy project that I led for a small AI software company is visualised in Figure 7.11.

Figure 7.11 Evolution of benefits and costs over time

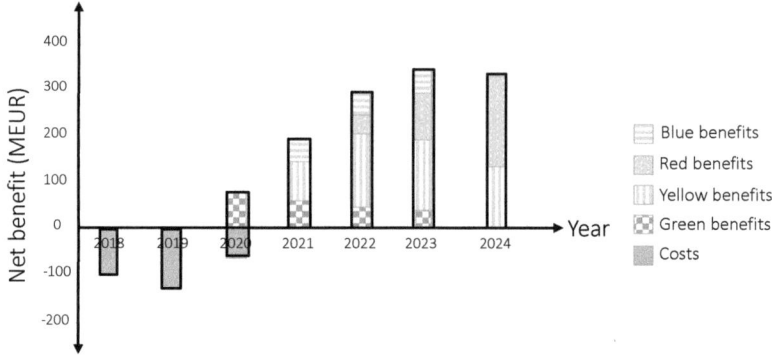

Often, not least when IT changes are involved (as they often are in more comprehensive changes), the project ends when certain benefits are realised. Other benefits may have *the potential to be realised* when we close the change, but they are not realised. My experience tells me that we rarely follow up benefit realisation in a systematic way after we close change initiatives or projects. In other words, we rarely ensure that the remaining benefits are realised. This in turn leads to fewer benefits being realised. Not all benefits will be realised unless we take certain actions (e.g. yellow, red). What we therefore need to do is to integrate the evaluation of change with the evaluation of business. Often, we are tracking the same objectives and measures. So, combining them is perfectly possible. However, it requires that the evaluation of benefits is followed up at some regular appropriate management, board, committee or similar meeting, once a month/quarter/year. The change manager therefore needs to hand over the benefit realisation to the business. This handover will be discussed in the next section.

Different large-scale changes are realised at different rates, so the frequency of monitoring benefits is difficult to give general advice on. What we do know, however, is that it cannot be a one-off phenomenon. We need to evaluate on an ongoing basis and over time. In some cases, weekly reconciliations may be justified, for example if there is a less deep and less broad change with relatively rapid benefit realisation. In other cases, quarterly monitoring may be sufficient.

Regardless of how we follow up, we benefit from setting a structure for follow-up at the very beginning of a change journey. It helps us ensure the kind of assessments we make of whether stakeholders have the basics in place. It also helps us to generate new activities on an ongoing basis that positively impact the conditions of our stakeholders.

Figure 7.12 shows an example where different follow-up meetings/forums are linked both to decision points and to time intervals between the major decision points in the revolutionary approach to change.

Figure 7.12 Follow-up structure over time

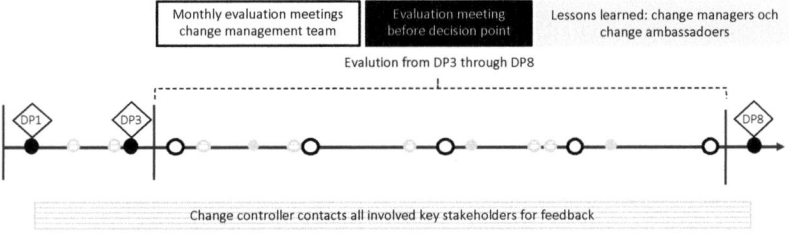

## Feedback to the business

Evaluation is important. However, it doesn't matter how much we evaluate if we don't also give feedback. It is through feedback, in all its forms, that we create the conditions for learning e.g. reinforce. We've already talked about how strong impact consequences have in relation to activators. We need to practice this when we lead change. I will in this context make a distinction between two types of feedback: that which comes from the change manager (individual-based) and that which we can build systems and structures for in the organisation (organisational). Both are needed in change management.

Feedback in change means information that helps us understand which behaviours worked, i.e. had the impact on an outcome in the way we wanted.

More rounds in the workplace led to more safety observations and, over time, fewer workplace accidents. However, it's not always so easy to see the connections, which means we have to chance, test, measure, evaluate and, based on the evaluation, feedback.

For the *individual-based* feedback, one of the most powerful tools we have as change managers is ourselves. I have not seen any organisation succeed in a major change where the change manager was disliked or 'not respected'. On the other hand, I have seen many organisations get quite far in their changes precisely because they have a person that many people appreciate leading the effort.

This ability to be appreciated is sometimes called *'likability'*[113] and is a powerful tool for a change manager. Likeability is often defined by various qualities: being honest, straightforward in communication, caring, compromising. Much of what I put into being kind, in other words. However, of course, since in this book we see the world through 'behavioural glasses', we want to understand what a change manager can do to be liked. (This doesn't just apply to change managers; it really applies to anyone who wants to influence others).

Behaviours that make us positively valued and that increase our ability to create results through others are quite general. The reason they can be general is that they contribute in one way or another to *psychological safety*[114] : an environment where respect, civility and reciprocity prevail. These are all key characteristics of organisations that succeed in turning ideas into new processes, products, business models or anything else that creates or redistributes value.

Asking questions is a typical good behaviour: questions about how the business is doing, how the stakeholders feel (or don't feel) about the change, what effects - positive and negative - they have seen from the change, how the chatter is going, etc. The beauty of questions is that they allow the recipient of the question to provide the answers. It creates a willingness to participate and contribute. It also gives us as leaders of change knowledge of what works and insights into what stakeholders are thinking about, experiencing and feeling. This helps us assess how we can help them in the change. After all, all change is achieved together. Therefore, we must also be willing to compromise when we have thought wrong and admit that we have made mistakes. Of course, we make mistakes sometimes. We all do.

Asking questions is an excellent way to provide *positive reinforcement*. Human beings like to talk about themselves; that is part of being a herd animal. It also helps us to make fewer mistakes in the future, provided we really listen to the answers. When we ask questions, we want to know which behaviours have produced which results. But maybe we don't see the behaviour when it happens, only the result. Asking about the behaviour then is a powerful tool. Maybe we don't see the result because it comes later, but we see the behaviour. Then we can also ask: 'I saw you just do that (whatever it is). I don't know the business in detail like you, but it seemed smart. Why did you do that? What do you think it creates?'

As change managers, we gain useful information and make ourselves more likeable by showing a genuine interest in how things are going. This in turn hopefully creates a greater willingness (reinforcement) in others to contribute to the change.

Other behaviours that make people likeable are keeping their word, listening actively, letting people speak to the point, speaking in a calm tone, looking the person they are talking to in the eye, standing by their opinion and still being prepared to challenge it. Expressions that reflect such behaviour are 'I think', 'let's discuss', 'that's one way of looking at it', and 'I understand'. It shows that we weigh arguments for and against things and talk to get others to share their experiences and learn from them.

We can also learn what makes us liked by understanding what makes us disliked. Behaviours that generally make us less liked are interrupting, raising our voices, demanding things, threatening, breaking promises, deceiving, belittling, pointing fingers, staring, talking in a moody way - faster or louder than necessary, speaking to persuade or to silence others. Common expressions that reflect this are 'I am in charge', 'I demand', 'you are wrong' and 'unthinkable'.

All these behaviours lead others to understand that we are not interested in getting along. We have the right answers, and we don't respect other points of view. We show no willingness to listen to others and feel no need to accommodate anyone. For a leader, this type of behaviour can have disastrous consequences.

> By behaving in different ways, we have different levels of impact. We are liked and respected to different degrees depending on how we act. As change managers, if we behave in a way that makes us easy to like, we instil trust in others, and gain more support for the change we want to bring about. Being 'kind' is an excellent starting point.

*Organisational* feedback is not about the change manager but about creating a system for giving feedback. Unfortunately, it sometimes matters little how good we as change managers (or leaders) are at giving feedback. We operate in a system. We as leaders cannot be everywhere, all the time. We have limited time. Finding ways where we can give feedback without being present is one way to give feedback with our limited resources.

When it comes to how we feed back the results of our changes, our imagination is often the bottleneck. I've been involved in both traditional and less traditional ways. Some traditional ways include using green and red magnets on a whiteboard to show how something is progressing, or not progressing. Line charts help us understand development over time. We can put flutter balls, which symbolise some part of the change, in a bowl in the coffee room.

I have also worked with different change groups to build houses of matches. Counted potatoes in a wooden box. I've also pasted up newspaper clippings with pictures of the ingredients needed to bake a sandwich cake. Each clipping symbolised a small step forward in the change and when all the progress had been made, pictures of all the ingredients required were on the wall. On Friday of that week, the sandwich cake also arrived. I hung a small plastic airplane on a string from the ceiling. For each bit of change progress, we moved the plane 20 cm on the 4-meter-long string. When we came to the end, we booked an agreed trip to a sister company in another country for project visits and experience discussions. Let your imagination run wild.

I believe very much in what we call *gamification*.[115] If we can have fun together, we will create better results in the short and long term. Change can be exhausting. Especially if they are large. We have more energy if we have fun. If the change manager can organise activities that make us want to join in and have some fun, he or she is likely to contribute to a successful change.

I also think it leads to the person being respected and liked. As I said, this also influences the results. If in no other way, at least by creating less resistance to change.

In terms of **evaluating and driving change**, it is useful to answer the following questions:

31. How and how often should we evaluate the change progress? That the prerequisites (expectations, competence, opportunity, reinforcement) are in place?

32. How and how often should we evaluate that benefits are realised (i.e. that actual improvements in organisational results are visible and can be measured)?

33. What concrete behaviours do we as change managers need to demonstrate to ensure that the prerequisites for change are in place (e.g. giving feedback, asking questions)?

34. How can we feed back the results of the change to a wider range of stakeholders in a systematic and educational way? To whom should we feed back what and with what frequency?

## Managing resistance to change

Realising various change activities and feeding back to the business aims to ensure that stakeholders have the basic prerequisites for behavioural change in place. However, we don't always manage to do that, no matter how careful we are.

> When the basic prerequisites are not in place, *change resistance* is created.[116] Understanding what these might be is particularly important when a change involves an obvious 'break' with the way things are in the organisation today, i.e. when the change is deep and broad.

We can talk about seven different types of resistance to change. Three of these we can categorise as *emotional resistance to change* and four we can categorise as *rational resistance to change*. The emotional ones are psychological resistance, cultural resistance and political resistance. The rational ones consist of so-called lock-in effects: investment lock-in, competence lock-in, systems lock-in, and agreements lock-in.

*Psychological resistance to change* is mainly associated with fear, anxiety or uncertainty about what the change might mean. If we are unaware of what a change means, it is natural to be anxious about how this will affect me. Will I be able to keep my job? Will I have a new boss? New role? New colleagues? This creates a resistance to trying to take on the new. The new is uncertain. What is uncertain frightens.

The *cultural resistance to change* is rooted in the culture of the organisation. Culture is a large and broad concept but often refers to the systems, norms and values that an organisation has built up over time. It typically represents things that are currently judged to be right or wrong by members of the organisation. Sometimes the organisation is just a function, department, country organisation or division. In other words, just a part of the larger organisation and then we can talk about subculture. A culture (and subculture) can also be strong. An organisation, regardless of size, that has had a relatively long period of success and/or a relatively low degree of change generally has a fairly high cultural resistance to change. 'We've been successful for 100 years, why should we change now?' is one of many arguments that illustrate a cultural resistance to change. I've definitely heard the 'we've always done that' or 'we don't do that here' argument more times than is reasonable.

In fact, this strong belief in one's abilities is so common that the phenomenon has been given its own name: the *Icarus paradox*, first described in a management context by Danny Miller, a professor of strategy at HEC in Montreal.[117] Icarus, as you know, was a figure in Greek mythology. He wanted to fly and managed to create wings of feathers and beeswax for himself. He became so enamoured of his ability to fly that he ignored his father Daedalus' warnings about flying too close to the sun. When Icarus got too close to the sun, the beeswax melted, his wings fell off and he fell - as is customary in Greek drama - to his death.

What we can learn from this story is both obvious and rational: we should not be blinded by our own excellence. What worked yesterday or today is not guaranteed to work tomorrow.

The *political resistance to change* is mainly related to organisational politics, power, and above all, positional power in the organisation. In traditional organisational hierarchies, power is associated with a certain position or a certain role. In organisational change, therefore, certain people often have something to gain from change. Others have something to lose from them. This may be the power or influence that comes with a particular title or something else that symbolises power or influence. People who guess, believe, or even reasonably assume that they will lose power, prestige or position in a change, have a reason to oppose that change for obvious reasons. After all, it will reduce their power. It is reasonable to assume that few want to feel degraded.

Since these three resistances to change are emotionally conditioned, they must be dealt with essentially emotionally. Emotional fears cannot be met with rational reasoning. Try to persuade a person afraid of flying with statistics about how few planes really crash and the probability that the particular plane they are about to take will crash. My guess is that it won't go well. Logical reasoning doesn't help the fearful. In fear, the frontal lobe, where our analytical thinking sits, is drained of blood. So, we can't reason logically when we're afraid. The blood needed in the brain to make it work has, thanks to evolution, been moved to our large muscle groups to prepare us to flee or fight.

Instead, when it comes to emotional resistance, we need to deal with it by discussing the fear or anxiety, the culture and the need for change, or the fact that some lose in power or reputation and others gain in power and

232

reputation. There is no other way than to talk about the change and let people accept that it will happen and have consequences. Helping employees understand and accept change through dialogue and conversation is the change manager's best tool for dealing with emotional resistance to change.

This reasoning differs from our remaining four types of resistance. On the contrary, the remaining ones deal with precisely rational resistance to change and resistance that can be explained as lock-in effects.

The first we call *investment lock-in*. If we as a management team, group or individual have invested a lot of time, resources, commitment or prestige in, for example, entering a new market in a new country or developing a process, it can be difficult to backtrack on this initiative. Loyalty to previous decisions often builds up and so there may be an inbuilt reluctance on our part as decision-makers to stop investing time, money or commitment in something where we have already invested a lot. This reluctance can manifest itself in many situations, even when it is obvious that we should back off. For instance, we can see how many international organisations originally based in north-western Europe remain in a particular geographical area despite the fact that it has proved almost impossible to conduct business in a way that is ethically defensible by the home country standards (e.g. bribery).

The good thing about resistance to change that arises from rational lock-in effects, as opposed to emotional change, is that they can be discussed. In some cases, we may even be able to assess in a reasonably objective way what is a good way forward. We may be able to answer how much more resources will be required for us to succeed and what the consequences will be if we don't. Often a simple business case for option A (give up) and option B (hold on) can give us an idea.

One way to create such a business case is to list the pros and cons of both. The descriptions should be concrete, and this probably requires 5-6 words. After that, we make a rating of how important these advantages and disadvantages are between 1 and 5 (1=not important at all and 5=completely crucial).

In Figure 7.13 below we can see a simplified example of a decision model for two options A vs. B'.

Figure 7.13 Decision model for continue investing in a new product line

| A. Continue development of a new product line | | | | B. Stop development of a new product line | | | |
|---|---|---|---|---|---|---|---|
| Pro | 1-5 | Con | 1-5 | Pro | 1-5 | Con | 1-5 |
| Possibilities to new revenue streams | 4 | Extensive costs over time | -3 | Better focus on existing clients | 4 | Long since new product launch | -2 |
| Large demand on existing products | 5 | New advanced partly known technology | -3 | Less complaints about resources | 2 | Existing revenue streams will decrease in 3-4 years | -4 |
| Possibilities to open a new market | 2 | Organisational unwillingness | -2 | | | | |
| Available competence | 4 | Weak support from the board | -3 | | | | |
| Sum | 15 | | -11 | | 6 | | -6 |
| A. Continue development of a new product line: | | | 4 | B. Stop development of a new product line: | | | 0 |

In this example, it concerns the further development of a new product line. Continuing to develop a new product line scored 4 and stopping scored 1. Since 4 is greater than 1, the starting point was to continue, which was done. What we need to note is that the model obviously *does not* determine which decision to make. That is not the purpose. The purpose is to give us an opportunity to discuss the factual issues we need to discuss to make an informed decision.

*Competence lock-in* means that we as an organisation have a reluctance to change because we currently have a certain competence (i.e. knowledge that we can apply and that give us competitive advantage today). It is often the case that organisations have, over a long period of time, developed expertise in a specific area, technology, market or similar. This is particularly evident when it comes to an organisation's *core competencies*. Core competencies are generally defined as a company's competencies that are difficult to imitate, can be used in several different ways and create a high value for the organisation's customers.[118] They are therefore important for the organisation's competitiveness. Changing ways of working or changing the organisation so that the competencies that have been built up and created success over a long period of time no longer fulfil the same function is

234

obviously fraught with uncertainty. Uncertainty leads to resistance. Should we abandon something that has been important for our competitiveness for the last 20 years? It is a perfectly reasonable question to ask and a result of resistance to change that is rooted in competence lock-in. Fortunately, we can discuss such a question.

Most organisations have different governance and support systems to run their business effectively. While IT systems may be what we think of when we say systems, there are other systems: management systems, quality systems or production systems and others that make up a set of rules, standards, processes, tools and procedures to help organisations improve.

*System lock-in* is built up by spending resources, i.e. time, money or materials, to operate within a particular system or standard. By doing so, we develop our success factors linked to this system. When, or if, we change to another system, it means changes in how we work, what tools or methods we use, and in some cases perhaps even what kind of people we need in the organisation. Moving from one system to another can be a major change. Anyone who has been involved in a change of an Enterprise Resource Planning system (ERP) in a large organisation knows how incredibly extensive these changes can be. For example, switching from Oracle to SAP, or from one version of SAP to another for that matter, involves a change in IT and processes. However, it also affects structures, competencies, and more. They are extensive. They require both different types and large amounts of change management resources to realise the result improvements. The same reasoning applies when we as an organisation move from being ISO certified to competing systems. It also means big changes for an organisation.

The fourth and final lock-in effect we call *agreement lock-in*. Most (if not all) organisations have contracts and agreements with various parties (stakeholders). These may be external parties: suppliers with whom we have contracts or customers to whom we have guarantee commitments. They can also be internal parties such as employees. Employment contracts are also agreements. Implementing a change that in one way or another means that we need to break contracts and agreements we have made creates resistance to change. In other words, there is a natural explanation for why we do not want to change if it means breaking a contract. Not infrequently, breaches of contract are associated with financial consequences. Terminating a supplier where our purchases are contracted to a certain number over a certain number of years costs breaking prematurely.

However, as with all lock-in effects, we can weigh the possible costs and negative effects of breaking agreements and make a rational assessment of whether it is reasonable or not. In addition to the potential costs, we should also not ignore the fact that the reputation and future attractiveness of the organisation may be negatively affected if we are perceived as an organisation that does not keep our agreements. 'Buying out' employees costs money and can also create a bad reputation. Clearly, we have the right to resist change if we are locked into agreements.

Whatever the type of lock-in effect that causes resistance to change, there is a logical or rational explanation for why it occurs and looks a certain way. In most cases, however, the conditions are in place to make a judgement about what is rational or smart to do going forward. In some cases, there may be a point, for example economic gain in the long run, to continue investing in something. In other cases, there may be an obvious economic loss in continuing. In the latter case, it is a matter of backing out as quickly as possible and trying to minimise the risks, even if this means that any investment made so far is to be regarded as 'money down the drain'.

Almost no matter what kind of change we lead, we will face resistance to change. What resistance and when depends on the magnitude and nature of the change and the organisation we are in. It is therefore difficult to give general advice on how we should face resistance to change. But I have mentioned one above. Listen to the business and be prepared to reassess your arguments. Once you have made up your mind to change anyway, there is another good advice:

"You must always build a 'golden bridge' for your opponent, so that he has a path to retreat." The words are those of Sun Tzu, whose thoughts from the 5th century BC are collected in nearly 400 maxims in the book *The Art of War*.[119] It's a little gem and a classic of strategy literature that can help us deal with challenges in organisations to this day: my take on this is that no one wants to lose face, feel stupid or feel left out.

> A good way to deal with resistance to change is to offer any 'opponents' a chance to back down in a dignified way. From a strategy perspective, it is always more important to achieve the change we want than to prove we are right (as if 'right' exists), so after being 'cold' in our analysis, we can be very 'warm' in our realisation.

This ties in with the reasoning throughout the book about being kind; that kindness is partly the difference between being intelligent and smart. We can thus trace these arguments back more than 2500 years. To me, that says something about how far Sun Tzu's shadow extends. More importantly, it tells me how critical this 'kindness' quality, of respecting others - even one's 'enemies' - is for anyone who wants to succeed in accomplishing something that requires a little more.

Thinking through what kind of resistance to change we might face and where it might come from prepares us for the work ahead. However, I do not believe in measuring and monitoring resistance to change. It quickly creates a focus on what is not working rather than what is working (and we want to focus on positive steps forward).

In our analysis, different types of resistance to change are likely based on expectations, competencies, opportunities or reinforcement not being in place. Then, as we reviewed above, we can work with these instead and ask questions about change resistance at follow-ups. One such example might be: what type of resistance to change do we think is the main reason why the Americas region does not have the opportunities in place? What should we do to remedy this? Trying to think about this at the beginning will help us to be better prepared.

---

In terms of **change resistance**, it is useful to answer the following questions:

35. What kind of change resistance might we face? From which stakeholder groups and key stakeholders is the most resistance likely to come? How can we meet that resistance effectively? Are 'golden bridges' needed?

---

## Hand over responsibility for realisation of benefits

Different benefits are realised at different locations in the business and over different time. To hand over the responsibility for realisation of benefits, we need to think about how much of the change and how much of the benefits are realised where, when and how.

If stakeholders have the basic prerequisites in place from the start, or if change activities have a positive impact on these prerequisites, we may be able to close a change relatively quickly. In other cases, we need to sustain the change over many years. During the lifetime of the change, we can link the evaluations to the different decision points we have set according to the revolutionary change approach. Sprints, for those more familiar with agile methods and concepts. As benefits are realised over time, at some point we need to hand over responsibility to the business.

By thinking about the *agency*, i.e. the ownership the change manager can take over the change as a whole, we gain insights into how and when a handover should take place.

238

One question to answer is where the boundaries of the change manager's responsibility lie. In other words, how much of the change and realisation of benefits can the change manager own and when must someone else take over.

A first step in sorting this out is to look at our *change message;* look at the wording about the change. I used to call this our *'Going from...to formulation'* where we describe the baseline or starting point and the goal. A second step is to think about where in the organisation the stakeholders who need to change their behaviours are. A third step is to think about which person in that organisation might be appropriate to follow up on the benefits. In some cases, this might be a controller, in others a line manager or a staff function. The fourth and final step is to ensure that the goals and metrics we set for the change are still relevant to track. That they can continue to be measured and monitored. Otherwise, the receiving organisation cannot continue to measure and feed back progress to the business. The ambition is that the beneficiary can continue to use the structure we have set up. I tis thus critical to measure the actual effects on results that changed employee behaviour has caused. This is however far from common in organisations.

In many organisations, there is often a lot of measurement of the business at both length and breadth. Meaningful and 'unmeaningful'. Assessing what is relevant for someone to continue to monitor by working with, for example, controllers from an early stage is an advantage. Then together we can ensure that the measurement, right from the start, is something that is in line with things we are already measuring and monitoring. This saves both time and frustration in the handover process. If it's a major change, then we will need to involve a finance function at some point; a rule of thumb is that sooner is better than later.

## Prioritisation of key performance indicators to track benefits

We need to prioritise key performance indicators for monitoring before handing them over to a beneficiary. During the change, we should therefore have identified a few things that we want to follow on an ongoing basis. Here we sometimes need to distinguish between measures that are of different nature. The internal perspective of quality, productivity, efficiency (e.g. time to market, lead time) may naturally land in production or with a process owner (to the extent they exist). Measures of a financial nature may naturally end up with an financial controller. Development-related measures linked to human resources (e.g. skills, vacancies in key positions) may be appropriate for an HR person. Only those who are involved in the business and have done the work properly will know who the recipient is and which measures. Regardless, it is good if we can find as natural an ownership as possible, even if it is not always easy.

A general advice on measuring change is that it should help us to track the evolution of change over time. Snapshots are less relevant. Trends and tendencies are more helpful. They teach us what works and what doesn't. We can see when an outcome is changing and perhaps link it to our activities.

We also need to ensure that what we measure does not conflict with existing business objectives and metrics. Many organisations have some form of balanced scorecard where the financial, customer/market, internal and development perspectives are represented (even if they are called other things). There is then a point in relating benefits to these and involving stakeholders early in the goal setting process.

Another general advice that can help in prioritising is to distinguish between *focused management* and *balanced control*. Focused control is about achieving significant movement in a specific area. Here we want to achieve as much and as fast a change as possible. It means proactivity and high activity on an ongoing basis. Balanced control is more about ensuring that the risks that arise in the business, because of the change, are adequately managed. This control is best managed by being handled reactively, when deviations or results that exceed or fall below minimum acceptable thresholds occur. By dividing these two we don't pay unnecessary attention to things that should not be in focus.

When we prioritise measures to hand over from change management, there are likely to be of both focused and balanced nature. In general, the balanced measures are often already being followed in the business. The focused measures are less common. An important task for change managers will then be to reconcile the objectives and measures that exist and ensure that those that are not currently monitored in the business, and which are an important part of the realisation of change, will be monitored going forward. By synchronising with other follow-up, the organisation will have fewer things to follow up in total. This helps us to focus on what is important.

In both academia and practice, there is relative agreement that too many targets and measures create confusion, weak governance (unclear expectations) or conflicts of objectives. It is difficult to make decisions on resource allocation and activities to be undertaken based on too many factors. What leads to what? How is everything connected? A starting point is that we can manage a business with about 10-20 objectives before it becomes unmanageable or conflicts between objectives arise. Sometimes 16 objectives, plus or minus a few, is also mentioned as a starting point for what we can manage.[120] And if we believe cognitive scientist George Miller, seven is more likely to be the number of variables people are generally able to take into account when making decisions.[121] So, no matter who we lean towards, we need to be economical with the number of targets and measures.

In practice, this means that if the business is already monitoring 16 things (targets, metrics), then it is full. If we still want to monitor the objectives of change, which I think we should, these need to be integrated and/or replace the existing objectives.

More is not better.

The person defining the objectives of a change needs to think about which objectives should be prioritised and which should be de-prioritised before handover. Prioritising is not the same as de-prioritising. Prioritising means that we leave everything as it is and put the 'everything' in an order of priority from 1 downwards. De-prioritising means that we remove parts of 'everything' altogether.

## Practical transfer of responsibility for benefit realisation

Since realisation over time is one of the change manager's responsibilities, we as change managers need to ensure that the work of realising the benefits continues even after the change is formally completed. An important part of this is to hand over responsibility for monitoring benefits to a beneficiary - often someone in the business. A 'handshake'. In practical terms, the change manager needs to identify a recipient organisation and person and get approval from that person that responsibility has been transferred. Until that happens, we cannot complete the change.

As we have seen before, some responsibilities for change may be handed over to the line, others to a finance department, or some other central management or support function. In the case of major changes, a possible suggestion is that the person or management team who has accepted responsibility for realisation follows up quarterly, monthly, or with whatever frequency is appropriate. Sometimes we need to continue to follow up for some or several years, depending on the time horizon of the change. These activities should then be included in the benefit realisation plan that the change manager is responsible for producing already with the goal analysis.

A *benefit realisation plan* should contain some kind of answers to the following questions: what is handed over? From whom to whom? When is it handed over? How is it handed over in concrete terms?

One example in this book is a project where I was project owner and chairman of the steering committee. This project aimed to improve an organisation's monitoring processes. An excerpt of the document that served as a basis for the handover is shown in Figure 7.14.

Figure 7.14 Structure and examples of handover of change

| Change | Baseline and target | Recipient | Position | Measure for evaluation | Feedback |
|---|---|---|---|---|---|
| Minimise manual labor in Excel before performance reviews | One employees work per year gives a direct benefit for the business | Business units 1-5 | Head of controlling for each Business unit | Reduced number of hours spent on manual labor in Excel | Quarterly, to BU-controllers from finance management team |
| Electronic report package used for performance reviews instead of binders | Cost for binders, paper and storage, and time for printing and copying devoted to support the business | Country organisations | Controllers in all BUs | Number of binders used for performance evaluation | Monthly, remove one post-it for each binder not used compared to last month |

In terms of handover, there are a few things to deal with. There is a formal responsibility from the change manager to the recipient to continue to monitor benefit realisation. For this to be possible, there needs to be a description of what the benefits are, how they are measured and how they will be realised over time so that the recipient has an opportunity to do this.

When to hand over depends on when the change manager's agency – ownership – for the change ends. This end may be at a given time, for example, because a person is taking over a new project, leaving that role. It may also be when a certain subset of the benefits (e.g. all green benefits) have been realised or when a defined organisational result has been achieved. It may also be that a system to enable new ways of working has a certain number of active users that determines the timing of handover. Note that system implementation – that the system is in place – *does not* qualify as change management. It is the use of the system, and the benefits because of the use, that we want to get at.

I think it is a good idea to formalise the transfer of responsibility. I usually try to hold a meeting with only handover on the agenda. At that meeting, any issues can be discussed and any documentation that will allow the beneficiary to continue the benefit realisation work can be handed over in a good way. My experience tells me that more and more benefits come if we do this. In the case of major and/or strategic changes, this handover is likely to need to be carried out in several rounds as items at decision meetings when we close a particular phase, or a particular project, sub-project, initiative or other. For example, this could be done at decision points 7 and 8 (according to the revolutionary change process). By having multiple handovers, we are less likely to lose potential benefits in the shuffle.

In conclusion, no matter what, when and how we hand over responsibility for the realisation of benefits to a beneficiary, a formal structure helps us to realise those benefits that are not realised automatically (all yellow, red and blue benefits). Often these are the major benefits of a change. Green benefits, direct savings are generally quite marginal.

---

In terms of **handing over responsibility of benefits realisation** to the business, it is useful to answer the following questions:

36. What should we hand over to the business? To which key stakeholders? When and how should these handovers take place?

---

# Summary: The work of the change manager

In this chapter, we have discussed the five functions of change managers: realising the benefits; managing stakeholders; developing knowledge and skills; evaluating and driving the change; and handing over to the business. We have also discussed how we can work practically within these.

**How can we realise benefits?**

★ Benefits are realised as employees develop their behaviours. Clear measurable benefits and continuous monitoring are musts if we are to realise the potential we see.

**How can we work with stakeholders?**

★ Stakeholder groups and key stakeholders can be involved, communicated with, informed and monitored. This can be done through various means such as working meetings, mailings, calls.

**How can we develop the skills of our stakeholders?**

★ Skills development can be done through e.g. training, supervision, walk alongs, manuals.

**How can we follow up and drive change?**

★ We can evaluate the progress of change by looking at the proportion of stakeholders who have basic prerequisites in place (i.e. expectations, competence, opportunity and reinforcement). We can also evaluate the realisation of benefits by looking at the specific performance measures in the business that should change as behaviours change.

**How can we hand over to the business in a way that enables continued benefit realisation?**

★ We can hand over different parts of the change to different parts of the business depending on what we hand over. For example, continued change work may be handed over to the line and some performance monitoring may be handed over to a finance department.

# Reflections: The work of the change manager

# 8. Organising change

Once we have clarified the functions of the change manager, a natural next step is to think about how we can organise ourselves.

Organisation is best thought of as two or more people who need to coordinate their work to achieve a common purpose or goal. In our notion of 'organisation' we like to link it to organisational structure, hierarchies, information pathways, responsibilities, span of control, etc. That's one way of looking at it, but there are others. *Organising is* really about coordinating activities that need to be carried out to achieve a common goal. We can decouple that from organisational structure.

Clay Shirky, author, writer and professor at New York University, writes eloquently about how we often confuse organisation with organising.

> We use the word "organization" to mean both the state of being organized and the groups that do the organizing... We use one word for both because, at a certain scale, we haven't been able to get organization without organizations; the former seems to imply the latter.[122]

To achieve change, we do not necessarily need to have or create an actual 'organisation'. However, we often need to organise ourselves, organise the different tasks that exist and allocate responsibility for different parts of the change to realise the benefits of the change. The change manager has one role, as we have seen, but several roles are important, especially in more comprehensive and strategic change.

In this chapter we will therefore describe how we can think about tailoring the organising of change and what roles different people may need to take in change work. A first starting point is that we should make a distinction between organisation and organising. When it comes to how we allocate responsibility for driving through change, the important thing is organising.

# Tailor organising

We need to organise ourselves when we can't achieve things on our own. Sometimes we even need to create a permanent structure: an organisation. No change manager can make change happen by himself. So, some kind of organising is a must.

It goes without saying that different changes require different organising and different organisation. Organisations differ - sometimes significantly.[123] Large organisations have different challenges than small ones. Public organisations have different problems than family-owned businesses. Family-owned companies are different from listed companies. Technology-intensive companies have different change challenges than companies that are heavily regulated due to, for example, capital adequacy requirements and banking secrecy. Giving general advice on how to organise ourselves around change is almost pointless.

However, as I argue throughout this book, there are a few issues that are worth thinking about. The questions about organising that I find help us to successfully realise change can be categorised under two headings: responsibilities and roles. These are closely linked to the functions we read about in the last chapter: realising the benefits; managing stakeholders; developing knowledge and skills; evaluating and driving the change; and handing over to the business.

Before we get into talking about specific responsibilities and roles in a change, I want to make two points. They are about whether change should be driven centrally or in the business and whether change should be driven as a project or not. Quite often these are interrelated.

## Change in the line business or centrally, as project or not

I generally believe in driving change in the line business. My experience tells me that we easily create as many problems as we solve when we drive key initiatives – change or not – from a centre. There is a tendency, especially in large organisations, not to be close enough to the business we want to change. When we drive change centrally, we often launch ready-made solutions. This reduces the ownership of the people who will adopt the solution to change their behaviour. Not infrequently, new ideas are received with a perception that they are completely unnecessary. Hence the importance of early and extensive involvement of (at least) key stakeholders.

Whether we drive the change centrally or in the business, we need to 'take' some of the line's time. Staff in the field need to be involved, alongside the work they do, in different types of meetings or workshops. In the line, resources are often scarce. Lending resources to change initiatives, or using them to drive change in the line, is rarely easy. Operations are often busy doing what they need to do. If a change manager can then mobilise change by taking responsibility for ensuring that those with wise ideas and a high level of trust are heard, this increases the likelihood that the change will be successful. One concrete thing to do is to help the line overstaff for a certain period ensuring key stakeholder can contribute without daily operations suffering.

When change is driven centrally, therefore, involvement becomes crucial. It also gets a bit more complicated because we as central people don't always know which people out in the field are good at their job and who we should involve. We also don't know what resources we can access because the line manager is very likely, and rightly so, not always willing to let his or her most skilled people prioritise development of the future over delivery in the present. To put it a little meanly, line managers sitting on human resources easily become an involuntary bottleneck or stopgap. This is also perfectly logical given their responsibilities. Therefore, if change needs to happen quickly, it is better to drive change on the ground. There will be less discussion before we get going.

That said, there are times when change is difficult to drive from the periphery. That is, *not* centrally. When it comes to major changes requiring central coordination and involving major changes in strategy, structure, processes or systems, and where the decision-making power of different units is limited, a central initiative is preferable. However, this obviously requires a high degree of involvement. Otherwise, we are back to the problem that central initiatives create as many problems as they solve.

When do we lead change in projects? The fact is that more and more change, especially of a strategic and wider nature in large organisations, is being driven in project form. Projects are a great way for us to reduce complexity. We can narrow down what we take on. By precisely delimiting ourselves, we can focus on smaller parts of a larger change in different sequences or different parts of the organisation. The project gives us some leeway to reprioritise direction and resources. We can run pilots and experiment with different approaches, solutions, designs, etc. before we push the button and impact many more. It is also more difficult to step back, redo and get it right if we have initiated deep change across the board and many are already engaged in change activities. In this way, organising into projects also reduces the risk of change. So, when we are uncertain about what objectives we are likely to achieve and what means we have at our disposal to achieve them, as is often the case in major transformations, the project form is not so bad after all.[124] Mind you, the all-critical involvement must then also be managed in the change project. We should also remember that then the project does not have deliverables as the main objective, like a traditional project, but realised benefits.

Sometimes changes can be so extensive that *one* project is not enough. Pushing through a change may require several different projects, packaged and managed in portfolios (or multi-projects). We typically do this when several projects have relatively few interdependencies and can be managed individually. However, at least one dependency always exists: access to resources in the form of skilled line staff (key stakeholders) who can contribute to the change. This is always a challenge in change. A truly crowded sector. Partly because it will be the same key stakeholders that we involve in many projects, and partly because we in the line often prioritise the present over the future - with some justification.

Sometimes several projects may also have several interdependencies. Then we need to coordinate the projects in some way. A portfolio of interdependent projects is sometimes called a programme. In larger projects e.g. EPR-projects, many technical and procedural components are often interdependent. In such cases, we can usefully organise ourselves with a programme management where the project managers and a programme manager coordinate the projects, their changes and their benefits. Programs also aim to realise benefits.

Whether we are driving wider changes such as projects, portfolios or programmes, project organisations can evolve over time. We were helped to understand this evolution by Greiner's model (Figure 3.3). Projects, portfolios or programmes often start with a few people. As we 'scale up', more resources and more dependencies are added, leading to crises. These crises, in turn, require the project organisation to change to resolve these crises: leadership crisis, control crisis, etc. So not only does a project organisation have to lead change in the business, where they generally do not have a clear mandate, the organisation that manages the change also must continuously change itself - in parallel with the change outside. This is no easy task (and that is why this book is comprehensive). From my perspective, it is no wonder that we often fail to realise our major changes. It is undeniably demanding.

In conclusion, minor changes that can be driven in line should, in my opinion, also be driven in line and not in project form. It is better if change becomes part of the day-to-day business. However, sometimes a central initiative is needed. What we then need to decide is whether it is enough to coordinate the change work in the line (keep together and support) or whether we need to centralise (move decision-making power upwards and towards the centre).

> The closer the business is to a change, the more likely it is that the change will be realised, as such closeness increases ownership of the change. And the greater the ownership, the greater the chance that the benefits will come, and in the next step, reach the customers or the business.

## Four types of responsibility

Whether we drive a change centrally or in the line business, as a project or as operations, there are different things we need to do: the tasks that are within the functions of the change manager (communicating, evaluating benefits, etc.) need to be done. Someone needs to have a responsibility for these tasks. However, there are different types of responsibility.

In the last chapter we discussed the functions of the change manager. What we meant then was responsibility for tasks that have a specific purpose. They should lead to some kind of result. Something should be achieved with benefit realisation and competence development. Managing stakeholders and following up and driving the change should lead to something, benefits. When we want to ensure that these lead to something, one person needs to own the responsibility for that function and its tasks.

> Sometimes it's not so easy to figure out whose responsibility something is. Two or more people may have to be responsible for different parts together to accomplish a task and/or deliver a desired result. When this is the case, it can help to look at different types of responsibility. When I say type of responsibility, I am referring to what the responsibility looks like, rather than what a person is responsible for.

In organisational design and governance, we sometimes distinguish between executive and non-executive roles, in this context, decision-making roles or positions.[125] This is particularly common in the governance of organisations with an Anglo-Saxon tradition. Boards in the US, for example, often have both executive and non-executive members. In the Nordics, we do not make this distinction as often. When it comes to major change and strategy work (and often otherwise in decision-making and governance issues), I think it helps to clarify that kind of responsibility.

If we believe that such clarification can help to explain responsibilities, we can develop the reasoning further. Making that distinction can then help us understand how different people contribute to change by being executive or decision making. Different people have different roles in an organisation, in its strategy, governance and management. Thus, different people and roles also have different responsibilities in the organisation's change work.

One breakdown, which is reasonably well established, particularly in project management, distinguishes four different types of responsibility. We can summarise these with the acronym RACI: responsible, accountable, consulted, informed.[126]

This division of responsibilities is described in Figure 8.1 and developed below.

Figure 8.1 Four types of responsibility

| R | A | C | I |
|---|---|---|---|
| Responsible | Accountable | Consulted | Informed |
| Who is doing the job? | Who ensures the job gets done? | Who needs to contribute? | Who needs to be informed? |
| This individual performs/coordinates the job, together with others (e.g., the consulted/s) | This individual owns the accountability for a job being done, and preferably a goal is attained | These individuals are involved to make sure a job is properly done | These individuals need to be informed about the job and the impact it has on them |

An *accountable* person is responsible for getting things done. That's where the buck stops. In change, this responsibility means that the performance improvements, i.e. benefits, we have identified and want to achieve are actually realised. An accountable person may often have a high level of responsibility in at least parts of the business to be changed and thus has both an interest in the success of the change and an influence on whether it does. Such roles are by definition key stakeholders to involve. On the other hand, it is probably not always the case that an accountable does the actual job.

Rather, the job is done by a *responsible*. The responsible is the person who leads the change operationally. If there are many projects, portfolios or parallel initiatives, the responsible is the one who holds this together. However, as we have said before, no one is capable of driving change all by themselves. Multiple stakeholder groups and key stakeholders need to be involved and communicated with.

These stakeholder groups and key stakeholders have a responsibility to be *consulted*. By consulted in this context, we mean people who can contribute their knowledge or experience, and who, because of this, have an explicit responsibility to contribute to a particular change.

Finally, we have a group of people who have a responsibility to stay *informed* about what is happening in a change. These are also the stakeholder groups we identified as people we want to inform in our stakeholder analysis, making our desire and this group's responsibility to ensure transmission of information reciprocal.

Another important point of the RACI model is that no one person should have two different types of responsibility for the same issue, challenge, decision or similar. If I am the responsible, someone else should be accountable. In simple terms, sitting on two chairs at the same time means conflict of interest: being both the doer and the enforcer.

In change, the change manager is often responsible. It is an executive function. It must be. The change manager must drive, sustain, follow up, manage, support and communicate. However, the change manager is not the where the buck stops. Instead, it should be a decision-maker, a person sitting on the actual resources who is accountable. When change is driven down the line, it should be a line manager. When change is driven as a project, it should be a project owner, sponsor or similar. In both cases it is beneficial that the person who owns accountability, is also managing at least some of the human resources that should contribute to the change.

However, when we look at the change as such, it is not obvious that the change manager is the responsible of a competence development intervention or an information dissemination. In these cases, a trainer (internal or external) may be more likely to deliver the development initiative, and a communicator (internal or external) may be more likely to ensure the quality of the information. In these cases, the change manager becomes the accountable rather than the responsible. Responsibility is therefore at different levels, just as in organisational hierarchies.

In sum, responsibility can therefore look different. There is a point in making this clear in changes. Exactly how these responsibilities are to be allocated needs to be discussed when initiating a change process. No one can drive through a change all by themselves. In this logic, everyone who might contribute in one way or another has some kind of responsibility, but of a different nature: as the main responsible party (R), as an accountable party (A), to provide input by being consulted (C) or to stay informed (I). You could see some examples of this in Figure 7.10 in the previous chapter.

## Roles in change work

Different people have different responsibilities. They also have different roles. As more organisations need to develop their capacity to manage and lead change, more and more organisations are employing more and more people with formal responsibility for doing just that (as responsible). At the same time, we are placing increasing demands on all employees to be able to manage and lead change and/or lead in change, which are two different things.

For me, *leading in change* means exercising leadership in a time and place where external and internal circumstances are constantly changing. Since the circumstances of all organisations are constantly changing in one way or another, all leadership involves leading in change. That is my conviction.

*Leading change*, that's something else. It is more clearly focused on driving through a specific change to achieve a specific improvement in performance. This is what a change manager should be engaged in. Unfortunately, the distinction between leading change and leading *in* change is not always so clear. 'Everyone is and should be a change manager in our organisation', I sometimes hear. This is a good idea, but it sharpens the need for clear roles and responsibilities in change management.

> The change manager is a specialist who spends most of his or her time leading change. A leader in change is a generalist who leads an activity in a changing world, and who does not spend most of his time leading change but leading a group, department, organisation, project or similar.

So how should we view the role of change manager? My reasoning does not mean that the person responsible for leading change must hold a *position* as a change manager. It can be. I have held that position for just over three years. However, even more often in my more than 20 years of professional life, it has rather been a *role* that I have assumed. One of many hats I have had to put on in various contexts, to use De Bono's 'hat-analogy'.[127] The hats that originally illustrate different ways of thinking (looking for the broad brushstrokes, asking for details, building on facts, drawing on one's emotions) help us to understand that in different situations we need to adopt different roles.

To illustrate: at a management team meeting we are not CFOs, marketing directors, HR directors or CEOs. We are members of the management team. That is our role there. We are to drive the company's or organisation's *common* agenda. That is our responsibility there. Then when we step out of the management team meeting and into a meeting with, say, auditors or customers, we are back in the role of CFO or marketing manager. Knowing what our role is in different contexts makes it easier for us to focus on what we are there to contribute.

Roles then become linked to the specific behaviours we need to exhibit in a particular context. In addition to my various positions as a change manager, management consultant or strategy head, I have had several different roles (hats) related to both more and less extensive changes of a more or less strategic nature. I have been a project owner, a management team member, a board member, chair of steering committees etc. Often the responsibility has been unclear at the beginning. A first step in clarifying responsibilities has been to separate the role I have been given in the change from the position I already hold in a clear way.

To be even more clear: A position is synonymous with an assigned post. A position is an organisational unit intended for one person only. In other words, a position is the outermost node in an organisational structure. It is often formalised by an agreement between two parties: an employer and an employee. We call this agreement an *employment contract*. A person's employment in an organisation is usually linked to one (1) position. This means that a position usually entails specific duties and responsibilities assigned to the person holding the position. Often a particular position may also be associated with one or more roles. In my experience, the position of Development Director (or similar) often has a role as chairman of some type of development board where decisions on major change initiatives are taken. The position of CEO may also include roles as chairman of the board of (some of) the subsidiaries. The Head of Communications has the role of a member of the management team. So could the HR Director, the Marketing Director, the Sales Director, etc. Related to change, the Head of the Programme Office (or similar) may have the role of convenor of the

Programme Council. The examples are many and show the importance of keeping roles and positions separate.

A role, on the other hand, is the behaviours an individual is expected to perform given a particular position in a particular context. In our case, the context is change management. Typical roles found in change management are then linked to the functions a change manager needs to ensure: realising benefits, working with stakeholders, developing competencies, following up and driving, and handing over to the business. A few common positions that in my experience take on roles in change (e.g. as change manager) are business development managers, strategy managers, management consultants (internal and external) and project managers.

Regardless of the different positions that take different contributions in change, we need several different roles. Roles that lead change and roles that support it. We'll look at these now.

## Change managing roles

The first role we look at is the *change manager* itself.

In change programmes or in major change projects or initiatives, which extend over time, there is an obvious value in formalising different roles. Sometimes so much so that they become positions. However, this is not a must. What is a must, however, is to have a clear organising and division of responsibilities for the different parts or elements of the change that need to be managed and coordinated.

> Depending on how broad the change is, how many different stakeholders will be affected, and the depth of change, how extensive behavioural changes are required by the stakeholders, different levels of change effort are required. The broader and deeper the change, the more time need to be spent on change management.

At some order of magnitude, the change is so great that someone must spend so much time that it becomes a full-time job. Sometimes even several people's full-time jobs. Sometimes for several years. When this is the case, it's not a bad idea for the change manager to become a position.

When a change is so extensive that it requires one or full-time staff is impossible to say. It is not possible to say that there must be a particular role or position in a particular change. However, as often, there are rules of thumb to follow.

One such rule of thumb is that if your change is 'reasonably broad and reasonably deep' then you need a half-time change management resource. And if it is broad and deep, you need at least one full-time resource.

So what is reasonably wide and deep? I like to think of it this way: if we need to change three out of five of the organisational elements (i.e. strategy, structure, processes, incentives and people), then it is likely to be reasonably deep. If all five elements need to change or if actual changes in strategy are included, then it is pretty sure to be deep. If there are more than 100 people from three or more different units, departments, business areas, divisions, companies, etc., the change is likely to be reasonably broad. If it is over five different organisational units and closer to 500 people than 100, I would say its broad. But the breadth can of course be much greater.

By way of comparison, one of the major change programmes I was responsible for involved 12,000 people in all the Nordic countries. We changed strategy (a little), processes and systems (a lot), structure (very little), incentives (a little) and human capital (quite a lot). In my team I had 6 full-time resources with specialist responsibilities in different areas of change management. I had one specialist for communication, one for competence development, one for business architecture, one for change controlling, and one for business case management. We managed to realise many of the benefits, but at the same time had to make many hard priorities. We could have been one or two more full-time people and still added value by prioritising the right change efforts. However, if there had been three more of us, we would probably have had to make up tasks and not make the best use of the organisation's resources. Had there been fewer of us, fewer of the benefits of change would have been realised. The change would probably have more costs than benefits.

When change is driven in projects, a rule of thumb is that for every full-time project management resource, approximately half a full-time change management resource is required. This assumes that it is a change project.

To take another real-life example: in a major IT-system project I was part of, large parts of the IT had to be replaced. This also meant that processes had to change, and competence had to be developed. It was large and extensive, and we organised the change as a project to be able to separate the changes and benefits from each other. There were eight projects in total, each with a full-time project manager and a portfolio manager holding the projects together. We were keen to have four full-time change management resources to ensure that the benefits were realised. We got two.

In the example above, the change was driven as a project. This is not always the case. However, when it is a project, there is an interface between change manager and project manager that is important to clarify when we work in change projects. In the introduction to the book, I defined project management simplistically as 'putting stuff on the dock' and change management as 'carrying the stuff in from the dock and making sure it gets used'. The RACI responsibilities of the project manager and the change manager need to be clarified. When change is so extensive that there is a project manager, the project manager is Responsible of the project, its deliverables and its benefits. The Accountable should be some form of steering committee chair. In this case, the change manager becomes the Responsible of the change activities. However, since these are only roles, a project manager, which is a relatively common position, can also assume the role of change manager. This will feel a bit messy until we sit down and map out the different responsibilities for different parts of the change work.

Organising is not the same as organisation. Role is not the same as position. Organising and role are less formalised in most organisations and are therefore perceived as more abstract.

In change management, it is crucial to sort these out. Change is usually expected to take place alongside day-to-day activities, operations. Operations is made up of organisation and positions, not organising and roles. When this is not sorted out, our change management resources are undersized, and fewer or smaller parts of the benefits are realised.

Anyone who has worked on change projects or change initiatives knows that allocating resources to change management is often a low priority. I believe one of the reasons why we see so many changes fail to realise the benefits they are intended to realise is that we have not sorted out the position-role issue and the organisation-organising issue. This scarcity of resources is a reason to be systematic in our change management efforts so that the resources we use create impact. Organising the change is then an issue.

If we want change, if it is important that the change realises the intended benefits, we often need to invest more in change management than we generally do. Change requires a systematic and structured approach to ensure that the organisation moves from one stage to another and that the benefits are thereby realised. It requires resources and these resources need to take on slightly different roles at different stages.

In addition to the change manager, who has a kind of overall role, we can talk about four roles linked to the change manager's function: one for benefit realisation, one for stakeholder management, one for competence development and one for monitoring and driving. Note that these roles can be assumed by one person, by two people, by four or by eight, etc. Note also that when we are change managers alone, without support resources, we need to wear all these roles (hats) simultaneously.

261

## Benefits realisation lead

A *benefits realisation manager* is responsible for ensuring that the benefits are realised in accordance with the purpose. In practice, this means ensuring that the change is properly designed and embedded, that the solutions developed work as intended and that they lead to the realisation of the changes.

The Benefits Realisation Manager is also responsible for developing a business case for the change and supporting the prioritisation of changes based on benefits and dependencies. Another important function is to keep the business case up to date by confirming benefits with the business and adjusting benefits and costs on an ongoing basis. Once the change is 'completed', the benefit realisation manager is also responsible for handing over to the business.

To do their job, benefit realisation managers need two documents: a business case, which describes the benefits and costs of the change, and a benefit realisation plan, which describes how these costs will be spent and benefits realised over time. Having worked as a broad controller or portfolio manager is not a bad background for this type of role.

## Stakeholder management lead

The person in the role of *stakeholder management lead* is responsible for the activities aimed at involving, communicating and informing about and around the change. In concrete terms, this may involve inviting and holding information meetings, communicating with key stakeholders, and supporting the identification, prioritisation, realisation and evaluation of various activities aimed at clarifying expectations and creating reinforcement. In addition to traditional analogue channels, this work can be enabled by digital channels and various types of communication and information activities on social networks, blogs, intranets, etc.

This work is planned, preformed, evaluated and updated in the context of the change plan in the form of involvement, communication and information activities that are initiated and evaluated. Several operational

262

communication managers with workshop experience have been invaluable as stakeholder management leads in changes that I have driven and in which I have played a part.

## Competence development lead

A *competence development lead* is responsible for ensuring that stakeholders who need to develop their competence and skills to learn new behaviours are given the opportunity to do so effectively. Effective for the individual (learning the right things) and effective for the organisation (with the limited resources available). Practical tasks include coordinating and supporting the development of principles, structure and guidelines for all competence development. It also involves supporting the design, planning, effectuation and follow-up of various competence development activities.

In larger changes, and not least in larger organisations, a person who is, for example, a training and development manager, can act as the client and owner of various training tools. That person may also be a primary contact with internal and/or external training providers. In my experience, an practised business-oriented training manager does an excellent job in this role. To manage their work, they may have a change plan with competency development activities.

## Change controller

In change, there is an obvious point in having a dedicated person to follow up the change and the benefits, and to drive the change. The role of such a person could be called a *change controller*. The role is similar to that of a benefit realisation lead but focuses more on the momentum of the change than on the realisation of benefits (which comes at a later stage).

The task of a change controller is to evaluate the progress of the change and support all those working on the change to drive it forward. In practical terms, this means regularly following up the change work to ensure that the right prerequisites are in place with the various stakeholders. This requires that there is a structure for evaluating change initiatives and their impact (e.g. as shown in Figures 7.7 and 7.8). This role therefore also includes being responsible for the materials and documentation (e.g. change plans) required to monitor the activity and inviting people to the various monitoring meetings that may be needed. It also includes recording and following up actions, decisions and cases related to the change in some form of log.

## Change support roles

In a change, there should be one or more people who take responsibility for driving the change. Some examples have been mentioned above. In addition to these leading roles, we also need supporting roles.

### Change ambassador

We have previously discussed how important it is to involve the business and to find support. For example, we have mentioned how important the named key stakeholders are to the successful realisation of change.

In some cases, particularly where major changes are involved, there is a benefit in formalising the responsibilities of one or more key stakeholders. Involvement then moves from a more passive mode: contributing knowledge at workshops and the like, to a more active mode: contributing on their own initiative, proactively, to clarifying expectations, identifying and trying to close competence gaps, creating opportunities or reinforcing the new more actively. This type of role can be called *change ambassador*.

A change ambassador is based in the business but spends part of his/her time acting as an information and communication bridge between the business and the change manager(s). This is often needed in all types of large-scale change but becomes particularly important when change is driven centrally and/or as projects. The role of ambassadors is to ensure that the business has *one* link with the change management. They can also make it clear to the business when the change is entering different stages and explain what the implications of these stages might be. Finally, they can represent the business to the change management. For example, they can check on the state of change within the business and help the change management with suggestions for change activities that can help the business move forward. They may also ask to be a standing item at the management team meeting for the specific business.

In many large organisations there are business development managers, project managers for development projects or similar who are more or less in the line business and who are responsible for development in the organisation they are based in. These are excellent people to use as change ambassadors.

## Super-user

Another role that can support change and is not a formal part of change management is super-user and trainer. In addition to change ambassadors in the organisation, there also needs to be a number of people with relatively deep expertise in different areas related to the change. If the change involves new methods, tools or systems for technology development, it is useful to try to identify key stakeholders who know these methods, tools and systems. Perhaps even those who are most skilled in using them in the way they are to be used. We call these *super-users*.

A super user works closely with both the business and the change management. Like the change ambassador, they are a natural channel for the business to turn to for support and assistance in the method(s), tool(s) or system(s) for which he or she is responsible. This helps the change management to ensure that end-users of the methods or systems get answers to the questions that arise in the operations. They become a support in getting the stuff lifted from the dock into use. A rule of thumb is to have at least two super-users per method, tool or system to reduce the risk of skills shortages if one of them leaves or takes on other tasks.

A super-user is responsible for monitoring the progress of his/her area over the change. They are involved on an ongoing basis to ensure that the design is right, that the right parts of the change are tested, that the benefits identified will be realised and point out any limitations/opportunities of the changes. While working with super-users helps the business to create good solutions, it is also an effective way of building competence in the organisation, for example in the system. It also makes the organisation less dependent on external support to solve challenges in the here and now. Super-users are thus often key stakeholders.

In addition, to the extent that super-users are able and willing, they can be used as *trainers* in the methods or tools. They have a good understanding of the business and the business requirements for the tools, and they know the tool and how it can be used to support the business. In other words, a trainer is a person with deep knowledge who can also pass it on to other people through the various competence development activities that the change requires.

## Support in the change after completed change

A central change management stops investing time when the change is completed according to the revolutionary change process. If nothing else, it often happens at what we have called in this book decision point 8 (in Figure 6.1). This usually does not mean that the benefits of the change have been realised. The change continues: more employees change their behaviours, use newly acquired skills, work in new organisational structures with new responsibilities to continue realising benefits. Super-users provide support even after a change is completed. However, after the change is completed, when the change management is no longer driving the change, super-users can still be part of a support function for the business to change.

This support function is typically something we set up already when we design, build and test solutions. After all, we know what needs to be changed, who has deep knowledge of the issues and can therefore provide natural support going forward. If these people in these positions are involved early on, they can contribute knowledge directly, allowing us to avoid problems that are otherwise likely to arise later in the change, during future pilots or roll-outs.

If we organise a function, we can make sure that we have slightly different levels depending on what needs to be changed. We can talk about four levels.

The first level of support consists of super users. The people in the business who know the change and the new solutions developed. These people can take note of, systematise and help solve the problems that the business reports. The super user can solve some problems directly while others need to be sent to the second level.

The second level of support is found within the organisation that owns or manages the process, tool or method that is affected by the change. Sometimes there is a quality or business development department that owns the processes, tools or management systems, etc. There may be process owners, system owners and/or system managers whose responsibility is precisely to update and improve the operation of its processes, systems and tools. These people constitute a good 'level two support'. In cases where IT changes are involved, it is useful if a representative from IT and one from the business decide on actions together. This is often defined in various maintenance management models (e.g. pm$^3$ or ITIL).

In some cases, there is a need for a third level. When the methods or tools are not owned and managed by the organisation itself, we may need to have a direct contact with the software vendor or methodology expert. This is particularly the case when major changes are involved in, for example, ERP, quality, management or production systems with a large IT component. When this is the case, this also needs to be formalised at a fairly early stage. It may be that the external party needs to be involved in the development work itself.

In terms of **organising**, it is useful to answer the following questions:

37. How do we need to organise change? Projects? Initiatives? In line? Centrally led?

38. What are the different responsibilities for change that we need to share? For different areas and issues? What types of responsibilities do we assign to whom?

39. What concrete roles do we need to ensure that someone has for the change to be realised and the benefits to become real?

## Background and experience for leaders of change

Those of you who have read this far realise now, if not sooner, that change - especially comprehensive and strategic change - is demanding. There are many things to keep track of. It requires a great deal of carefulness, patience and improvisation that is not required when we are doing 'business as usual'. It also requires a great deal of humility and sensitivity towards all those who contribute to making the change real. In short, it requires a little more.

The Roman emperor Augustus can serve as an illustration. Augustus, who was the adopted son of Julius Ceasar and emperor from 27 BC to 14 AD (for 42 years), is widely regarded as the founder of the Roman Empire and the greatest emperor of Rome of all time. During his reign, that empire stretched from Hamburg in northern Germany to the Nasser Lake in southern Egypt, and from the Portuguese and Moroccan Atlantic coasts in the west, to Israel, Palestine, Lebanon and well into Syria in the east. His legacy included the Pax Romana, a two-hundred-year period of relative peace during which fire services, policing, infrastructure, and financial and social reforms could be realised. These were likely contributing factors to the empire's greatness.

One of the reasons he succeeded in making these extensive changes is said to be partly because he exhibited the virtue the Romans called *clementia*. In Roman mythology, Clementia is the goddess of grace and gentleness. August was less autocratic. Among other things, he refused to take his place as dictator, unlike both Julius Caesar and Sulla who represented him. He also had 80 silver statues, erected in his honour, melted down. Paying attention to others and trying to understand what others are going through seems to have been important. I think it's just as important today.

Leading a major change is demanding. It's a balancing act to be both like Malcolm X and my mother. However, it's not magic. It's not about populating space in two weeks or splitting atoms in the garage in your spare time. It's not necessarily complex, abstract or elusive. It can be, and it may require some analysis and sorting out initially, but usually it's not the complexity that's the hard part. What is difficult is that it is precisely demanding. It requires resources (more than we generally have) and patience and stamina to persevere (also more than we generally have). It also requires an ability to engage others and listen to their perspectives (something we generally do too little of). Personally, I don't know of anything as exacting in the world of work as leading strategic and comprehensive change, but I don't know of much that is as instructive either.

One person I brought into a large change programme, Maria, often said about change that "many feel called but few are chosen" (to refer to Matthew 22:14). It's a good simile. The meaning of the expression is that of all those who set out to do the task, few succeed. It is certainly true in change management. We've seen it in research, too - in study after study. However, what's so amazing is that anyone can become good at it.

All it takes to be a good change manager is a great deal of deliberate practice and patience: work on, stop, reflect on how we can be even better, work on, succeed, fail, stop, reflect. Again and again. In fact, this is the (un)secret recipe for all deep knowledge. It's easy to understand in theory, but hard to cope with in practice.

As a final tip, I believe that change produces better results, achieves more benefits, if we as change managers are genuinely interested in the business we want to change. We need to let the day-to-day challenges of the business 'wash over us'. If we don't, we risk creating other, new, just as many, and perhaps worse problems than the old ones we tried to solve. In my experience, once I start to get to grips with a business and understand the actual challenges it faces, my interest grows as I learn more. Humans are fundamentally curious, so I don't think I'm alone in this.

So, if you find it difficult to generate genuine interest initially, there may be a point in acting as if you are interested. Walk about. Ask questions. Many. Often. To different stakeholders. I think, interest comes with learning. A lack of interest is perhaps more a lack of knowledge of the parts and how the parts create a whole.

And should it be the case that we fail to generate interest over time, despite talking to people and trying to build a deeper knowledge of the system and its elements, then we are probably not the right person in the right place in that particular case. Perhaps someone else should take over, if possible? It is not a failure to admit that we do not have or are failing to acquire the interest or knowledge to do something properly. It is so sometimes. To then show the kind of maturity required to recognise that, I think, is anything but a failure. Not to acknowledge this, on the other hand, is a failure.

In the gangster movement there is the term 'studio gangsters' and in the military there is the term 'armchair generals', both of which are used to condescend to other people's lack of 'real world' experience. We may have views on both terms and their origins, but they illustrate an important point

270

that also applies to change. It is in 'the real world' that things happen, not in the studio or at the desk. It is also in action that organisational change is realised. My belief is that change cannot be driven from the desk. A good change manager must understand how the business works.

Often the change manager (especially the centrally placed one) has to be a bridge between the central, e.g. management, board or staff functions and the business. The change manager needs to help translate the often ill-defined ambitions of a management team or board into concrete changes in the day-to-day running of the business that will help them perform better in the here and now.

> Change must be operational, must involve the business. In change - and in all management - it is impossible to be strategic without being operational. Understanding the operational, the business, is a prerequisite for being strategic. Operational and strategic are not opposites. The opposite of strategic is 'un-strategic'. The opposite of being operational is 'un-operational'. People who do not understand the operational automatically become un-strategic. They cannot make judgements about how resources should be used effectively.

To paraphrase the concepts of the gangster rap and the military, I don't think we need more 'Powerpoint change managers' who 'only work strategically'. As change managers, we need to get out into the real world - to the business and the customers. There is no other way to ensure that the change we want to bring about creates real benefits.

# Summary: Organising change

In this chapter we have discussed how we can think about tailoring the organising of change, what roles we need in the work and the different responsibilities associated with these different roles.

**How can we think about tailoring the organising of change?**

★ Organising is not the same as organisation. We always need to organise, but we don't always need a 'formal' organisation. Change can be driven in line or centrally, in projects or in operations. The less need for central coordination, the better. Change happens in the business and should, as far as possible, be a natural part of all activities - not a 'side project'.

**What different roles might we need to play in the change process?**

★ All change needs someone to own and lead the change: a change manager. This is primarily a role. But it can also be a position. In addition to this role, there may be one or more benefit realisation lead (working on monitoring, business case management and handover to the business), stakeholder management lead (e.g. working on information and communication) and competence development lead and change controller. In addition to these 'leading' roles, there may be a need for 'supporting' roles during the change and after the leading roles are no longer in place. These may be ambassadors, super-users and trainers who have been involved in the change process.

**How do we allocate responsibility between different people and/or roles to drive change?**

★ Different roles may have different responsibilities in different parts of the change. The Accountable is responsible for making something a reality (e.g. an objective is achieved, a decision is taken). The Responsible ensures that this 'something' becomes a reality. The Consulted is responsible for contributing knowledge to the work on this 'something'. Informed is responsible for gathering information about this 'something'.

# Reflections: Organising change

# 9. Summary and conclusions

We have now reached the point where we can do no more than draw conclusions and lessons from what we have read and try to understand how we can apply it in everyday life (if we have not done so on an ongoing basis).

I am *not* of the opinion that there is an absolute truth. Unambiguous truths are hard to find in the disciplines of how people and organisations work. Or almost any discipline (ask a quantum physicist about Schrödinger's cat). However, I also don't believe that the whole world and everything in it is a social construct and that we can't know anything about anything. There are things we can say are more 'likely true' than others. These things are based on science and proven experience. Some things are better substantiated, researched and discussed than others, and therefore have a higher credibility than those things that have not been subjected to the same critical scrutiny and cumulative evolution over time.

There are proven and researched ideas and methods about what it takes to successfully lead change: what is not about leading the business, but about changing the business. These are the things I have tried to convey in this book. If you start from them, from the model, method or logic I present, you will hopefully avoid some of the mistakes that are otherwise relatively common.

Roger Bacon, a 13th century scientific theorist, mathematician and astronomer, wrote in his *Opus Majus* that:

> Reasoning draws a conclusion, but does not make the conclusion certain, unless the mind discovers it by the path of experience.[128]

This means that your reasoning, and what you have learned so far, may well be valuable. However, it is not until you have experienced what you've learned and seen how they apply in your 'real world' they can be confirmed as 'true for you'. It is also only then that they really stick, and in Bacon's words are 'certain'.

275

I like to talk about three levels of knowledge: the first level is about knowing what something is or what it looks like. We can take a bicycle as an example. It has a handlebar, two wheels, a frame, a chain and so on. The second level is about knowing what the bicycle is used for and how. It is a means of transport, you sit on the saddle, you pedal on the pedals and you can influence the speed with that, and turn with the handlebars, etc. The third level is about getting on the bike, finding your balance, starting to pedal and actually riding. To do this, you need to be active. Behave. Practice. Experience ensures the conclusions.

In this book, I've made sure that there is an opportunity to exercise (ride a bike). While reading the book, we can work on a change we are facing or in the middle of (hence the questions that have come up continuously). However, in a book we can only put the emphasis on levels one and two.

You now know what change is and what it looks like (level 1). You know how different methods and tools for managing change can be used to create a more effective, creative or successful organisation (level 2). For you to become a master of change, your next step in development is practice, practice, more practice, and in parallel with practice, deliberate reflection (level 3).

So, my final advice in this book is this: get on your bike, ride and reflect. You may fall a few times at first - if you don't fall, you are probably not challenging yourself enough. However, over time you will become more experienced and eventually really good at cycling.

## Least effort for real change

In 2010, I was appointed Change Manager in a listed global group. I was the first to be coded with that position in the HR system of that organisation. In that position, I was responsible, among other things, for how one of the subsidiaries with 10,000 employees would drive through major changes. One part we spent a lot of time on was benefit realisation. As a consultant, before

I joined that company, I had developed business cases where benefits were not always realisable. I didn't know any better. I had also, as a procurer of consultancy services, seen far too many business cases with benefits that I was pretty sure would not be realised. So, I and one of the teams I led wanted to be thorough in our work. After all, change is not the goal. Result improvement is.

When I presented the ideas about the change method, the model, the tools, etc. (which was an early version of what is in this book) to the subsidiary's management team, I received the following comment from a vice president:

> Pontus, this is absolutely right! Of course, this is how it has to be done in order to really reap the benefits. Of course! However, can't we just cut back a little - in some places? This is a lot of work.

I am occasionally met with similar questions and requests - although more rarely nowadays actually - and I wanted to respond. My answer to the director in question was:

> Well, it's probably possible to remove some elements, simplify a bit and make some things a bit less thorough... However, it has to be a bit case by case...

So far he was satisfied (and I meant every word), but I continued:

> ...but we should remember that if we don't do it properly, it's associated with risk - just as everything is, when we don't do things properly. In this case, it means a risk that we will have costs for the change and fewer, or at worst no, benefits. Without a doubt, we get less leverage on the investment.

Unfortunately, he wasn't quite as happy anymore. However, what I said is true. That's the risk. Therefore, it must be the answer. The more we neglect, the more likely it is that benefits will fall away. Part of the story is that I got to keep my seven full-time change management resources in a change programme with a total budget of EUR 40 million.

It is a pity that we often want to dodge doing things properly, although I logically understand the reason. It seems expensive to spend a lot of resources on change management. It's sometimes hard to understand the value of something as fuzzy (in many people's opinion) as change management. I'm no better. Earlier in my working life, I also saved on change management resources. Now I don't.

And I do not see the same reasoning when it comes to more scientific or technical areas. How would it sound if politicians or other health care executives asked: 'Do surgeons have to stand and wash their hands for so long? It takes a lot of time!' Or if the management of a construction company asked: 'Do we have to let the concrete in the bridge dry so long before we can lay asphalt and start driving with an overturn?' or 'Do we have to calculate the buoyancy of ships so carefully?' 'Does the algorithm for self-driving cars have to be so detailed? Can't we just drive once!?'. You get the point.

> Just because there are no purely 'technical' or 'physical' constraints evident in change work, it does not mean that less rigorous work has less impact on the outcome. While much is uncertain about what we know about strategy, change and management, there is also much that we know with good support.

There is therefore a point in thinking of change work as having precisely technical or physical limitations. If nothing else, as a thought exercise.

If we take the practical consequences of this, two conclusions become clear:

* If you must change e.g. because of survival, a crisis or new laws, or if you are convinced that you will go through with the change, do it for real. Do it seriously.
* If you don't need to change or suspect you won't have the energy or the ability to do it for real, don't bother. Again, do it seriously.

These conclusions are not silly principles to adhere to in change management as a kind of *change philosophy*.

> The wise change manager (and the smart organisation) learns to prioritise fewer changes and push them through, one at a time and as quickly as possible. This is more effective than stiffly prodding 10 change initiatives at once. And from a strategy perspective, more effectively realised changes lead to greater success over time.

Experienced change managers know which rules they can break and when, and in which changes, without exposing themselves to unnecessary risk (missed benefits). So, an experienced person can duck a few things. The person leading a change for the first, second or third time cannot. Or those who don't know what rules they are breaking. That is the difference between an experienced and a less experienced change manager. It is also the experience that determines how successful we are in our change work. And it is that experience that we should pay for when we hire and engage change managers. We need to take change seriously.

## The absolute essence of the book

The shortest version of what is written in this book is the following:

Organisations are under pressure to change. They must change to remain relevant in a constantly changing world. If you want to make real change and create an organisation that is better equipped for the future, you need a systematic and structured approach to move your organisation from where you are today, to where you want to be tomorrow. We call such a systematic approach change management.

In terms of change management, there is support in both proven experience and scientific research for the following behaviours:

* Identify the organisational outcomes we want to influence and get an idea of how much we want to influence them, i.e. define the benefits.

* Specify which behaviours of which employees affect these results positively and negatively, so we know which behaviours we want to influence.

* Involve the key stakeholders and critical mass of the organisation required to change the behaviours that deliver the desired performance improvements.

* Involve these stakeholders as early as possible to allow them to take ownership of our common change. Ask many people if they understand where we are going and how they can contribute and ask often.

* Perform skills development interventions targeted at improving the specific behaviours that affect the outcomes we want to improve and evaluate the impact of the interventions.

* Create a business case built on benefits that are the effects of changed employee behaviours. Set the benefits against the costs associated with changing these employee behaviours.

* Check with the business and any management team/steering committee on an ongoing basis to ensure that they believe in the solution and the benefits the change will bring. Update the business case based on the input from the reconciliations.

* Ensure that your change activities are targeted at clarifying expectations, developing competencies, creating opportunities and/or reinforcing the deficit behaviour of one or more stakeholders. Otherwise, change resistance is created.

* Evaluate and reflect on an ongoing basis on the change activities carried out and their impact on the change, and on the results (realisation of benefits).

★ Generate change activities based on what evaluations show has worked - not what you think needs to be done in advance. Don't plan too much; plans quickly become invalid. When planning, plan from the end, decide what will be delivered when and count backwards. Then decide what to do here and now.

★ Offer feedback in an educational and appealing way - preferably visually - to the business as to what is happening in the change work, what results it has produced so far and how the people in the business can help.

If you do this, you have a good chance that the improvements in results that are the purpose of the hard work of change will be realised.

## The collective battery of questions

To try to help us carry out these change behaviours, we have looked at different questions throughout the book. These questions help us to work with change systematically. We do a work preparation for our change. A work preparation that increases the chances of getting the effect of our change efforts.

By thinking through and answering these questions, we are well prepared to tackle our changes. Answering these questions does not mean writing an essay, or some long winding justification with background and a thousand different motives. That would leave us stuck at our desks again. It is counterproductive. After all, we should be spending time out in the field in the businesses we want to change. When we have thought things through, a few short notes are really enough. In some cases, maybe just 10 words. However, if there are fewer words than that, there is a risk that the descriptions become too superficial to support the realisation of the change. But there may be cases that require more extensive thought and a slightly longer explanation. Different challenges we face need different levels of detail in solutions. With experience we learn what requires what.

So, whatever the magnitude of the overall change effort, the purpose of the questions is to help us think through the change from start to finish. If we do that, we won't get lost as easily. We don't lose sight of the obvious. We are not starting a change that cannot possibly go anywhere. We become more effective in our use of change resources.

> So, when you are faced with a possible change: answer all the questions. Do it quickly and 'half-heartedly' the first time. Put it aside for a day. Go back and re-evaluate and refine your initial answers. After a couple of rounds, a couple of three days, it's often pretty clear what we're facing. Change is an iterative process, thought and action must support each other - also in the very beginning.

You will find the collective battery of questions on the next page.

If you get stuck in your work and need some input or support, just get in touch. **I'll help you.**

## Figure 9.1 Questions to answer in a change

|  |  |  |
|---|---|---|
| Change pressure | 1 | What are the main reasons why we want to change the organisation? |
| | 2 | What in the business environment creates pressure for change? What in the industry? What in the organisation? What in the employees? |
| | 3 | How do these different pressures for change interact? |
| | 4 | What is the change we want to bring about - at the 'headline level'? |
| Results and behaviours | 5 | What concrete results do we want to affect with the change (e.g. profitability, customer satisfaction, productivity, innovation)? |
| | 6 | Have we covered financial, customer and market, internal and development objectives and understood their relationships? |
| | 7 | In which direction do we want to influence the results? Increase or decrease? How much? Until when? |
| | 8 | What concrete behaviours do we need to change to influence outcomes? |
| | 9 | How do these behaviours sound when they are specified, i.e. measurable, observable, reliable and active? |
| Scope and stakeholders | 10 | How big is our change? How deep? How broad? |
| | 11 | Who are our stakeholder groups and named key stakeholders? |
| | 12 | Which stakeholders impact our ability to realise change? Which of these stakeholders do we need to influence to realise the change? |
| | 13 | Which stakeholders do we need to involve in the work? Communicate with? Inform? Monitor continuously? |
| Attacking change | 14 | How is our change mainly driven through? Revolutionary or evolutionary? |
| | 15 | What, which parts, stages or elements of the change, need to be driven revolutionarily? Which parts, stages or elements of the change need to be evolutionary? |
| | 16 | What, which parts, stages or elements of change are likely to be mainly unsteady? How should we think about the timing of these? |
| | 17 | What, which parts, stages or elements of the change are likely to be essentially steady? How should we think about the speed of these? |
| | 18 | How can we combine revolutionary and evolutionary change strategies to best drive our change and its various parts? |
| The work of the change manager | 19 | What measurable benefits – changes in organisational performance – do we see from the change? (compare with questions 5 and 6 on organisational performance) |
| | 20 | What and how big are green benefits? Yellow? Red? Blue? What is the distribution between the different types of benefits? |
| | 21 | What control do we have over change? How far can we push it without a mandate from others? Identify, analyse and define, generate proposals for solution, decide on solution, realise, evaluate and reflect, feed back and adjust? |
| | 22 | How likely is it that we will succeed in realising the change, i.e. ensure that the benefits are delivered to customers or the business? |
| | 23 | What is the realisability of change based on its scale? Level of involvement – the right people and the right number? Support from 'management' (if needed)? |
| | 24 | How well are the basic prerequisites for change in place among stakeholders? How likely are we to succeed in getting these conditions in place in our change work? |
| | 25 | What is the message of change and its different parts? The idea of change? The change description? The examples of benefits? The change summary? Do the elements form an understandable and logic whole of the change? |
| | 26 | What specific change activities (e.g. mailings, meetings, training) do we know from the start that we need to carry out? When approximately should they be carried out? |
| | 27 | Which stakeholders are participants and/or beneficiaries of these specific activities? In what order should they be considered? |
| | 28 | What are the major competence gaps? In which stakeholder groups and key stakeholders do we see these? What are the best formats for competence development to close these gaps? |
| | 29 | When and how will we evaluate the success of stakeholder competence building activities? |
| | 30 | How should we create structures and procedures to disseminate knowledge continuously and across the organisation? |
| | 31 | How and how often should we evaluate the change progress? That the prerequisites (expectations, competence, opportunity, reinforcement) are in place? |
| | 32 | How and how often should we evaluate that benefits are realised (i.e. that actual improvements in organisational results are visible and can be measured)? |
| | 33 | What concrete behaviours do we as change managers need to demonstrate to ensure that the prerequisites for change are in place (e.g. giving feedback, asking questions)? |
| | 34 | How can we feed back the results of the change to a wider range of stakeholders in a systematic and educational way? To whom should we feed back what and with what frequency? |
| | 35 | What kind of change resistance might we face? From which stakeholder groups and key stakeholders is the most resistance likely to come? How can we meet that resistance effectively? Are 'golden bridges' needed? |
| | 36 | What should we hand over to the business? To which key stakeholders? When and how should these handovers take place? |
| Organising change | 37 | How do we need to organise change? Projects? Initiatives? In line? Centrally led? |
| | 38 | What are the different responsibilities for change that we need to share? For different areas and issues? What types of responsibilities do we assign to whom? |
| | 39 | What concrete roles do we need to ensure that someone has for the change to be realised and the benefits to become real? |

# Notes and inspiration for further reading

Some of you may want to dive deeper into the 'ocean of knowledge' that deals with strategy, change and strategic change. For your help, I have listed the sources I noted in the book. While they provide a picture of where an argument is coming from, it may provide some inspiration for further reading.

In some cases, they are classics, in others, alternative sources. Unfortunately, since much research is behind expensive subscriptions to scientific journals, I have tried to supplement these sources with those that are available to everyone. In some cases this is easy because some scientists are good at popularising their research and publishing books. In other cases, unfortunately, this is not the case, but with a bit of persistence and finesse, we can usually find a little something about almost anything on the worldwide web. Keywords like 'summary' and 'pdf' usually help.

Notably, several books and articles provide inspiration and explanations beyond the specific notes and chapters under which they are organised.

---

### Foreword

[1] Ohmae, K. (1982). *The mind of the strategist: The art of Japanese Business*. McGraw-Hill

[2] Nadle, M. (1965). Malcolm X: the complexity of a man in the jungle. *Village Voice*, February.

[3] See e.g. https://en.wikipedia.org/wiki/By_any_means_necessary [Last accessed 20220329].

### 2. Change?

[4] Berdyaev, N. (1947/1976). *The beginning and the end*. Preager Publishers.

[5] See e.g. Daft, R. L. & Becker, S. W. (1978) *Innovation in Organizations*, Elsevier; Hage, J. (1980) *Theories of Organization*, Wiley; International Organization of Standards (2019) *Innovation management - Innovation management systems - Guidance* (ISO standard 56002:2019E). https://www.sis.se/api/document/preview/80012916/. [Last retrieved: 2022-09-14]; Rehn, A. (2017). *Innovation*. Liber

[6] See e.g. Hamel, G. (1997). *Strategy as revolution*. Harvard Business Review (July-August); Freeman, C. (1974). *The economics of industrial innovation*. Penguin Books.

[7] Christensen, C. & Overdorf, M (2000). Meeting the challenge of disruptive change. *Harvard Business Review* (March-April).

[8] Schumpeter, J.A. (1934). *Theory of economic development*. Harvard University Press.

[9] D'Aveni, R., Dagnino, G. & Smith, K. (2010). The age of temporary advantage. *Strategic Management Journal*, 31(13), 1371-1385; Grant, R. M. (2003). Strategic planning in a turbulent environment. *Strategic Management Journal*, 24(6), 491-518.

[10] Wernberg, J. (2018). Går allt verkligen fortare? Teknologisk förändring, entreprenörskap och experiment. I Anderson, M. & Eklund, J. (Eds). *Navigera under osäkerhet: entreprenörskap, innovationer, och experimentell policy*. Entreprenörskapsforum.

[11] Schwab, K. (2016). *The Fourth Industrial Revolution*. World Economic Forum.

[12] See e.g. Ciravegna, L. & Michailova, S. (2022) Why the world economy needs, but will not get, more globalization in the post-COVID-19 decade. *Journal of International Business Studies,* 53, 172-186; Lewinson, M. (2021). *Outside the box: how globalization changed from moving stuff to spreading ideas.* Princeton University Press.

[13] Moss Kanter, R. (1985) *Change masters: innovation and entrepreneurship in the American corporation.* Free Press.

[14] Lieberman, M. & Montgomery, D. (1988) First mover advantages: a survey, *Strategic Management Journal,* 9(SI) 41-58; Robinson, W. & Sungwook, M. (2002) Is the first to market the first to fail? Empirical evidence for industrial goods businesses, *Journal of Marketing Research,* 39(1) 120-28.

[15] See, e.g., Chandler, A. (1962). *Strategy and structure: Chapters in the History of the American Enterprise.* MIT Press; Porter, M. (1996) What is Strategy? *Harvard Business Review,* Wadström, P., Schriber, S., Teigland, R. & Kaulio, M. (2017). *Strategy: the arena, the deal, the ways of working, the responsibility, the intent.* Liber.

[16] See e.g. Barney, J. B. (1986). Strategic factor markets: expectations, luck, and business strategy. *Management Science,* 32(10), 1231-1241; Grant, R. M. (1991). The resource-based theory of competitive advantage: implications for strategy formulation. *Knowledge and strategy,* 33(3), 3-23;, 1319-1350; Wernerfelt, B. (1984). A resource-based view of the firm. *Strategic Management Journal,* 5(2), 171-180.

[17] See e.g. Ansoff, H.I., Declerck, R.P. & Hayes, R.L. (1976). *From strategic planning to strategic management.* John Wiley and Sons; Goold, M. & Campbell, A. (2002). *Designing effective organisations: how to create structured networks.* Jossey-Bass; Hamel, G. (2014). Bureaucracy must die. *Harvard Business Review,* November; Miles, R. E., & Snow, C. C. 1978. *Organizational Strategy, Structure, and Process.* McGraw-Hill.

[18] See e.g. Danielsson, U. (2021). *Världen själv.* Fri tanke.

[19] See e.g. Damanpour, F. (1992). Organizational size and innovation. *Organization studies,* 13(3), 375-402; Cohen W. & Levin, R. (1989). Empirical studies of innovation and market structure, in Schmalensee, R & Willig, R. D. (Eds.), *Handbook of industrial organisation,* II. Elsevier; Gilder, G. (1988). The revitalization of everything: the law of the microcosm. *Harvard Business Review,* 66(2), 49-61.

[20] Wadström, P. (2022). *Advaning strategy through behavioural psychology.* Kogan Page.

[21] Maguire, S. & Redman, T. (2007). The role of Human Resource Management in information systems development. *Management Decisions.* 45(2), 252-264; Mintzberg, H. (1987). Crafting strategy. *Harvard Business Review* (July); Buchanan, D. A., & Boddy, D. (1992). *The expertise of the change agent.* Prentice Hall; Todnem, R. (2005). Organisational change management: a critical review. *Journal of Change Management.* 5(4), 369-380.

[22] See e.g. Anderson, K. A. Kramppe, R. & Tesch-Romer, C. (1993). The role of deliberate practice in the acquisition of expert performance, *Psychological Review*, 100, 363-406; Ericsson, A., Prietula M. & Cokely, E. (2007). The making of an expert, *Harvard Business Review.*

[23] See e.g. Åhlström, P. (red) (2010). *Verksamhetsutveckling i världsklass.* Studentliteratur.

[24] See e.g. Kind, S. & Knyphaussen-Aufsess, D. z. (2007). What is 'business development' - the case of bio-technology. *SBR*, 59(April), 176-199.

[25] See e.g. Gersick, X (1991) Revolutionary change theories: a multilevel exploration of the punctuated equilibrium paradigm. *The Academy of Management Review*, 16, 10-36; Tushman, M. L. & Romanelli, E. (1985). Organizational evolution: a metamorphosis model of convergence and reorientation. *Research in Organizational Behavior* 7, 171-222.

[26] See e.g. PMP (2003). *PMP project management professional study guide.* McGraw-Hill Professional; APM (2019) *APM body of knowledge.* Association of Project Management.

[27] Mankins, M. & Steele, R. (2005). Turning great strategy into great performance. *Harvard Business Review*, July-August; Zook, C. (2001) *Profit from the core.* Harvard Business Review Press.

[28] Pettigrew, A. & Whipp, R. (1991) *Managing change for competitive success.* Blackwell Business.

[29] Rogers, P., Meehan, P. & Tanner, S. (2006) *Building a winning culture*. Bain & Company.

[30] Bashin, S., Burcher, P. (2006) Lean viewed as a philosophy. *Journal of Manufacturing Technology Management*, 17(1), 56-72; Berggren, I., Lindkvist, J. (2001) *Projects - Organization for goal orientation and learning*. Studentliteratur; Burnes, B. (2009) *Managing change*. Prentice-Hall; De Waal, A. A., Counet, H. (2009). Lessons learned from performance management implementations. *International Journal of Productivity and Performance Management*, 58, 4, 367-390.

[31] Kotter, J. (1996) *Leading change*. Harvard Business School Press.

[32] Duckworth, A. L., Peterson, C., Matthews, M. D. & Kelly, D. R. (2007). Grit: perseverance and passion for long-term goals. *Journal of Personality and Social Psychology*, 92(6),1087-1101.

[33] Bandura, A. (1978). Self-efficacy: toward a unifying theory of behavioural change. *Advances in Behaviour Research and Therapy*, 1(4), 139-161; Baumeister, R. F., Bratslavsky, E., Muraven, M. & Tice, D. M. (1998). Ego depletion: is the active self a limited resource?. *Journal of Personality and Social Psychology*, 74(5), 1252-1265; Ryans, D. G. (1939). The measurement of persistence: an historical review. *Psychological Bulletin*, 36(9), 715-739.

[34] Becket, S. (1964). *The unmentionable*. Gebers.

## 3. Pressures for Change Large and Small Ways

[35] Kandel, E. (2006) *In search of memory: the emergence of a new science of mind*, W.W. Norton and Company.

[36] See e.g. Eden, C. (1992) On the nature of cognitive maps. *Journal of Management Studies*, 29(3), 261-265; Fiol, C. M. & Huff, A. S. (1992) Maps for managers: where are we? where do we go from here? *Journal of Management Studies*, 29(3), 267-285; Tolman, C. E. (1948). Cognitive maps in rats and men. *Psychological Review*, 55(4), 189-208.

[37] See e.g. Blanchard, O. (2000). *Macroeconomics*. Prentice Hall.

[38] See e.g. Augilar, F. J. (1967). *Scanning the business environment.* MacMillan.

[39] Hai, T. N., Van, Q. N., & Thi Tuyet, M. N. (2021). Digital transformation: opportunities and challenges for leaders in the emerging countries in response to COVID-19 pandemic. *Emerging Science Journal*, 5, 21-36; Priyono, A., Moin, A. & Putri, V. N. A. O. (2020). Identifying digital transformation paths in the business model of SMEs during the COVID-19 pandemic. *Journal of Open Innovation: Technology, Market, and Complexity*, 6(4); Sein, M. K. (2020). The serendipitous impact of Covid-19 pandemic: a rare opportunity for research and practice. *International Journal of Information Management*, 55, 102164.

[40] See e.g. Naisbitt, J. (1982). *Megatrends: ten new directions transforming our lives.* warner books.

[41] See e.g. Bade, R. & Parkin, M. (2001) *Foundations of Microeconomics.* Addison Wesley Paperback.

[42] Porter, M. (1980) *Competitive Strategy*, Free Press.

[43] https://assets-global.websitefiles.com/5f47edc7df93400f850fdd8d/61405c693dc5173aac5665ab_Elkjop_Arsrapport_2021_A4_onepage.pdf [Last retrieved: 2022-09-14].

[44] https://www.annreports.com/apple/apple-ar-2021.pdf [Last retrieved: 2022-09-14]

[45] See e.g. Baines, T., Ziaee Bigdeli, A., Bustinza, O. F., Shi, V. G., Baldwin, J. & Ridgway, K. (2017). Servitization: revisiting the state-of-the-art and research priorities. *International Journal of Operations & Production Management*, 37(2), 256-278.

[46] Greiner, L. (1972) Evolution and revolution as organisations grow. *Harvard Business Review.*

[47] See e.g. Bales, R. F., Mills, T. M., Roseborough, M, & Strodtbeck, F. L. (1951). Channels of communication in small groups. *American Sociological Review*, 16, 461-468; Callahan, C., Owen, S., & Renzulli, J. (1974). Fluency, flexibility and originality as a function of group size. *Journal of Creative Behavior*, 8(2), 107-113; Diehl, M., & Strobe, W. (1987). Productivity loss in brainstorming groups: Toward the solution of a riddle. *Journal of Personality and Social Psychology*, 53, 497-509; Hare, A.P. (1952). A study of interaction and consensus in different sized groups. *American Sociological Review*, 17, 261-267; Wheelan, S. (2009). Group size, group development, and group creativity. *Small Group Research*, 40(2), 247-262.

[48] See e.g. Dunbar, R. I. M. (1992). Neocortex as a constraint on group size in primates. *Journal of Human Evolution*, 20, 469-493.

[49] See e.g. Gross, R. (2015). *Psychology: the science of mind and behaviour*, 7th ed., Hodder Education; Thorndike, E. (1898). animal intelligence: an experimental study of associative processes in animals. *psychological monographs: general and applied*, 2(4), i-109.

[50] Wadström, O. (2020). *Att förstå att påverka beteendeproblem*. Psykologinsats

[51] Bandura, A. (1977). *Social learning theory*. Prentice-Hall.

[52] Moxley, R. (2004) Pragmatic selectionism: the philosophy of behaviour analysis. *The Behavior Analyst Today*, January. Cengage Learning.

[53] Levinthal, D. & March, J. (1993). The myopia of learning. *Strategic Management Journal*, 14, 95-112.

**4. Organisational Performance and Behavioural Change**

[54] Carlyle, T. (1829/1885). Signs of the times, in *Critical and Miscellaneous Essays* (1827-1855). Chapman Hall.

[55] See e.g. Reichheld, F. (2003). The one number you need to grow. *Harvard Business Review*, December.

[56] See e.g. Baer, D., Wolf, M. & Risley, T. (1968). Some current dimensions of applied behaviour analysis. *Journal of Applied Behavior Analysis*, 1, 91-97; Sulzer-Azaroff, B. & Meyer, G. (1991). *Behaviour analysis for lasting change.* Wadsworth/Thomson Learning; Sundel, M. & Sundel, S. (1999); *Behavior change in the human services: an introduction to principles and applications*, 4th ed., Sage Publications.

[57] See e.g. Lindsley, O. R. (1991) From technical jargon to plain English for application. *Journal of Applied Behavior Analysis*, 24, 449-458.

[58] Wadström, O. (2020). *Att förstå och påverka beteendeproblem.* Psykologinsats.

[59] See e.g. Digman, J. M. (1990). Personality structure: emergence of the five-factor model. *Annual Review of Psychology*, 41, 417-40; McCrae, R. R. & Costa, P. T. (1987). Validation of the five-factor model of personality across instruments and observers. *Journal of Personality and Social Psychology*, 52(1), 81-90; Rothmann, S. & Coetzer E. P. (2003). The big five personality dimensions and job performance. *SA Journal of Industrial Psychology*, 29, 68-74.

[60] Clelland, D. C. (1961). *The achieving society.* Free Press.

[61] Braksick, L. (2007) *Unlock behaviour, unleash profit.* McGraw-Hill Wadstrom, P. (2022). *Advancing Strategy through Behavioural Psychology: create competitive advantage in relentlessly changing markets.* Kogan Page.

[62] See e.g. Herzberg, F. (2009). *One more time: How do you motivate employees?* Harvard Business School Press; Latham, G. P. (2003). Goal setting: A five-step approach to behaviour change. *Organizational Dynamics*, 32(3), 309-318. Locke, E. A., & Latham, G. P. (1990). *A theory of goal setting and task performance.* Prentice Hall; Skinner, B. F. (1979). *The shaping of a behaviourist.* Knopf; Vroom, V. H. (1994) *Work and motivation.* Jossey-Bass.

[63] Daniels, A. (2001) *Bringing out the best in people.* McGraw-Hill.

[64] Skinner, B. F. (1969) *Contingencies of Reinforcement.* ACC, Meredith Corporation.

[65] Wadstrom, O. (2020). *KBT och lite till: 49 års erfarenheter som beteendeterapeut.* Psykologinsats.

[66] Daniels, A. (1989) *Performance Management*. Performance Management Publications.

[67] Wu Tang Clan (2000): Protect Ya Neck (The Jump Off) [Recorded by Wu Tang Clan, produced by Diggs, R. F.] On The W. Loud Records: New York City.

[68] See e.g. Komaki, J. & Minnich, M. R. (2001) Developing performance appraisals: criteria for what and how performance is measured. In Johnson, C. M., Redmon, W. K. & Mawhinney, T. C. (Eds.) *Handbook of organisational performance: behaviour analysis and management*. The Haworth Press.

[69] Abernathy, W. (1996). The sin of wages: where conventional pay systems has led us, and how to find a way out. PerSys Press; Wadstrom, O. & Ekvall, D. (2013). Sportsmanship, achievement, development. Psychology paper.

**5. Change magnitude and stakeholders**

[70] Brin, S. (2005). Search Engines, Technology, and Business. Guest Lecture, UC Berkeley, (October 3).

[71] Wadström, P., Schriber, S., Teigland, S. & Kaulio, M. (2017). *Strategi: arenan, affären, arbetssätten, ansvaret, avsikten*. Liber.

[72] Fleming, L. & Sorenson, O. (2003). Navigating the technology landscape of innovation, *Sloan Management Review*, 44(2), 15-23; Henderson, R. & Clark, K. (1990). Architectural innovation: the reconfiguration of existing product technologies and the failure of established firms, *Administrative Science Quarterly*, 35(1), 9-30; Schilling, M. A. (2000). Towards a general modular systems theory and its application to interfirm product modularity, *Academy of Management Review*, 25(2) 312-334.

[73] Galbraith, J. K. (2001) *Designing organisations: an executive guide to strategy, structure, and process, Revised.* Jossey-Bass.

[74] Chandler, A. (1962). *Strategy and structure: chapters in the history of the American enterprise*. MIT Press.

[75] See e.g. Kathuria, R., Joshi, M. & Porth, S. (2007). Organizational alignment and performance: past, present and future. *Decision Sciences*, 45(3), 503-517; Lawrence, P. & Lorsch, J. (1967). *Organization and environment: managing differentiation and integration.* Harvard University; Likert, R. (1961). *New Patterns of Management.* McGraw Hill; Miller, D. (1986) Configurations of strategy and structure: towards a synthesis. *Strategic Management Journal*, 7(3), 233-249; Wu, L.-F., Huang, I. C., Huang, W. C. & Du, P.-L. (2019). Aligning organisational culture and operations strategy to improve innovation outcomes: an integrated perspective in organisational management. *Journal of Organizational Change Management*, 32(2), 224-250.

[76] Donaldson, T. & Preston, L. (1995). The stakeholder theory of the corporation: concepts, evidence, and implications, *Academy of Management Review,* 20(1) 65-91; Freeman, R. E. (1984). *Strategic management: a stakeholder approach.* Cambridge University Press.

[77] Rhenman, E. (1968) *Industrial democracy and industrial management.* Tavistock.

[78] Moreno, J. L. (1934) *Who Shall Survive?* Beacon House.

[79] Hagan, T. & Smail, D. (1997) Power-mapping: background and basic methodology. *Journal of Community & Applied Social Psychology*, 7(4), 257-267.

[80] Brown, S. & Eisenhardt, K. (1997) The art of continuous change. *Administrative Science Quarterly*, 42, 1-34; Chesbrough, H. W. & Appleyard, M. M. (2007). Open innovation and strategy. *California Management Review*, 50(1), 57-77; Dachler, H. & Wilpert, B. (1978). Conceptual dimensions and boundaries of participation in organisations. *Administrative Science Quarterly*, 23(1), 1-39; Vaara, E., Rantakari, A. & Holstein, J. (2018). Participation research and open strategy. in Seidl, D., Whittington, R. & von Krogh, G. (Eds.), *Cambridge handbook of open strategy.* Cambridge University Press; Whitehurst, J. (2015). *The open organisation.* Harvard Business School Publishing.

[81] See e.g. Centola, D., Becker, J. & Brackbill, D. & Baronchelli, A. (2018). Experimental evidence for tipping points in social convention, *Science*, 360(6393), 1116-1119; Marwell, G. & Oliver, P. (1993). *The critical mass in collective action.* Cambridge University Press; Schelling, T. (1978). *Micromotives and Macrobehaviour.* Norton.

[82] Gladwell, M. (2000). *The Tipping Point: how little things can make a big difference*. Little Brown.

[83] See e.g. Karakaya, E. & Lundberg, S. (2020). Diffusion, In *International Encyclopedia of Human Geography*, Ed. Kobayashi, A. Elsevier; Rogers, E. M. (1962). *Diffusion of innovations*, Free Press; Tarde, G. (1903). *The laws of imitation* (E. Clews Parssons, trans.) H Holt & Co.

[84] Mendelow, A. L. (1991) Environmental scanning: the impact of the stakeholder concept. In *Proceedings from the second international conference on information systems*, Cambridge.

## 6. Tackling Change

[85] Dewey, J. (1916). *Democracy and education: an introduction to the philosophy of education*. MacMillan.

[86] Mintzberg, H. & Waters, J. A. (1985). Of strategy: deliberate and emergent. *Strategic Management Journal*, 6(3), 257-272.

[87] Skinner, B.F. (1976). *About behaviourism*. Random House.

[88] Garud, R., Van de Ven, A. (2002). Strategic change process. In Pettigrew, A., Thomas, H. & Whittington, R. *Handbook of strategy and management*, 206-231. Sage Publications.

[89] See e.g. Beer, M. & Nohria, N. (2000). *Breaking the code of change*. Harvard Business School Press.

[90] See e.g. Freeman, C. (1974). *The economics of industrial innovation*. Penguin Books; Hamel, G. (1997). Strategy as revolution. *Harvard Business Review* (July-August); Marx, K. & Engels, F. (1848). *Manifesto of the Communist Party*. Office of the "Educational Society for Workers".

[91] See e.g. Gilbert, C. (2005) Unbundling the structure of inertia: Resource versus routine rigidity, *Academy of Management Journal*, 48(5), 741-63; Howard-Grenville, J. (2005). The persistence of flexible organisational routines: the role of agency and organisational context, *Organization Science*, 16 (6), 618-36.

[92] See e.g. Aldrich, H. (1999). *Organizations evolving.* Sage; Imai, M. (1986). *Kaizen: the Key to Japan's competitive success.* McGraw-Hill; Nelson, R. R. & Winter, S. (1982). *An evolutionary theory of economic change.* Belknap press; Quinn, J. B. (1978). Strategic change: logical incrementalism. *Sloan Management Review,* 20(Fall), 7-21.

[93] Barnes, S. (1987). *Bohica.* Daring Books.

[94] See e.g. PRINCE2, https://www.axelos.com/certifications/propath/prince2-project-management; Impact Management Project IMP, https://impactmanagementproject.com/; Practical Project Management PPS, https://www.tietoevry.com/se/tjanster/affars-och-teknikradgivning/pps/pps-modellen/, PROPS (now XLNP) https://semcon.com/sv/erbjudanden/project-excellence/ [Last retrieved 20220508].

[95] See e.g. Collins, B. E. & Guetzkow, H. (1964). *A social psychology of group processes for decision making,* Wiley; Hinsz, V. B. (1990). Cognitive and consensus processes in group recognition memory performance, *Journal of Personality and Social Psychology* 59(4), 705-718; Jackson, S. E., May, K. E. & Whitney, K. (1995). Understanding the Diversity of Dynamics in Decision Making Teams. In Guzzo, R. A. & Salas, E. (Eds.), *Team effectiveness and decision making in organisations,* Wiley; Rochford, L. & Rudelius, W. (1992). How involving more functional areas within a firm affects the new product process. *Journal of Product Innovation Management,* 9(4), 287-99; Priem, R. L. Harrison, D. A. & Muir, N. K. (1995). Structured conflict and consensus outcomes in group decision making, *Journal of Management,* 21(4), 691-710; Shaw, M. E. (1932). A comparison of individuals and small groups in the rational solution of complex problems, *American Journal of Psychology* 44, 491-504.

[96] Simon, H. A. (1982). *The sciences of the artificial.* MIT Press.

[97] Beer, M. & Nohria, N. (2000) Cracking the code of change. *Harvard Business Review,* May.

[98] Moss Kanter, R. (1985) *Change masters: innovation and entrepreneurship in the American corporation.* Free Press; Tushman, M.L. & O'Reilly, C.A. (1996). Ambidextrous organisations: managing evolutionary and revolutionary change. *California Management Review,* 38, 8-30.

[99] Mintzberg, H. & Westley, F. (1992) Cycles of organisational change. *Strategic Management Journal*, 13, 39-59.

[100] See e.g. Peters, T. (1993). *Liberation management.* Pan

[101] See e.g. Cohen, W. H. & Levinthal, D. A. (1990). Absorptive capacity: a new perspective on learning and innovation. *Administrative Science Quarterly*, 35(1), 128-152.

[102] See e.g. Tushman, M. L., Newman, W. H. & Romanelli, E. (1986) Convergence and upheaval: managing the unsteady pace of organisational evolution. *California Management Review*, 29(1), 29-44.

[103] Lewin, K. (1951). *Field theory in social science.* Harper-Row.

[104] Kotter, J. (1996). *Leading Change.* Harvard Business School Press.

## 7. The Work of the Change Manager

[105] Pierce, A., Schultz, D. & Joshi, S. T. (2000). *The unabridged Devil's dictionary*, 6th ed., University of Georgia Press.

[106] Hassner-Nahmias, A. (2009) *Who is a change manager?* Doctoral dissertation, Bond University; Gold Coast, Australia; Rothwell, W. J., Hohne, C. K. & King, S. B. (2007). The change manager, 121-146. *Human Performance improvement*, Elsevier.

[107] Dahlgren, L., Lundgren, G. & Stigberg, L. (2000). *Increase the benefits of IT!* Ekerlids Verlag.

[108] J. C. Harsanyi, J. C. & Selten, R. (1988) *A general theory of equilibrium selection in games.* MIT Press; Nash, J. F. (1950) Equilibrium points in N-person games. *Proceedings of the National Academy of Sciences of the United States of America*, 36(1), 48-49.

[109] Slater, R. (1987). *Portaits in silicon.* MIT Press

[110] Quiller-Couch, A. (1916). *On the art of writing.* Dover Publications.

[111] Reed, R. & DeFillippi, R. J. (1990). Causal ambiguity, barriers to imitation, and sustainable competitive advantage, *Academy of Management Review* 15(1), 88-102.

[112] Wadström, P. (2021). How non-executive strategy professionals strategize. *Journal of Strategy and Management*, 15(1), 16-37.

[113] See e.g. Horai, J., Naccari, N., & Fatoullah, E. (1974). The effects of expertise and physical attractiveness upon opinion agreement and liking. *Sociometry*, *37*(4), 601-606; Reysen, S. (2005). Construction of a new scale: the reysen likability scale. *Social Behavior and Personality: an international journey*, 33(5), 201-208.

[114] See e.g. Edmondson, A. (1999) Psychological safety and learning behaviour in work teams. *Administrative Science Quarterly*, 44(2), 350-384; Newman, A., Donohue, R. & Eva, V. (2017). Psychological safety: a systematic review of the literature. *Human Resource Management Review*, 27(3), 521-535.

[115] See e.g. Deterding, S., Dixon, D., Khaled, R. & Nacke, L. (2011). From game design elements to gamefulness: defining gamification, MindTrek '11: In *Proceedings of the 15th International Academic MindTrek Conference: Envisioning Future Media Environments*, September, 9-15, Tampere, Finland: ACM; Zichermann, G., & Linder, J. (2013). *The gamification revolution: how leaders leverage game mechanics to crush the competition*. McGraw Hill.

[116] See e.g. Argyris, C. (1990). *Overcoming orgazational defiences: facilitating organisational learning*. Prentice Hall; Krüger, W. (1996) Implementation: The core task of change management, *CEMS Business Review*, 1, 77-96; Oliver, C. (1991). Strategic responses to institutional processes. *Academy of Management Review*, 16(1), 145-179; Senge, P. (1990). The leader's new work: building learning organisations. *Sloan Management Review*, 32(1), 7-23.

[117] Vermeulen, F. (2009). Businesses and the Icarus paradox. *Harvard Business Review*, October; Miller, D. (1990). *The Icarus paradox*. HarperBusiness.

[118] See e.g. Prahalad, C. K. & Hamel, G. (1990). The core competence of the corporation, *Harvard Business Review*, 68, 79-91; Prahalad, C. K. & Hamel, G. (1996) *Competing for the Future*, Harvard Business School Press.

[119] Sun Tzu & Giles, L. (1910/2000). *The Art of War*. Allandale Online Publishing

[120] See e.g. Hope J. & Frazer, R. (2003). *Beyond budgeting: how managers can break free from the annual performance trap.* Harvard Business Press; Kaplan, R. & Norton, D. (1992). The balanced scorecard. *Harvard Business Review*, 70, 71-79.

[121] Miller, G. A. (1956). The magical number seven, plus or minus two: some limits on our capacity for processing information. *Psychological Review*, 63(2), 81-97.

## 8. Organising Change

[122] Shirky, C. (2009). *Here comes everybody: the power of organizing without organisations.* Penguin Books.

[123] See e.g. Burns, T. & Stalker, G. (1961). *The Management of Innovation.* Tavistock; Fang, C. Lee, J. & Schilling, M. A. (2010). Balancing exploration and exploitation through structural design: advantage of the semi-isolated subgroup structure in organisational learning. *Organization Science*, 21(3) 625-42; Miles, R. E. & Snow, C. C. (1986). Organizations: new concepts for new forms, *California Management Review*, 28(3), 62-73.

[124] Cochrane J. R. & Turner, R. A. (1993) Goals-and-methods matrix. *International Journal of Project Management*, 11(2), 93-102.

[125] See e.g. Barnard, C. I. (1968/1938). *The functions of the executive.* Harvard University Press.

[126] See e.g. Project Management Institute (2000) *A guide to the project management body of knowledge* (PMBOK Guide 5th ed). Project Management Institute.

[127] De Bono, E. (1985). *Six thinking hats.* Little Brown and Company.

## 9. Summary and Conclusions

[128] Bacon, R. & Burke, R. B. (1962). *Opus majus.* Russell & Russell.